A
DRAGON
APPARENT

NORMAN LEWIS

Travels in Cambodia, Laos, and Vietnam

D1579291

ELAND BOOKS, LONDON
&
HIPPOCRENE BOOKS, INC., NEW YORK

Published by
ELAND BOOKS
53 Eland Road London SW11 5JX
&
HIPPOCRENE BOOKS, INC.,
171 Madison Avenue, New York, NY 10016

First published by Jonathan Cape 1951
© Norman Lewis 1951

ISBN 0 907871 00 3
First issued in this paperback edition 1982
Reprinted 1984, 1987
All rights reserved

Printed and bound in Great Britain
by Redwood Burn Ltd, Trowbridge, Wiltshire

Cover Illustration © Tony Ansell
Cover Design © Patrick Frean
Map © Reginald Piggott

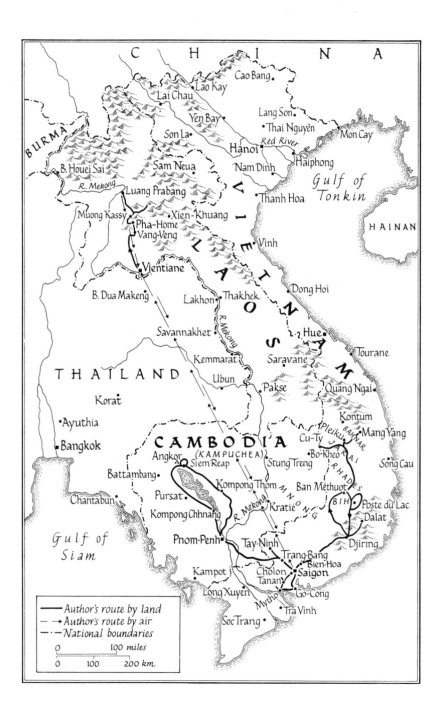

C H I N A

BURMA

Cao Bang
Lao Kay
Lai Chau
Yen Bay
Lang Son
Son La
Thai Nguyên
Mon Cay
Hanoi
Red River
Haiphong
B. Houei Sai
Sam Neua
Nam Dinh
R. Mekong
Thanh Hoa
Gulf of Tonkin
Luang Prabang
Muong Kassy
Xien-Khuang
HAINAN
Pha-Home
Vang-Veng
Vinh
Vientiane
Dong Hoi
B. Dua Makeng
Lakhon
Thakhek
R. Mekong
Savannakhet
Hue
Kemmarat
Saravane
Tourane
THAILAND
Ubun
Pakse
Quang Ngai
Korat
Kontum
Mang Yang
Ayuthia
Pleiku
Cu-Ty
Bo-Kheo
Song Cau
Bangkok
CAMBODIA
(KAMPUCHEA)
Angkor
Siem Reap
Stung Treng
Ban Méthuot
Battambang
Kompong Thom
Poste du Lac
Pursat
R. Mekong
Kratie
Dalat
Chantabun
Kompong Chhnang
Pnom-Penh
Tay-Ninh
Trang-Bang
Djiring
Gulf of
Siam
Bien-Hoa
Kampot
Cholon
Saigon
Tanan
Long Xuyen
Go-Cong
Soc Trang
Mytho
Tra Vinh

—— Author's route by land
--→ Author's route by air
—·— National boundaries

0   100 miles
0   100   200 km

CONTENTS

ILLUSTRATIONS

Publisher's Note

The photographs used in the first edition are lost. The present issue uses imperfect reproductions in the belief that readers will prefer them to none at all.

BIOGRAPHY

Norman Lewis has written 12 novels and 6 non-fiction works. Of the latter, his two travel books, *A Dragon Apparent*, and *Golden Earth* (travels in Burma) – both best-sellers in their day – describe his journeyings in the Far East at a time when the countries he visited were passing out of the reach of the ordinary traveller, and which will never again be seen as they were then.

His novel, *The Volcanoes Above Us*, based on personal experiences in Central America in revolt, sold 6 million copies in paperback in Russia – enormously to his surprise, he says, as the book expressed no political point of view. *The Honoured Society*, a non-fiction study of the Sicilian Mafia, was serialized in 6 installments on the *New Yorker*, and his best-selling novel *The Sicilian Specialist*, incorporating at that time undisclosed facts about the Kennedy assassination, was removed from sale in some American cities following a Mafia ban. *Naples '44*, a recently published war-diary, which received high critical acclaim, describes his adventures in British Intelligence in the Italian South.

Norman Lewis regards his life's major achievement as the world reaction to an article written by him entitled *Genocide in Brazil*, published in the *Sunday Times* in 1968. This led to a change in the Brazilian law relating to the treatment of Indians, and to the formation of *Survival International*, the influential body, with branches in many countries, dedicated to the protection of aboriginal people.

Lewis relaxes by his occasional travels to off-beat parts of the world, which he prefers to be as remote as possible; otherwise he lives with his family in introspective, almost monastic calm, in the depths of Essex.

PREFACE TO 1982 EDITION

The ancient civilizations of Vietnam, Cambodia and Laos were already falling into decay when I travelled through South-East Asia prior to writing this book. Inevitably degeneration had followed contact with the West, and the invasion and subsequent colonization by the French; yet much of the charm and the grandeur of the past had survived in these countries, protected by their remoteness and the dense rain-forests and mountain ranges covering half their area.

The central plateau of Vietnam was peopled largely by tribes of Malayo-Polynesian origin, living in spectacular long-houses, whose existence had barely been noticed until the coming of the Japanese. These Moïs, as they were called, were living as their ancestors had probably lived for thousands of years when I visited them, and although the French had carried off some hundreds for forced labour in the tea-plantations, they had otherwise been left alone, to live their complicated, highly ceremonial and – to an outsider like myself – idyllic lives. The long houses accommodating a whole village, shown in this book, no longer exist. They were bombed to nothingness by the B.25s in the Vietnam war, and such of the population who survived were forced into the armies fighting the Nationalist Viet Cong, who were revenged on them in due course when the US abandonment of the country took place.

With the exception of these gracious and endearing people, the population of Vietnam, Cambodia and Laos were Buddhist, and therefore in essence gentle, tolerant, and addicted to pleasures and satisfactions of a discriminating kind. Just as in Japan, popular excursions would be made in certain seasons to admire trees in blossom. There were night-scapes in Saigon to be visited only when the moon was in a certain phase, and rich mandarins – still existing in those days in what remained culturally a province of China – would pay for white herons to be released across the sky when the party was seated in readiness for this aesthetic experience. At five in the evening, when one took the breeze on the waterfront in Saigon, stalls were put out with soft drinks of many colours, and one chose refreshment as much for its auspicious colouring as its taste. There was a right way in Vietnam to do everything, a gentle but persuasive protocol, full of subtle allusions, and nuances in gesture and speech that evaded the foreign barbarian. The Europeans corrupted but failed to barbarize Indo-China, and many of them who lived there long enough were happy enough to go native and cultivate what they could of the patina of the old civilization. Laos was considered the earthly paradise of South-East Asia, although Cambodia ran it a close second. So much was this realized by French officialdom that the competition for a posting to either country was strenuous. Many a wily administrator manoeuvred his way to a position in Ventiane or Luang Prabang, where he instantly married a Laotian wife, set up a shrine with joss-sticks to the lares of his house, and spent much of his leisure decking out Buddha caves with fresh flowers.

Both of these oases of decorum and charm were to be devastated and debauched in the Vietnam war, when as many bombs were showered among the shrines and the pagodas of these small countries as were expended in all the bombings put together of the World War in Europe.

Protocol demanded that visits be made to the rulers of these countries. I was warned to present myself at the palace of King Norodom Sihanouk, who later demoted himself to prince, and succeeded in holding the French, and after them the Americans, at bay for so many years. He was a gentle, softly-spoken young man, and we sat side by side on a sofa, deploring the inroads made by the West on the traditions of his country. In that year, despite his protests, a cinema had opened in Pnom Penh, and his subjects who flocked thither to see *Arsenic and Old Lace* forsook the ancient shadow play forever, while temple dancers ceased to have appeal for those who had been entertained by Fred Astaire and Ginger Rogers in action.

Some dignitaries were more formal in style. The Emperor Bao Dai liked visitors to crawl into his presence, or at least make a token obeisence by falling on one knee, but these were experiences I managed to evade. Many surprises awaited the traveller. A reputedly ferocious war lord could find nothing to talk about but the cultivation of chrysanthemums. An ex-governor of South Vietnam received me with what was regarded as charming informality while seated upon a close-stool ornamented with dragons. The Pope of the Cao Daï, the universal religion which included Joan of Arc, Victor Hugo and the Duc de la Rochefoucauld among its saints, appeared briefly in an entourage of white robed 12 year-old girls, said to have formed his harem.

General des Essars, was in command of French troops in Cambodia, and I had two meetings with him, the first a formal one at his headquarters, and the second totally informal in the romantic and justly famous opium den run by Madame Shum, where he was accustomed to settle his nerves by smoking two pipes of an evening. Whereas on the first occasion the General had been brimming with confidence and euphoria, on the second, sedated and perhaps somewhat dispirited by his two pipes, he saw a vision of the future that left him no better than resigned in his frame of mind. He had 2,500 Cambodian troops under his command, and he accepted the fact that nothing would ever turn them into fighters. Their religion, he said, had knocked all the aggression out of them. What could you expect in a country where every man-jack of them had done a year in a monastery, where they taught you that 'thou shalt not kill' had to be taken literally?

At the root of the trouble, said the General, lay the fact that Buddhism deprived the people of South-East Asia of the motives we Westerners understood and admired. If the aim in life was nothing more than to acquire virtue, what was the point of any form of competitive endeavour? If people only bothered to gather possessions for the spiritual benefit of giving them away, why then work hard? Why go to war?

And this was largely true. There were pagodas everywhere, full of monks who lived by begging, each of them holding a five-day festival once a year. A festival was always going on somewhere to provide villages in search of virtuous poverty with an opportunity for showering gifts on all comers, and shedding their burden of surplus wealth. Pnom Penh must have been the world's only city where a man taking a taxi sometimes found himself offered a tip by the driver.

It was of course, improper to take life in any form, however lowly. Devout Cambodians allowed mosquitoes to feast on their blood, and handled leeches tenderly when they fastened on them in the rice-paddies. A monk once reproved me for crushing a cockroach underfoot, with the warning that this might have been my grandfather in reincarnation. Villages obliged to live by fishing got round moral objections by 'rescuing the fish from drowning', and it was agreed that if they subsequently happened to die there could be no harm in consuming their flesh. All along the banks of the Mekong one saw the live fish laid out for sale, tied with decorative ribbons, often fanned by conscientious sellers, occasionally even solaced by the music of a bamboo flute.

Even in the gently, melancholic Autumn of those days there were guerrillas in the jungles and mountains, who had gone there to take up arms against the French, but they caused little inconvenience to the pacific traveller. The Issarak (freedom fighters), as they were called, went into action with guitars slung on their back, involving themselves in not particularly bloody clashes, reminiscent of the ceremonial wars between Italian City States, when a day of battle might produce a single casualty. Travelling along jungle trails in areas known to be under Issarak control, I was careful to restrict such movement to the hours of the afternoon, when they could be relied upon to be taking their siesta. At the lengthy festival of the New Year, the fight was called off, and everybody went home for a week or so to worship at the ancestral shrines, engage in ritual gambling, feed the monks, and to sleep.

Later the real war was unleashed, to be conducted in secret by radio through the U.S. Embassy in Pnom Penh. South Vietnam was already a wasteland, deluged by high-explosives, poisons and fire. Mr. Kissinger had said that the dominoes were falling, so now it was the turn of Cambodia and Laos, delivered to the greatest holocaust ever to be visited on the East. It consumed not only the present, but the past; an obliteration of cultures and values as much as physical things. From the ashes that remained no phoenix would ever rise. Not enough survived even to recreate the memory of what the world had lost.

What could these people have suffered to have transformed the sons and brothers of General des Essars' reluctant conscripts, formed in the ambulatories of monasteries rather than on the barracks' square, into those terrible and implacable warriors who flocked to the standards of the Khmer Rouge?

BACKGROUND

INDO-CHINA lies immediately to the south of China proper and to the east of Burma and Siam. On a world-map it is no more than a coastal strip, swelling out at its base — the rump of Eastern Asia. It is purely a political entity; originally the French colonial possessions corresponding to the conquered Empire of Annam, and its tributaries. This temporary union is in the process of dissolution.

The Indo-Chinese countries contain the scattered remnants of as many races as those of Europe, but they are inextricably jumbled up in a jig-saw of racial islands and enclaves, from which only three nations emerge: Vietnam, Cambodia and Laos. Of the total population of 25 millions, 17 millions are Vietnamese. The Cambodians and Laotians are peoples in monastic retirement; non-participants, as followers of a contemplative and renunciatory religion, in the march of progress. The population of the whole of Indo-China is concentrated in a few fertile valleys and deltas, leaving the greater part of the country unpopulated, jungle-covered, and looking much the same as China itself must have looked several thousand years ago, before the deforestation began. The interior is neither completely mapped, nor completely explored. It abounds with game: elephants, tigers, deer and many kinds of cattle, which, having known only hunters armed with cross-bows, may be closely approached and slaughtered with the greatest ease from cars on the jungle tracks.

Pacification of the Moïs of Central and Southern Vietnam — those bow and arrow tribes which in the early part of the last century were believed to be the only human beings with tails — was only undertaken in 1934. Certain tribes of the remote interior have not yet submitted to French authority.

The early history of Indo-China is that of primitive aboriginals — Mongolians in the north and Malayo-Polynesians in the south —

coming respectively under the influences of their great civilized neighbours, the Chinese and the Indians. From the latter union two brilliant and neurotic civilizations were created: those of the Khmers and the Chams. Both of them, after much precocious accomplishment, overtaxed their strength in wars, and collapsed. The Chams were first compressed and then absorbed by the southward movement of conquerors from China — the Vietnamese; while the remnants of the Khmers, listless and degenerate, were crowded back by the same people to the Siamese frontier. Scrupulous Vietnamese peasants still burn paper rent for the benefit of the spirits of long-vanished peoples, whose land they now possess.

The first Europeans to arrive in Indo-China — the missionaries and traders officially classified by the Vietnamese authorities as 'red-haired barbarians' — were dazzled by the people's virtues and enchanted by their hospitality. 'Whereas all the other Eastern Nations,' said the Jesuit Borri, writing in 1622, 'looking upon the Europeans as a profane people, do naturally abhor them, and therefore fly from us when first we come among them: In Cochin-China it falls out just contrary: for they strive who shall be nearest us, ask a thousand Questions, invite us to eat with them, and in short use all manner of Courtesie with much Familiarity and Respect . . . This loving and easie Disposition is the Cause of much Concord among them, they all treating one another as familiarly as if they were Brothers, or of the same Family . . . and it would be look'd upon as a most vile action, if one Man eating any thing, tho' never so little, should not share it with all about him, giving every one about him a bit.'

Borri and his successors, however, soon found causes for criticism. As a sign apparently that something was Rotten in the State, the devil frequently manifested himself, under horrific forms. Once called out with crosses, Agnus Deis and relics to confront him, Borri was only a matter of instants too late and saw three prints of his feet 'above two spans long, with the Marks of a Cock's Talons and Spurs'. The laws, too, were shockingly severe. Men and women received sound thrashings in the streets for slight breaches of good manners and then knelt to thank the mandarin who had ordered the punishment. A high official found guilty of delaying the presentation of a petition to the Divine Emperor was beheaded on the spot. But in other ways there was a barbarous penal insufficiency, of which the newcomers were equally unable to approve. The maximum prison sentence was three years, which, if the prisoner had aged parents to look after, could be served under some kind of parole system at home; while thieves who pleaded dire necessity were sometimes pardoned.

It was to correct these moral weaknesses that proselytizing pressure was brought to bear, and when the Vietnamese showed themselves intractable, the principle of religious tolerance was imposed by force of arms. In 1858, after a gradual extension of their influence over fifty years, the French began the outright conquest of the country. The annexation of Vietnam — at that time known as Annam — was followed by requests from Cambodia and Laos to be taken under French protection. The Cambodians' decision is said to have been much influenced by the French assurance that they would be allowed in future to keep for themselves all the white elephants they captured — animals of peculiar sanctity which previously they had been obliged to surrender to the Vietnamese Emperor.

During the last war the Japanese were allowed to occupy Indo-China without opposition, and the French collaborated with them until March 1945. At that time, after observing the success of allied arms in the West, the Japanese decided to intern the French authorities and to set up a puppet Vietnamese state headed by the Emperor Bao-Dai. This government collapsed with the defeat of Japan and was replaced by a purely nationalist one, the Viet-Minh, headed by Ho-Chi-Minh. The Emperor Bao-Dai abdicated and, after remaining for a short time as 'adviser' to the Ho-Chi-Minh Government, finally left the country. Shortly after, a French expeditionary corps disembarked at Saigon, and the present war began.

After five years of fighting the French have re-occupied most of the large towns, the major part of the Tonkinese rice-growing delta in the north, and about half that of Cochin-China, in the south. The Viet-Minh control about four-fifths of Vietnam and the coastline of Cambodia, by which the free passage of arms is assured between Siam and their Southern Army, in Cochin-China. Although the strength of the army of the Viet-Minh is unknown it is believed to amount approximately to 100,000 men, and to be slightly numerically inferior to the French forces which oppose it. It is increased by an incalculable number of partisans who are to all intents and purposes inoffensive peasants during the daytime hours. The Viet-Minh is well supplied with small arms and automatic weapons, mostly purchased in Siam and the Philippines and has recently obtained up-to-date artillery from China.

In 1949 'independence within the French Union' was granted to the three countries of Indo-China, and the ex-Emperor Bao-Dai, recalled from self-imposed exile, was created head of the French-sponsored Vietnamese State. It is now apparent that this move has not been successful in its intended effect, which was to rally Vietnamese dissidents under the banner of the Emperor, and thus put an end to the war.

After four years of virtual stalemate, the military situation is again fluid. Viet-Minh leaders assured me in the spring of 1950 that by the autumn of that year they would launch an all-out offensive in an attempt to drive the French from the country before the rains broke in June 1951. When, in January 1951, the proofs of this book were being corrected, the promised offensive was already four months old, and in the north the Viet-Minh, having occupied most of Tonkin, were closing in on Hanoi. It seems certain that before the book appears further important changes will have taken place.

CHAPTER I

SAIGON AND THE VIETNAMESE

IN 1949, a curtain which had been raised for the first time hardly more than fifty years ago in China, came down again for a change of scene. Low-grade clerks in air and shipping offices all over the world were given piles of leaflets and told to stamp the word 'suspended' over such place names as Shanghai, Canton and Kunming. Later they used the 'service discontinued' stamp. If you had wanted to go to China it was too late. You would have to content yourself with reading books about it, and that was as much of the old, unregenerate China as you would ever know. At this moment the scene shifters were busy, and they might be a long time over their job. When the curtain went up again it would be upon something as unrecognizable to an old China hand as to Marco Polo. And when this day came you had a feeling that curious travellers might find themselves restricted to state-conducted tours, admiring the marvels of reconstruction – the phoenix in concrete.

Now that China had passed into the transforming fire, it seemed that the experience of Far-Eastern travel, if ever to be enjoyed, could no longer be safely postponed. What then remained? Which would be the next country to undergo this process of change which was spreading so rapidly across Asia, and which would have to be seen now, or never again in its present form? I thought that Indo-China was the answer, and it was all the more interesting because, compared to the other Far-Eastern countries, so little had been written about it.

In the middle of January 1950, deciding to risk no further delays, I caught an Air France plane at Paris, bound for Saigon.

On the morning of the fourth day the dawn light daubed our faces as we came down the skies of Cochin-China. The passengers were squirming in their seats, not sleeping and not waking, and the air-hostess's trained smile came stiffly. With engines throttled back the plane dropped from sur-Alpine heights in a tremorless glide, settling in the new, morning air of the plains like a dragonfly on the surface of a calm lake. As the first rays of the sun burst through the magenta mists that lay along the horizon, the empty sketching of the child's painting book open beneath us received a wash of green. Now lines were ruled lightly across it. A yellow pencilling of roads and blue of canals.

A colonel of the Foreign Legion awoke uneasily, struggling with numbed, set facial muscles to regain that easy expression of good-fellowship of a man devoted to the service of violence. Becoming interested in something he saw below, he roused a friend, and they rubbed at the window and peered down. We were passing over a road that seemed to be strangely notched at intervals. 'The defence towers,' murmured the colonel, smiling with gentle appreciation. A few minutes later there was another moment of interest as we passed above that gauzily-traced chequer-board of fields and ditches. Down there in the abyss, unreal in their remoteness, were a few huts, gathered where the ruler-drawn lines of roads crossed each other. From them a wisp of incense curled towards us. To have been seen so clearly from this height it must have been a great, billowing cloud of smoke. There was a circle of specks in the yellow fields round the village. 'Une opération,' the colonel said. Somehow, as he spoke, he seemed linked psychically to what was going on below. Authority flowed back into the travel-weary figure. With the accession of this priestly essence he dominated the rest of the passengers.

Beneath our eyes violence was being done, but we were as detached from it almost as from history. Space, like time, anaesthetizes the imagination. One could understand what an aid to untroubled killing the bombing plane must be.

It was a highly symbolical introduction to South-East Asia.

In air travel, first impressions are stifled in banality. At Saigon, the airport — a foretaste of the world-state, and as functional as a mortuary — was followed by a bus-trip down Napoleonic boulevards to an internationalized air terminal. Then came the hotel; an unpalatial palace of the kind that looms across the road from French railway stations. So far the East was kept at bay. Grudgingly conceded a room, I flung open the shutters for a first impression of the town from a high vantage point, flushing as I did a covey of typical London house-sparrows.

Saigon is a French town in a hot country. It is as sensible to call it — as is usually done — the Paris of the Far East as it would be to call Kingston, Jamaica, the Oxford of the West Indies. Its inspiration has been purely commercial and it is therefore without folly, fervour or much ostentation. There has been no audacity of architecture, no great harmonious conception of planning. Saigon is a pleasant, colourless and characterless French provincial city, squeezed on to a strip of delta-land in the South China Seas. From it exude strangely into the surrounding creeks and rivers ten thousand sampans, harbouring an uncounted native population. To the south, the once separated China-town of Cholon has swollen so enormously as to become its grotesque Siamese twin. There are holes in the urban fabric roughly filled in with a few thousand branch and straw shacks, which are occasionally cleared by accidental fires. The better part of the city contains many shops, cafés and cinemas, and one small, plain cathedral in red brick. Twenty thousand Europeans keep as much as possible to themselves in a few tamarind-shaded central streets and they are surrounded by about a million Vietnamese and Chinese.

I breakfasted, absurdly, but after a twenty hours fast, on a long, saffron-coloured sole; pleased that the tea served with it should have a slightly earthy, hot-house flavour. This finished I went out into the mild, yellow light and immediately witnessed a sight which compensated one for Saigon's disappointingly Westernized welcome. There was a rapid, silently-swirling traffic in the streets of bicycle rickshaws mixed up with cycles; a bus, sweeping out of a side-street into the main torrent, caught a cyclist, knocked him off and crushed his machine. Both the bus driver and the cyclist were Chinese or Vietnamese, and the bus driver, jumping down from his seat, rushed over to congratulate the cyclist on his lucky escape. Both men were delighted, and the cyclist departed, carrying the wreckage of his machine and still grinning broadly. No other incidents of my travels in Indo-China showed up more clearly the fundamental difference of attitude towards life and fortune of the East and the West.

But still impatient with Saigon's centre, I plunged quickly into the side-streets. I was immediately arrested by an agent of the customs and excise, well-dressed in a kind of tropical knicker-bockers, who told me politely that from my suspicious movements he believed me to be trafficking in foreign currency. Marched discreetly to the Customs House I was searched and then, when no gold or dollars were found, shown registers by the disappointed and apologetic officials to prove by the great hoards recently recovered that they rarely misjudged their man.

From this happening it was clear that Europeans rarely leave the wide boulevards where they belong, that if they sometimes take short cuts they do so purposefully, and that to wander at haphazard looked very much to the official eye like loitering with intent. For all that, it was my intention to spend my first day or two in the Far East in just such aimless roamings, collecting sharp first impressions while the mind was still freshly receptive; before the days came when so much would no longer surprise, would be overlooked, would be taken for granted. The business of organizing the journey through the country could be attended to later.

It was clear from the first moment of picking my way through these crowded, torrid streets that the lives of the people of the Far East are lived in public. In this they are different from people in almost any other part of the world. The street is the extension of the house and there is no sharp dividing line between the two. At dawn, or, in the case of Saigon, at the hour when the curfew is lifted, people roll out of bed and make for the pavement, where there is more space, to perform most of their toilet. Thereafter they eat, play cards, doze, wash themselves, have their teeth seen to, are cupped and massaged by physicians, visit fortune-tellers; all in the street. There is none of the desire for privacy that is so strong in Europe and stronger still in the Islamic countries. Even the better houses seemed to consist on the ground floor of one large room in which the family lived communally while visitors drifted in and out through the open doors.

People took small snacks at frequent intervals, seating themselves at wayside booths decorated with painted glass screens that had perhaps been imported from Japan, as the subjects were Japanese: scowling Samurai and winged tigers. Great store was set by the decorative presentation of food. Diaphanous baby octopuses were suspended before acetylene lamps. There were tasteful groupings of sliced coxcomb about cured pigs' snouts on excellent china plates. Roast chickens and ducks, lacquered bright red, were displayed in heraldic attitudes, with gracefully arched necks, or completely flattened-out, like kippers. There were segments of pigs, sundered with geometrical precision which, after the de-naturalizing art to which they had been submitted, seemed with their brilliant, glossy surfaces as unreal as the furnishings of a toy butcher's shop. Here the appetites were solicited under frivolous rather than brutal forms.

One wondered about the origin of some of the delicacies; the ducks' heads fried in batter and the webbed feet of some wading bird or other. Were they the fruit of a laborious empirical process, appealing to palates of extraordinary refinement, since in either case fleshy sustenance was practically non-existent? Or were they, as a Vietnamese suggested, along with such traditional Chinese dishes as edible birds' nests and sharks' fins, the last resort of famine-stricken populations who gradually developed a taste for what, in the original emergency, they probably ate with the greatest repugnance? If this hypothesis is correct some of the results show an ironic twist. Bears' paws, once probably thrown to the beggars by the hunter, are now only within the reach of millionaires in the most exclusive Chinese restaurants. Saigon merchants have to pay about £50 per kilogram for first quality sharks' fins, imported from West Africa, and the birds' nests harvested from the islands of the Vietnamese coast contribute notably to the cost of the arms bought by the Viet-Minh, within whose territory this source of wealth is located.

Many people when making their purchases preferred to gamble for them with the merchants, and for this reason a bowl of dice was at the disposal of customers on most stalls. A double-or-quits basis was employed, with the odds arranged slightly in the merchant's favour. House-wives are said to gamble consistently for their shopping on days shown as favourable in their horoscopes, which means that on slightly more than fifty per cent of such occasions they return home empty handed and with the house-keeping money gone. Even the children gambled for their sweets, using miniature dice in charmingly decorated bowls. Before making a throw the child usually invoked good luck in a musical phrase, consisting, as it happened, of the first four notes of the Volga Boat Song.

Gambling is the besetting sin of the Vietnamese. It is a national mania, assuming at the great feast of the New Year almost a ritual aspect, since a day is set aside upon which the Vietnamese of all ages and ways of life gather together to stake their possessions on the fall of the dice. The underlying motive seems to be religious in character; an act of submission to destiny and with it a sacrifice; a propitiation and an expression of faith.

Since the belief in the uncontrollable gods of Fortune seems uppermost among Vietnamese credences, there is a universal demand for revelation of the future. There was an amazing variety of arrangements by which this demand was catered for. After the bashful and hesitant European tribute to the sciences of prediction, with its association of afternoon tea and church fêtes, this display of the seemingly innumerable methods of augury was an astonishing spectacle. There were any number of splendid mountebanks, unbelievably endowed to play their parts, with wise, ancient faces and the straggling, white beards of Chinese sages. Before them on the pavement were set out the instruments of their art, the cards, the curiously shaped stones, the bowl of sand, the mirrors of catoptromancy, the divining bird. Behind them the walls were spread with backcloths covered with astrological charts, diagrams of the fateful parts of the human body, the bald heads and childishly drawn faces of phrenologists the world over, the signs of the Zodiac, and the equally picturesque Chinese years which are symbolized by animals.

But to these legitimate methods of advertisement a new and, to me, improper element had, in many cases, been added; one that involved a confusion of function and an inexcusable distortion of the very essence of prognostication. This was the implication, in pictorial form, that fate can be cheated. There were warning sketches of the misfortunes that awaited those who failed to patronize the fortune-teller. Calamity had been brought up to date, for these wretched persons were being blown to pieces by a significantly mushroom-shaped explosion. Those on the other hand who had taken the precaution to keep informed of what the fates had in store for them, seemed to have been able to do something about it, since they were to be seen clasping members of the other sex under a token moonlight, or riding in what were recognizably American cars. It all seemed most illogical. If the future has been decided, then we will be atomized or achieve life's crowning success in the shape of an American car. One can't have it both ways. But perhaps a soothsayer dealing in such immutabilities would lose his business through his competitor, installed no more than three or four yards away along the street, who could show that there was some way of rubbing out the writing of destiny and that one could avoid the bombs and have the car, even if one's horoscope had arranged for it to be the other way round.

23

The Vietnamese are fascinated by dentistry, and I should imagine that the dentist's is one of the most crowded professions. Hard by the charts of the fortune-tellers, and at first sight easy to confuse with them, were those of the dentists; heads shown in cross-section, macabre and highly coloured, with suggested arrangements of gold teeth. Few races can resist embellishing the jaw with gold, and to the Vietnamese a good number of gold teeth, arranged according to accepted standards, are a discreet evidence of prosperity as well as showing a proper pride in one's appearance. The fact is that teeth left in their natural, white state have always shocked Vietnamese susceptibilities by their resemblance to the fangs of animals. Until quite recently — and even now in some country districts — they were camouflaged with black enamel. One of the old Emperors, receiving in audience a European ambassador, is said to have exclaimed in ungovernable horror, 'Who is this man with the teeth of a dog?' This mild phobia provides innumerable citizens with an artistic means of livelihood. Sometimes the teeth of both jaws are completely framed in gold, and neat shapes, often playing-card symbols, are cut in the front of the framing of each tooth, thus laying bare a minimum expanse of the original bone.

In order of popularity after the dentists come the portrait photographers. It is interesting to observe that the beautiful Vietnamese ladies, shown as specimens of the photographer's art, are less oriental than caucasian. By local standards their lips are thin and that slightly prognathous appearance, so noticeable throughout the Far East, is avoided. Only the narrow, shallow-set eyes with the Mongolian fold of the lids reveal the origin of these faces. One wonders whether those features of the oriental appearance which we regard as most typical, and perhaps least attractive, are also least attractive to them . . . or whether this is yet another instance of the all-powerful effect of the cinema for standardization.

There is no doubt that here, as elsewhere throughout the world, the films have been devastating in their influence. In these streets cinema posters had been plastered up wherever a space could be found. The subjects were bloody and horrific; a torture scene with the victim's bowels being wound out on a windlass; soldiers being hacked to death on the battlefield or blown to pieces by bombs. Always blood. Rivers of blood. When a more domestic setting was depicted, it was with a sexual motive, the male being shown in full evening dress, the woman or women in cami-knickers. These were the products of Eastern studios. The imported products, as I learned later, were nearly all Wild Westerns and their description has so much affected popular imagination as to have become almost synonymous with the movies themselves. The tendency now is not to say, 'I'm going to see a film,' but, 'I'm going to see a Far Western' or, as it becomes in Vietnamese or Chinese, a *Pá-Wé*. Buffalo Bill and his successors have been exhumed, or perhaps remade, to satisfy this local taste. One's eye is constantly assaulted by scenes of Far Western pseudo-history, interpreted by a Far Eastern imagination, in which ferocious cowboys, armed with the tommy-guns the white man is always supposed to have possessed, do terrible slaughter among small, slant-eyed and rather Vietnamese-looking Indians.

The variety of the scene was endless, and in the end exhausting. Retiring to a Chinese café, I was received by a waitress who advanced with a damp towel, held in a pair of forceps. This I took and following the example of the other patrons, wiped my face and hands with it. I ordered beer and was served a bottle with a snarling tiger on the label. It was very weak and slightly perfumed. The young lady left the change, a small pile of filthy notes, on the table. I learned later that particularly dirty notes are given to encourage customers to leave them as a tip. She then returned and joined the rest of the staff who were listening respectfully to the radio playing, 'When Irish Eyes are Smiling'. This was sometimes overwhelmed by the penetrating soprano of a Chinese crooner, broadcast from the gramophone shop over the way. Looking in its window a few moments before I had noticed among the portable gramophones and the saxophones several neatly fitted crocodile cases containing silver-mounted opium sets for the chic smoker. Many small pink lizards, with black, bulging eyes, dodged about among this splendid window display.

While I sat in the café a funeral passed. It was preceded by a man with a flute and another with a drum. The hearse was so enormous that it passed with difficulty through this narrow street. The children of the family played happily about the coffin and the principal mourners in white robes were half carried and half dragged along behind. Among the officiants was a man carrying a bowl of cigarettes for the benefit of passing spirits. Apart from the funeral the traffic in this street was limited to ponies and traps on their way to market, with bundles of ducks hanging from their axles, their heads gently stroking the surface of the road.

A yard or so from the café door a herbalist had set up a stall and was selling the small, ugly, dried-up corpses of such animals as lizards, anonymous organs hideously pickled in bottles, desiccated insects, a great selection of animals' teeth, and horns of all shapes and sizes. He also had bottles of mixture, cough cures and elixirs. The advantages of taking these were illustrated in series of pictures, on the comic-strip principle. Patients with chronic coughs were shown as deserted by all. Romance in Viet-Nam seemed to be as insecurely founded as the makers of dentifrice believe it to be in Europe. And only with his cough cured was the sufferer seen once again in the arms of his loved one. There was a medicine too that seemed to cure mediocrity, because a course of this turned the investor from a loafer into a public speaker at the microphone.

It was all very entertaining to a stranger completely fresh from the West, but from the experiences of these few hours I had learned one disturbing thing. This was that as a European I had been invisible. My eyes never met those of a Vietnamese. There was no curious staring, no gesture or half-smile of recognition. I was ignored even by the children. The Vietnamese people, described by early travellers as gay, sociable and showing a lively curiosity where strangers were concerned, have now withdrawn into themselves. They are too civilized to spit at the sight of a white man, as the Indians of Central America do sometimes, but they are utterly indifferent. It is as if a general agreement has been reached among them that this is the best way of dealing with an intolerable presence. Even the rickshaw coolie, given, to be on the safe side, double his normal fee, takes the money in grim silence and immediately looks away. It is most uncomfortable to feel oneself an object of this universal detestation, a mere foreign-devil in fact.

CHAPTER II

THE UNIVERSAL RELIGION

THE first important task of the visitor to Saigon on a journalistic or literary mission is to present his credentials at the Office of Information and Propaganda. The reason for this is that only through the sponsorship of this office will he be able to move about the country, as tourist accommodation rarely exists in the hinterland and, in any case, a circulation permit is required before any journey can be made.

On the second day after my arrival I therefore presented myself at the office in question and was received by the director, Monsieur de la Fournière. I was prepared for a certain amount of official discouragement of a project which involved travelling over as much as I could of a country where a war was in progress. At best I hoped for permission to visit one or two of the larger towns, travelling possibly by plane. At worst I feared that I might be told quite flatly that I could not leave Saigon. I was therefore amazed to find this interview going entirely contrary to my expectations. The consistent contrariness of travel is one of its fascinations, but usually it is the other way round. The difficulties and frustrations turn out to be worse than one had feared.

The director was young, expansive and enthusiastic. I had hardly begun to outline my hopes before he took over. Far from being surprised that anyone should want to travel about the country at such a time, he seemed to find the idea both reasonable and praiseworthy. Taking up a firm stance before a wall map, he began to demolish distances and dangers with bold, sweeping gestures and in rapid, idiomatic English. The outlines of the journey were sketched in, in a few firm strokes.

'Laos first, I suggest,' said the director. 'An earthly paradise. Can't imagine it, if you haven't been there. I say, first, because you

28

want to get there before the rains wash the place away. Probably be just in time. Otherwise you might find yourself stranded.'

'Mean travelling by plane,' I suggested.

'No,' the director said. 'Planes can't take off. More likely to find yourself cut off until they rebuilt the bridges at the end of the year. That is, unless you could get to the Mekong. That's why it's better to go now. No point in taking unnecessary chances.'

The director drew a short, firm line on the map with his pencil. 'First stage – Dalat. Centre of the elephant-hunting country. Go and see the Emperor. Might get him to take you on a trip. Better to go by convoy though. You're sure to find it more interesting than by air. Attacks getting infrequent these days. Anyway, nothing venture, nothing have.'

I agreed, enchanted with the breathtaking novelty of this attitude in an official. The director plunged on confidently through half-explored jungles towards the central plateaux. 'You aren't looking for a luxury tour I suppose? That is, you don't mind pigging it with soldiers occasionally?'

We hovered over Kontum. 'Malarial,' the director said. 'Rather nasty type too. Nothing to worry about though, if you keep moving. Normal hazards, that is . . . The Viet-Minh? – Well naturally you'll inform yourself on the spot. No sense in putting your head into the lion's mouth.'

We now turned our faces to the west. The director thought that it wasn't advisable to go further north, as some of the tribes hadn't made an official submission, and, in any case, the country wasn't accurately mapped. Of course, one might jolly one of the local administrators into getting up a little expedition on the side. He hesitated, evidently toying wistfully with the prospect, before putting it, reluctantly, from his mind and turning a Balboan eye to survey the few hundred miles of jungle and swamps separating us from the border of Siam.

'We want to get to the Mekong River somehow or other. Probably find a soldier or professional hunter going somewhere, in a

29

Jeep. What we call a *moyen de fortune* ... Paksí, now, that's an idea.'
With a wave of the hand the director vanquished the many bands
of vulgar pirates, as the French call them, which infest that area.
' ... or if not Paksí, Savannakhet?' Soaring above the degrees of
latitude separating these alternatives, the director whisked us back
to our cross-roads in Central Annam and set us off in another
direction, clearing with an intrepid finger a track subsequently
described as *digéri* by the jungle. 'Once you get to Mekong — ' the
director shrugged his shoulders. The adventure was practically at
an end, for only a thousand miles or so in a pirogue had to be covered
before reaching Saigon again. ' ... unless you happen to hit on a
moyen de fortune going north to Vientiane. Then, of course, if you
felt like it, and the opportunity came along, you could get across
country to Xien Khouang in the Meo country ... perhaps from
there up towards the frontier of Burma or of Yunnan.'

It was evident that the director was loth to return from these
exciting prospects to the drab dependabilities of Saigon, where the
moyen de fortune had no place.

Moyen de fortune. The phrase was beginning to touch the imagination. It was one that rang continually in my ears from that time on.
It became the keynote of my journeyings.

It was the duty of a subordinate, a Monsieur Ferry, to clothe the
director's flights of creative fancy with the sober trappings of
organization. Ferry's first glance at the suggested itinerary produced a pursing of the lips. As for the *terra incognita* to the north and
west, he couldn't say. No doubt the director knew what he was
talking about. It was his job to see that I got to Dalat, where a
Madame Schneider would take charge of me and pass me on to a
Monsieur Doustin at Ban Méthuot. After that — well — it would all
depend upon the direction I chose, and, of course, local conditions.

Monsieur Doustin, a very knowledgeable man would see to all
that. Ferry presented me with the three maps of the country,
physical, ethnographical and geological, that are given to all official
visitors and journalists. These were followed by a collection of

publications; special numbers of French magazines devoted to Indo-China and government papers on the contemporary economic and political situation. It was a highly intelligent and efficient method of presenting the French point of view, and I was mildly surprised to find that such a breadth of interests was taken for granted in the visitor.

Above all it was reassuring to gather that any aspects of this journey that might have savoured of the conducted tour looked like disappearing as soon as one was a reasonable distance from Saigon, to be replaced by the fickle and planless dispositions of fortune.

Ferry went with me to the office of the bus company that ran the service to Dalat. He was disappointed to find from the seating plan that all the best places had been sold. The choice seats were those that flanked the interior aisle, because, if the convoy happened to be attacked, you were protected in this position, to some slight measure, by the bodies of those who sat between you and the windows. I had a corner seat at the front of the bus, which afforded an excellent field of vision, accompanied, of course, with the maximum vulnerability on two sides.

Since I would have a few spare days in Saigon, Ferry had an attractive suggestion to put forward. On the following day, M. Pignon, the High Commissioner and foremost French personality in Indo-China, was to pay an official visit to the Pope of the Cao-Daïst religion, at his seat at Tay-Ninh, some fifty miles away. For this occasion, a strong military escort would be provided, and as it was a great opportunity to escape the boredom of life, hemmed-in in Saigon, anyone who could possibly do so would get themselves invited. For a journalist, it was only a matter of applying.

From Ferry's description, Cao-Daïsm sounded extraordinary enough to merit investigation. There was a cathedral, he said, that looked like a fantasy from the brain of Disney, and all the faiths of the Orient had been ransacked to create the pompous ritual, which had been grafted on an organization copied from the Roman

Catholic Church. What was more to the point at the present time, was that the Cao-Daïsts had a formidable private army with which they controlled a portion of Cochin-China. The French tolerated them because they were anti-Viet-Minh, and therefore helped, in their way, to split up the nationalist front. There were also militant Buddhist and Catholic minorities among the Vietnamese, all of whom scrapped with each other as well as the Viet-Minh, but these lacked the florid exuberance — and the power — of the Cao Daïsts. Ferry thought that it might help in extracting the maximum benefit from the experience, if I spent a few hours reading the subject up. He, therefore, presented me, on behalf of his office, with a work entitled, *Histoire et Philosophie du Cao-Daïsme* (*Bouddhisme rénové, spiritisme Vietnamien, religion nouvelle en Eurasie*), by a certain Gabriel Gobron, whose description as European representative of the faith, sounded, to my mind, a faintly commercial note. Gobron was also described as having 'quitted his fleshly envelope of suffering in 1941'.

I returned to the hotel at about seven-thirty, switched on the enormous ceiling fan and went to open the window. The square below was brightly lit and the sky was still luminous with the aftermath of sunset. As I pushed open the window, there was a momentary, slight resistance, and a violent explosion thumped in my eardrums. Across the square an indolent wreath of smoke lifted from the café tables and dissolved. Two figures got up from a table, arms about one another's shoulders and reeled away like drunkards who have decided to call it a night. Other patrons seemed to have dropped off to sleep with their heads on the tables, except for one, who stood up and went through a slow repertoire of calisthenics. A passer-by fell to his knees. Now, after several seconds, the evening strollers changed direction and from all quarters they began to move, without excitement, towards the café. I went down to see if there was anything to be done, but already the wounded were being tended in their cramped attitudes and the discipline of routine was

32

taking charge. Waiters snatched the seemingly wine-stained cloths off the tables. A boy with a stiff broom and pail came out and began scrubbing at the spotted pavement. An officer, one hand bound up in a napkin, sat clicking imperiously for service with the fingers of the other. Within ten minutes every table was full again. This hand-grenade, one of eight reported to have been thrown that evening, caused fifteen casualties — a Saigon record to date. The mortar-fire in the suburbs did not start until after ten o'clock.

Before going to sleep, I set myself to the task of extracting the doctrinal kernel in Gobron's book from its formidable husk of metaphysical jargon. I learned that Cao-Daïsm was officially founded in 1926, originating among one of the many groups of Cochin-Chinese spiritualists. The favoured congregation were informed, through the agency of an instrument known in English as the planchette, or in French as *la Corbeille-à-bec* — a platform-like device carrying a pencil upon which the hand is rested — that they were in touch with Li-taï-Pé sometimes known as the Chinese Homer, who, in the Tang Dynasty, after 'the burning of the books', re-established Chinese literature.

Li-taï-Pé began by announcing that he was the bearer of a most important message to mankind from the Lord of the Universe. He explained that he, Li-taï-Pé, in his capacity of minister to the Supreme Spirit had at various epochs and in different parts of the globe founded Confucianism, The Cult of the Ancestors, Christianity, Taoism and Buddhism. (In later messages Islam was added to this list.) The establishment of these religions, the Sage said — each of which took into consideration the customs and psychology of the races for which they were separately designed — took place at a time when the peoples of the world had little contact with each other owing to the deficient means of transport. In these days things were very different. The whole world had been explored and communications had reached a stage when any part of the globe was only a few days removed from any other part. The time had

33

clearly come, through his intervention, to bring about an intelligent re-organization, a syncretism of all these only superficially diverse creeds in a harmonious and cosmopolitan whole. The divinely inspired amalgam was to be called after the name Cao-Daï, by which the Founder of the Universe had stated that he now wished to be known.

At this early period the objects of the religion, as summarized by Li-taï-Pé, were 'to combat heresy, to sow among the peoples the love of good and the practice of virtue, to learn to love justice and resignation, to reveal to men the posthumous consequences of the acts by which they assassinate their souls'. It seems later to have been realized that the combating of heresy was an anomaly in a religion aiming at a fusion of existing doctrines, and it was abandoned.

A calendar of saints, while in the process of formation, is still meagre. It includes Victor Hugo, Allan Kerdec, Joan of Arc, de la Rochefoucauld, St. Bernard, St. John the Baptist and the Jade Emperor. These frequently communicate by spiritualistic means with the Cao-Daïst leaders, giving their rulings on such important matters of ritual as the offering of votive papers on ancestral altars. It would seem that in oriental spiritualism a curious prestige attaches to 'guides' of Western origin, paralleled, of course, by the Indian chiefs, the Buddhist monks and the Chinese sages, that play so prominent a part in equivalent practices in Europe.

From the philosophical point of view, Cao-Daïsm seems to be encountering some difficulty in its efforts to reconcile such contradictory tenets as Original Sin and Redemption with the doctrine of the soul's evolution through re-incarnation. The prescribed rites are strongly oriental in character: regular prostrations before an altar, which must include ritual candlesticks, an incense burner, offerings of fruit and a painting showing an eye (the sign of the Cao-Daï) surrounded by clouds. Occidental converts are excused by the Pope from ritual prostrations, which 'for the moment may be replaced by profound reverences'.

In Cochin-China it is a respected convention that all organized movements of persons shall start well before dawn. The intelligent intention behind this practice, which has been remarked upon by all travellers in the past, is to permit as much of the journey as possible to be covered in the coolest hours. What happens in practice, at least in these days, is that various members of the party cannot find transport to take them to the agreed place of assembly and have to be fetched; while others are not awakened by the hotel-boy, who may not have understood the arrangement, or may, on the other hand, be employing this means of passive resistance towards the hated European. In one way or another, the precious minutes of coolness are frittered away and it is dawn before one finally leaves Saigon. In this case further delays were introduced by the many security measures, the halts at road-blocks, the slow winding of the convoy round obstacles, the waiting for telephoned reports of conditions ahead from major defence-posts on the route. While we dawdled thus the sun bulged over the horizon, silhouetting with exaggerated picturesqueness a group of junks moored in some unsuspected canal. For a short time the effect of the heat was directional, as if an electric fire had been switched on in a cool room. But the air soon warmed up and within half an hour one might have been sitting in a London traffic block in a July day heat-wave.

The convoy was made up of about twenty civilian cars and was escorted by three armoured vehicles and several lorries carrying white-turbanned Algerians. The foreign visitors had been carefully separated. I rode in a Citroen and was in the charge of an English-speaking functionary, a Monsieur Beauvais, whose task it was, I gathered, to provide a running commentary of the trip, throwing in, occasionally, in accordance with the official line of the moment, a few words in praise of Cao-Daïsm. In this he was somewhat frustrated by a colleague sitting in the front seat, who, being unable to speak English and assuming that I did not understand French, contributed an explosion of disgust, salted with such expressions as *merde* and *dégolasse*, whenever he overheard a mention of the words Cao-Daï. However, even from the French point of view it did not really matter, as the official attitude was just then in the process of switching round once more. Beauvais, too, soon stopped worrying about his official job. What he was really interested in was English literature and in particular English civilization as presented by John Galsworthy, which contrasted so nostalgically with the barbarous life of a government employee in Cochin-China.

As soon as the convoy was really under way it began to travel at high speed. Except where we were forced to slow down for road-blocks the Citroen was doing a steady sixty m.p.h. The deserted paddy-fields through which our road ran were the colour of putty and the sunshine reflected blearily from the muddy water. As we passed, congregations of egrets launched themselves into the air, rising straight up in a kind of leap, assisted with a few indolent wing-beats and then settling down uneasily in the same place again. There were distant villages, raised on hillocks above the water, and solitary villas — Mediterranean-looking, with their verandas and flaking stucco, except for the china lions in the garden, grinning at us absurdly, and the roof with its facetious dragon or sky-blue ceramic dolphins. Sometimes such houses had been burned out. There were no signs of human life. The populace had evidently received orders, as for the passage of the Son of Heaven, or of one of the Divine Emperors, to keep indoors. Sometimes, at what I suppose were considered danger points, lines of Vietnamese auxiliaries stood with their backs to the road, rifles at the ready. At short intervals we passed beneath the watch-towers; squat structures, made of small Roman-looking bricks, shaded with Provençal roofs, and surrounded with concentric pallisades of sharpened bamboo staves. In theory, the whole length of the road can be swept by machine-gun fire from the towers, whose defenders are also supposed to patrol the surrounding area. These pigmy forts lent a rather pleasant accent, a faintly Tuscan flavour, to the flat monotony of the landscape.

After about thirty-five miles we entered Cao-Daï territory, in which, according to my official guide, complete tranquillity had been restored. His friend said something about bandits and rats, and spat out of the window. I asked why the towers were even closer together and why machine-gunners squatted behind their weapons which were pointed up every side-road. Monsieur Beauvais said there was no harm in making sure, sighed, and brought the subject back again to the amenities of upper-class, rural England.

Our first Cao-Daïst town was Trang-Bang, where a reception had been arranged. There seemed to be thousands of children. For miles around, the countryside must have been combed for them. They had been washed, dressed in their best and lined up beside the road, clutching in one hand their bunches of flowers of the six symbolical colours and giving the fascist salute with the other. The spontaneous acclamations were tremendous and the children, who all looked like jolly, china dolls, were, I am sure, enjoying themselves enormously, without having the faintest idea what it was all about. Monsieur Beauvais seemed much embarrassed by the fascist salute, from which his friend, however, derived grim pleasure.

The notables of Trang-Bang, dressed in their best formal silks, were on the spot to mix with the visitors. In this country, which owes all its civilization to China, the best years of one's life are its concluding decades. The dejection that encroaching age stamps so often in the Western face — the melancholy sense of having outlived one's usefulness — are replaced here with a complacency of spirit and a prestige that increases automatically with the years. Cao-Daïsm was founded by retired functionaries and professional men, who see to it that no one who is not a grandfather ever manages to get his foot on the bottom rung of the ladder. Going up to one of these happy old men, I complimented him on the appearance of the children, who were still cheering and saluting. The old man's face crinkled in a smile of ineffable wisdom. He explained that it was the result of a vegetarian diet. Vegetarianism, he explained, was one of the tenets of the Cao-Daïst faith.

'Of course, we don't insist on our converts making a sudden break with their bad habits. We start them off with a meatless day a week and gradually improve them until a full release is attained.'

'And have all your people attained a full release?'

'Almost miraculously, yes,' said the old man delightedly. 'They turned their backs on the squalid past, almost overnight. Why, even five-year-old children implored their parents never to let them see meat or fish again. It was a wonderful experience.'

We chatted pleasantly for some time. My friend informed me that he was a fourth grade official of the Cao-Daïst Legislative Corps, a lawyer with the rank of Bishop, and that he expected shortly to be promoted to Inspector-General of the third grade, carrying the dignity of Principal Archbishop. After that the way remained clear to the final attainable splendour, the culmination of all the efforts of his mature years, the rank of Cardinal-Legislator – only five grades removed from the Pope himself. There would be many more austerities to be practised before that glittering goal could be reached, but what did it matter? At his age one could do without almost anything. That was the best of it, the old man pointed out, smiling gleefully. All those abstentions – the renunciation of relations with one's wife, for instance – they came into force only in the higher grades. The turn of the screw was put on gently, so that by the time you had to give things up for the Kingdom of God, you were pretty well ready to give them up anyway. It was all so humane.

It might have been, but what about the children with all this voluntary abnegation, practised almost as soon as they were out of the cradle? The answer was given by a Cao-Daïst doctor of the ninth grade and a member of the Charity Corps, in which he had reached the rather low rank of *fidèle-ardent*.

'We suffer from malnutrition in all its forms,' he said. 'Just look at the children, Look at the condition of their skins. Covered from head to foot with sores, most of them.'

I told him that those I saw looked the picture of health.

'Well, naturally,' the doctor said. 'You don't expect them to put the pellagra cases in the front line, do you?'

Beauvais was embarrassed once more, before we left. There was a burst of heavy mortar-fire. Beauvais thought it was miles away and that the wind was carrying the sound in our direction. But there was no wind in Cochin-China — at least while I was there.

At Tay-Ninh we were first received by the administrator, dressed in a gorgeous old mandarin's coat of dull blue silk, on which the yellow flowers and medallions were seen rather faintly, like the watermarks on superior stationery. The administrator had a small, aged face which, in the local manner, he kept under conspicuous control. Whenever he smiled, which in the course of his duties he did frequently, he laid bare a row of ivory hearts in the background of his gold-framed teeth. Having welcomed, with unquenchable vitality, each member of the visiting party — a task occupying at least half an hour — he darted away, and reappeared with an amateur ciné-camera with which he exposed a few feet of film on each of the principal French dignitaries. Champagne and biscuits were now served, and as polite interest in one's surroundings seemed to be encouraged, I wandered through the ground-floor rooms of the administrator's typically European villa.

The administrator had thought fit to advertise the modernity of his outlook by furnishing his house in Western style. The tables, with their Liberty runners, the chairs, the Indian rugs, the thick, greasy glaze of the pottery, recalled a Tottenham Court Road show-room. But progressive Easterners of this type find it almost impossible to prevent a dash of the local flavour intruding itself into the flat and tasteless 'good taste' of their European décor. Even when the interloper is without other merit, I find it at least piquant. In this case the administrator had decorated one of his otherwise impeccable Heal walls with the pictures of the four vices. Here, where the reproduction Van Gogh sunflower should have been, were the stern warnings, to be seen on sale in all Saigon art shops, to the gambler, the drunkard, the opium smoker and the voluptuary. The administrator had probably been taken in because the technical production of these masterpieces was typically Western and curiously photographic in its flat, bluish monochrome. But the subjects themselves, gentle, contemplative almost, and not in the least horrific, were as Vietnamese as pictures of Highland cattle are English. The only detail I can remember of these somnolent transgressions was the fine mosquito-net with which the bed in the last scene was equipped. Viet-Nam needs a Rowlandson or a Hogarth to deter its sinners. Gin Lane in oriental guise would sell a million copies.

The next item on the programme was a visit to the cathedral, where, according to the description of the ceremonies I read in next day's paper, His Holiness, Pope Pham-Cong-Tac, whose name means 'the Sun shining from the South', awaited us, beneath the golden parasol, attired in his uniform of Grand-Marshal of the Celestial Empire. He was carrying his Marshal's baton, at the sight of which, according to Cao-Daïst literature, all evil spirits flee in terror.

Physically, the Pope looked hardly able to support the weight of his dignity. He was a tiny, insignificant figure of a man, with an air of irremediable melancholy. His presence was, in any case, overshadowed by the startling architectural details of the cathedral, for the design of which he himself had been responsible.

From a distance this structure could have been dismissed as the monstrous result of a marriage between a pagoda and a Southern baroque church, but at close range the vulgarity of the building was so impressive that mild antipathy gave way to fascinated horror. This cathedral must be the most outrageously vulgar building ever to have been erected with serious intent. It was a palace in candy from a coloured fantasy by Disney; an example of fun-fair architecture in extreme form. Over the doorway was a grotesquely undignified piece of statuary showing Jesus Christ borne upon the shoulders of Lao Tse and in his turn carrying Confucius and Buddha. They were made to look like Japanese acrobats about to begin their act. Once inside, one expected continually to hear bellowing laughter relayed from some nearby Tunnel of Love. But the question was, what had been Pham-Cong-Tac's intention in producing a house for this petrified forest of pink dragons, this hugger-mugger of symbolism, this pawnbroker's collection of cult objects? Was he consciously catering to the debased and credulous tastes of his flock? Or could it be that visible manifestations of religious energy on the part of men who have lived lives entirely divorced from art must always assume these grotesque forms?

In support of the latter theory it is significant that the founders and directors of this movement were all men who had spent most of their lives in the harness of a profession or in the civil service. To have been successful as they had been in these walks of life would have left them little time to cultivate taste, if they happened to have been born without it. I was interested, subsequently, to note in the ensuing ritual that, although the Governor of South Viet-Nam kowtowed energetically before the altar, no attempt was made to induce Monsieur Pignon, the High Commissioner, to do so. Profiting by the experiences of even the Emperors of China and Annam with foreign ambassadors, the Cao-Daïsts have recognized the seemingly congenital disinclination of Europeans to performing the kowtow, so that Western converts are excused this form of devotional exercise. Monsieur Pignon did, however, consent to hold lighted joss-sticks between his clasped fingers and incline his head, even if somewhat distantly, before the massed symbols of Lao-Tse, Confucius, Buddha and Jesus Christ.

The siting of the Cao-Daïst Rome at Tay-Ninh was by no means accidental. A few miles from the town a single symmetrical mountain humps up suddenly from the plain, rising from what must be practically sea-level to 3000 feet. As there is not another hillock for fifty miles in any direction to break the flat and featureless monotony of Cochin-China, this darkly forested plum-pudding silhouette is quite remarkable. In a part of the world where every religion has its sacred mountain, such an eminence is obviously irresistible. Consequently it has been since dimmest antiquity a place of revelation. Its slopes are said to be riddled with caves, both natural and artificial, housing at one time or other the cult objects of numerous sects. It was most unfortunate from my point of view that the holy mountain itself was possessed not by the Cao-Daïsts but the Viet-Minh. This prevented a most interesting visit, although it was in any case improbable that revolutionary iconoclasm had spared the relics of those ancient beliefs.

But there were other survivals of Tay-Ninh's notable past to be seen in the streets of the town itself; pathetic-looking groups of Chams in the penitents' robes of the rank and file of the Cao-Daïst faithful. At the end of the Middle Ages the Annamese, moving southwards from China, had overwhelmed, absorbed, digested the brilliant civilization of Champa. Now only a few particles of that shattered community remained. They were scattered about in a few isolated villages in Cochin-China and Cambodia, and here they had clung to their holy place.

These Chams were aboriginal Malayo-Polynesians, the only group of that race to have accepted the civilization of Indian colonizers in the remote past. They made a great impression upon Marco Polo, but judging from the account of the Dominican, Gabriel de San Antonio, who visited them in the sixteenth century, there was a nightmarish element in their civilization. It was brilliant but unbalanced and psychopathic, like that of the Aztecs. The Chams could place themselves in the vanguard of the technical achievement of their day, devise new agricultural methods, undertake vast irrigational projects, encourage the arts and sciences. And yet one half of the racial mind never developed. Stone age beliefs, like grim Easter-Island faces, were always there in the background. On certain days, San Antonio says, they sacrificed over six thousand people, and their gall was collected and sent to the King, who bathed in it to gain immortality.

These degenerate survivors of that glittering, sinister past were Brahmanists or Muslims, or both combined. The metaphysical appetite of South-East Asia is insatiable and its tolerance absolute. The modern Chams find no difficulty in worshipping the Hindu Trinity, *the linga*, the bull of Siva, a pythoness, Allah — who is believed to have been an eleventh century Cham king — plus Mohammed and a number of uncomprehended words taken from Muslim sacred invocations and regarded as the names of deities, each with its special function. They are inclined to give their children such names as Dog, Cat, Rat to distract from them the attentions of evil spirits. For this reason there were several Cham kings named excrement. One assumes that the Chams will have little difficulty in adding to their already enormous catalogue of rituals and credences those few new ones imposed by the Cao-Daïsts.

From the newspaper account I learned that on leaving the cathedral, 'preceded by a unicorn, a dragon and a band playing *une marche précipiteuse*, escorted by a numerous suite carrying the car of the Buddha, the portraits of Sun-Yat-Sen and Victor Hugo, and the statue of Joan of Arc', we marched to the Vatican. The streets, said the account, were lined with adepts dressed in togas of red, blue, yellow and white. In the general commotion I must have missed some of this. I should have much enjoyed the processional unicorn, which I failed to see either then or at any other time. I recall, however, the dragon; a fine capering beast which on its hind legs leaped up into the air and tossed its head most desperately to the jerky rhythm of fife and drum. The report failed to mention a guard of honour of the Cao-Daïst army, equipped with well-made wooden imitation rifles. When I mentioned the matter of the toy guns, I was told that it was out of respect for the sanctity of the surroundings.

The Vatican was the administrator's villa all over again, except that His Holiness had an evident liking for grandmother clocks. Fanned by turkey's feathers, hosts and guests exchanged lengthy platitudes of goodwill, which at random were broken off for a stroll in the garden, or a visit to the champagne bar, and then renewed without the slightest embarrassment, as if no interruption had taken place.

At the banquet which followed, I sat next to a Cao-Daïst colonel, who informed me, with a secret, knowing smile, that he was head of the secret police of this Universal Religion of the Age of Improved Transport. The meal was vegetarian and although the French visitors had been told that they could order eggs if they wished, no one dared to do so. There were seven courses, six of which were based on soya, which I first mistook for some kind of overstewed and tasteless meat, that had, somehow or other, been served by mistake. The Colonel and I got on very well together and helped each other liberally to soya. Although intoxicants are equally forbidden to the Cao-Daïst faithful, I noticed many of the dignitaries present stretching the point, and the Colonel, himself, had several helpings of red wine, after which he genially discussed the technique of his profession.

On my left was a young man who asked me if I was familiar with the works of Victor Hugo. I nodded, without emphasis, barely remembering the first lines of a poem beginning: Mon père, ce héros au sourire si doux —

'I am a re-incarnation of a member of the poet's family,' the young man said. I congratulated him and asked if he also wrote. The modest reply was that he would have considered it an impertinence to do so after the tremendous reputation of his kinsman, who, after all, was generally admitted to be the greatest poet who ever lived. Did I, by the way, realize that the master's sublimest works had been written after his death, or, as he put it, since dis-incarnation? My informant then went on to explain that he was the official editor of Victor Hugo's posthumous work, a task simplified by the fact that only certain of the highest ranking members of the hierarchy were permitted mediumistic contact with such saints as Li-Taï-Pé, Joan of Arc and the poet. All Victor Hugo's communications were given in verse and this, plus his life's work, would ultimately form a corpus to be memorized by candidates for high office. Much intrigued by this adaptation of the old Chinese system of literary examinations for the mandarinate, I asked for a sample of the poet's most recent production and was given the account of the Creation as described in a seance to the Ho-Phap, or Pope. I reproduce a few lines.

HO-PHAP (*referring to Victor Hugo's use of the word 'water' in his description of the creation*):

> Est-ce bien la forme de l'eau parlée dans la genèse chré-
> tienne?

VICTOR HUGO:

> Oui, c'est cette sorte de gaz qu'on appelle hydrogène,
> Plus ou moins dense qui fait la partie la plus saine,
> Dire que l'Esprit de Dieu nage au-dessus des eaux,
> C'est à ce sens qu'il faut comprendre le mot,
> Avec son astral qui est de lumière,
> Il anime par sa chaleur ces inertes matières,
> Une couche d'oxygène produit, se met en action,
> Le contact des deux gaz donne une détonation.
> — Mais vous avez, Ho-Phap, une crampe à la main,
> Renvoyons notre causérie pour demain.

At the very hour when these junketings were in progress at Tay-Ninh, French troops were under fire from Cao-Daïsts in the Province of Mytho, about seventy miles to the south. The French said that the Cao-Daïsts had turned to banditry and that a battle had developed when they had called upon them to give up their arms. The Pope, Pham-Cong-Tac, promptly repudiated all responsibility, pointing out that the insurgents had left his fold and joined one of the eleven schismatic sects that refused to recognize his authority. The schismatic sect can be as politically useful to the Cao-Daïsts as a racial minority elsewhere.

CHAPTER III

SUNDAY DIVERSIONS

BACK in Saigon I had a day to spare before the real journey began. It was Sunday, and in the morning I walked slowly to the Jardins Botaniques. Clusters of Vietnamese beauties on bicycles were bound in the same direction, floating, it seemed, rather than pedalling, as the trains of their silk gowns trailed in the air behind them. The robes worn by Vietnamese ladies recall those of ancient China, before the sumptuary laws imposed by the Manchus. White silk is the material preferred, and as Vietnamese girls are always utterly immaculate and addicted to swan-like movements, the whole effect is one of unearthly elegance. The park was full of these ethereal creatures, gliding in decorous groups through the shady paths, sometimes accompanied by gallants, who, in their cotton shirts, shorts and trilby hats, provided a sadly anticlimactic spectacle. The girls thus arrayed belonged to the classes which included shop assistants and all ranks above. Domestic servants, or *boyesses*, as they are pleasantly known by the French, were dressed just as charmingly, but more simply, in pyjamas only. It is curious that members of the lower social strata are permitted to protect themselves from sunstroke by conical straw hats, whereas the bourgeoisie, although employing every hair-style, from an uncontrollable torrent of tresses reaching to the waist to a permanent wave, do not allow themselves a head-covering. In passing it should be observed that the kind of coolie-straw that a girl wears for her best is a beautifully made piece of headgear, of lacquered, semi-diaphanous material, lightly stitched over a framework of circular ribs. It is held in position for Sunday strolling with a strap of silk with a bow at each end and a third bow under the chin. The result is extremely coquettish and I felt sure that the shop girl or typist must regret being prevented, by her social position, from wearing such a becoming adornment.

Photography is a popular excuse for these decorous *fêtes-champêtres* of Saigon. There were several accepted backgrounds for portraiture which were in constant use. The archaeological museum is housed in a pagoda-like building and a group of legendary maidens loitered constantly in the vicinity, awaiting their turns to be photographed, caressing the snout of one of the decorative dragons. Another favoured site was the lake verge. The water had dried away leaving a few inches of liquid coated with a patina of scum, through which unsupported lotus flowers thrust a yard into the air. There was a punt, a standard photographic property, which could be set adrift only with great difficulty, in which the lady to be photographed balanced herself, looking mysterious and rather forlorn, while the photographer camouflaged the painter with lotus leaves before taking his shot. The moment the exposure had been made, the punt was hauled in, another lady floated into photogenic position while her predecessor drifted away at the side of her escort.

The natural history of the Jardins Botaniques is charming rather than exciting. One does not look for sinister manifestations of nature-in-the-tropics in a public park, but I was surprised at the absence of all troublesome insects, such as wasps or flies. A few undistinguished butterflies fluttered about, looking like those to be seen on any English heath. There were few flowers, but sprays of purple blossoms, with thick velvet-looking petals, sprouted from the trunk and thicker branches of one of the trees. Since it was a local tree, there was no way of discovering its name. The only trees labelled were exotic specimens from Dakar and Madagascar, so presumably one would have to go to these places to study the vegetation of Indo-China. Cranes were building their nests in the topmost branches and a beautiful and very Chinese sight they made, with the sun shining through the lavender-grey plumage of their wings against the pale green foliage. Somewhere, too, just above my head, wherever I went, but always invisible, a bird produced tirelessly a single, mournful note. It was as if a cuckoo had flown into a great, hollow jar and there repeated incessantly the first note of its call. This was a sound which later I was to realize is hardly ever absent from the background of Indo-China.

The deportment of the Vietnamese in such places is beyond reproach. There is a gently-repressive, Sunday-school atmosphere. Docilely, the visitors admired the caged deer; threw dice for ice-cream — folding the paper containers and stowing them in their pockets; viewed in silent satisfaction their choice of the eight original films of 'Charlot', shown by a 9.5 mm., hand-cranked cinema contraption, rigged up on a bicycle; patronized the fortune-tellers, who counted their pulses and examined their eyeballs with magnifying glasses before disclosing the edicts of the fates; bought tributes of artificial flowers from a kiosk bearing on its pale blue awning, for decorative purposes only, the words, 'Employez le pâté et savon dentifrice de . . .' the manufacturer's name having been removed.

It was all very delightful and civilized.

Down by the river, where I went in the afternoon, the feeling was very different. Half the Vietnamese population of Saigon lives on the water and whenever I happened to be in Saigon, and had an hour or two to spare, I used to go there to enjoy the spectacle of the vivid, turbulent life of the common people. In my many walks along the river bank, I never, except within fifty yards of the *Cercle Nautique*, saw another European.

The original reason for taking to the water must have been that it was just as cheap to build a small sampan as a hut, the risk of fire was lessened, and there was no question of ground rent. Moreover, if one liked an occasional change of scene, nothing was easier than to move. The temperature on the river is quite a number of degrees cooler than in the town and one can take a dip whenever one feels like it. The laundry problem is facilitated for the womenfolk, and by keeping a few lines in the water one can occasionally catch a fish. All in all, there seems to be no real excuse for living anywhere else. Owing to the immense population now living in sampans on the Chinese

facing: WATER-PEDDLERS ON THE CHINESE CREEK

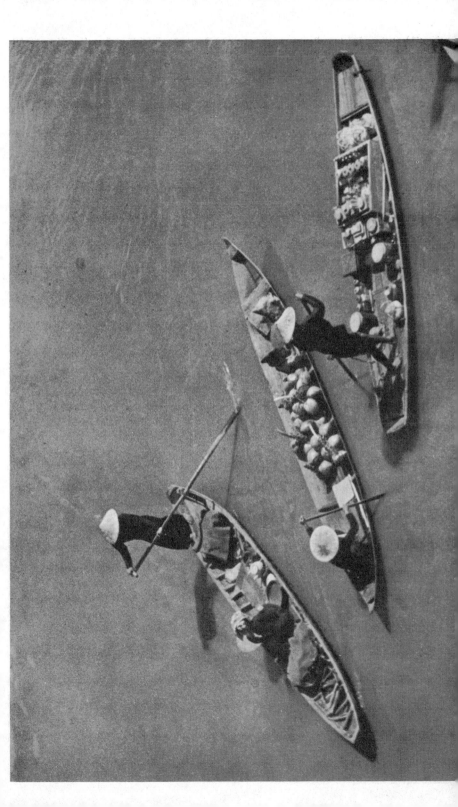

Creek and its tributaries, numerous floating services have come into being to cater for them. There are sampan-restaurants, with cauldrons of noodle soup; water sellers who carry drinking water in the white-enamelled bottoms of their boats; shops of all kinds, and, of course, river-borne magicians.

To reach the quay-side meant a walk of not more than five minutes up the main street, the Rue Catenat. It was five o'clock, and by this hour possible to risk the sun and walk out in the open, along the water's edge, where the dockers were loading and unloading cargoes. A quarter of a mile away, across the river, was no-man's-land. One could go there during the daytime, but at night the Viet-Minh sometimes appeared and fired mortar-shells into the centre of the town. Previously, the further bank had been clustered with huts, but the French had cleared them away, thus aggravating the refugee problem. At about this time the dockers had their evening meal and the owners of the eating booths had accordingly set a long line of tables. On each table stood three bottles, one of Tiger beer flanked on each side by brilliantly coloured mineral waters. Awaiting the customers, in bowls of attractive designs, were semi-hatched eggs with small apertures cut in their sides to allow of choice in the degree of incubation.

I walked on to the waterfront café at the Point des Blageurs and sat down to enjoy the scene in comfort. The animation with which I was surrounded was, in its way, different from and more intense than anything I had experienced before. One has been accustomed to crowds, to the spectacle of vast gatherings of people in the streets, in places of entertainment, in railway stations or restaurants. But such crowds have all been, more or less, engaged in a similar kind of activity. Here it was the diversity of occupation that was so remarkable. There must have been many hundreds of people in sight, all busily living their own lives and most of them independently of the actions of others in their immediate neighbourhood.

There were several junks moored just off-shore. They had gardens on their decks, with domestic pets, a few cocks and hens, a

49

canary in the cage, and flowers growing in packing cases. Somebody was constantly pottering round these deck-gardens, watering the flowers or looking to see if the hen had laid an egg. Through openings in the junks' sides one could observe incidents from the domestic routine. Occasionally a naked child came flying through in an attempt to land on top of another child, splashing about in the water beneath. There were people sprawled about under the canopies of fifty sampans, playing cards, dicing, chatting, sleeping. People came ashore and exercised pigs on leads along the water-front. A score of anglers drooped motionless over their lines, the most singular of these being one who tried his luck through a manhole cover in the street. Professional fishermen worked from sampans, lowering into the water large triangular nets at the end of levers. One would have expected this process occasionally to produce a spectacular fish; but not so. I never saw anything longer than three inches come out of the water. The prawn fishers seemed to have better luck. They worked up to their knees in black slime, groping about with their wicker baskets in the mud. It was filthy work, but they at least caught prawns. Women, if they were not cooking, were washing themselves, leaving no part of their persons unvisited, but completing the process in such a way that not an unwonted inch of their form was displayed. For no particular reason that one could see, people fidgeted continually with junks and sampans, shifting them here and there, and then replacing them in exactly the same position as before. In doing so they narrowly avoided collisions with lightermen who were ferrying passengers to and from the ships in the port. Hawkers passed incessantly, drawing attention to their wares with melodious cries or the beating of appropriate gongs. They were ignored by innumerable loafers who hung about, giving advice on a dozen gambling games that were in progress. In the background musical-comedy river-boats thrashed slowly past. They had triple decks and tall narrow funnels, their balustrades were as ornate as the balconies of New Orleans, and they were smothered in red Chinese characters.

CHAPTER IV

A CONVOY TO DALAT

THE Dalat convoy left at 5 a.m. Suspecting — as indeed proved
to be the case — that the hotel boy would not call me, I lay
awake most of the night, perspiring gently, listening to the
occasional explosion of distant mortar bombs and to the rumble of
army trucks patrolling the streets. I was travelling in a shirt and
shorts, and my bag was packed with the bare essentials for a journey
of unknown length: a pair of long trousers and a jacket for formal
occasions (if any), a mosquito net, anti-malarial tablets, insect-
repellent cream and a camera. A French acquaintance had suggested,
in all seriousness, that I should carry a pistol; not so much for self-
defence as to be able to Save The Last Bullet for Myself, should I
fall into the hands of the Viet-Minh. This suggestion I had rejected.
I was carrying a travelling permit obtained for me by the Office of
Information, importantly styled, 'Ordre de Mission', in which I
was described as 'Lewis Norman, Écrivain Anglais, habilité par
Mm. Jonathan Cape, Thirty Bedford Square'. This paper had to be
frequently renewed, the description suffering in consequence both
compression and distortion. In the end I became 'Louis Norman
Thirsty Bedford', and it was under this agreeable title that I finished
my journeyings.

At 4.30, feeling not particularly refreshed, I got up, dressed
quickly and went down into the square to find a *cyclo*. As usual,
there were three or four, drowsing over their handle-bars, outside
the hotel. I sat down in the chair, arranging my bag awkwardly
under my legs and we pushed off. As *cyclos* are not supposed to
understand French one does not give them verbal directions. They
just pedal straight ahead and one flaps with either hand when the
time comes to turn.

We found the civilian part of the convoy in the process of assembly behind the red-brick cathedral. The spectral figures of my fellow-passengers lurked by the bus, leaving it until the last possible moment before getting in. I was the only European present and no one took the slightest notice of me. In these times the whites preferred to travel by air.

The bus was equipped internally to carry about twice the number of passengers one would have supposed from its external dimensions. This had been achieved, quite simply, by fitting seats that would have accommodated a ten-year-old child in comfort and by arranging it so that one's legs were clenched firmly by the seat in front. I thanked heaven, in the circumstances, that I was travelling with the silent and introverted Vietnamese and not, for instance, a busful of excited Arabs. The travellers were dressed in their workaday clothes of black calico, except for the driver, who wore black satin pyjamas embroidered with the Chinese characters for good luck, and a most expensive looking, golden-brown, velour hat. He was about five feet in height and weighed, perhaps, eight stone; physically somewhat ill-endowed, it seemed, to control this overloaded juggernaut. Very sensibly, I thought, watching him hauling on his mighty wheel, a notice pinned to his back asked passengers, in two languages, not to distract his attention by talking to him.

Sitting next to me was a well-preserved lady in middle age. Her hair was arranged in a complicated chignon, set off with jewelled pins in the form of small daisy-like flowers. Having neglected her fine set of teeth, the white bone was showing slightly through their coating of black enamel. She was heavily perfumed with jasmine and as most of the female passengers showed a predilection for such pungent attars, the atmosphere of the bus was soon heavy with a funereal sweetness. My travelling companion carried a small box, like a powder compact, from which, shortly after we moved off, she selected betel nut and began to chew. At quite long intervals she leaned over me and shot a thin stream of juice through the window. When later we stopped I noticed that the wind-carried splash of orange betel against the blue side of the bus was, in its way, not undecorative.

Before and behind us the convoy stretched as far as the eye could see. It seemed to be composed entirely of the lorries of Chinese merchants. They looked like motorized covered wagons with their tops of plaited bamboo. Their sides were painted with the usual Chinese characters for good fortune, peace, longevity and riches. It was a bad thing in an attack, they said, to be sandwiched between Chinese lorries, which were said to panic in the most unphilosophical manner at the first shot fired. At each end of the convoy there were armoured cars, and on the rare occasions when the road was wide enough, they came fussing along the line of the convoy, like hens marshalling nervous chicks. The trouble was that the road rarely permitted the passage of two vehicles abreast and, naturally enough, it was in the narrow sectors, where the convoy might be spread out over five miles of road, with the armoured cars wedged in immutable position, that the ambushes took place.

For the first thirty or forty miles out of Saigon we were still in the flat, rice-growing country. We passed many solitary villas by the roadside – the 'big-houses' of Cochin-China, with dragons of smoky-blue china undulating like sea-serpents across their roofs and a menagerie of ceramic lions and elephants in their gardens. Vietnamese animal figures are never intimidating in their aspect. Their expressions are always genial, even flippant, and one suspects that the intention is humorous as well as ornamental. The rooftops seemed to be the favourite place to assemble china figures of all kinds; perhaps because they would be silhouetted in this way to the best possible effect. The best examples included jovial, bearded philosophers in the act of beating tambourines, with one leg skittishly raised, or else ogling ladies who enticed them coquettishly. Souvenirs of family visits to the seaside perhaps. Who knows? At all events most of the houses were deserted, or had been requisitioned by the military; but where the family remained there was invariably a platform on a pole placed somewhere near the front door with offerings to the spirits: a bowl with rice, a pot of tea, joss-sticks, even a packet of cigarettes.

This was the Borri country, where the first Jesuit missionaries had set out upon their labours, enchanted with the civility of their reception, although perturbed by the prevalence of devils. 'They walk about the Cities so familiarly in human Shapes, that they are not at all fear'd but admitted into Company.'

The villages were stockaded, with strong points at the angles of the fortifications. Inside there were towers and *miradors* as they are called locally; structures like oil derricks supporting a machine-gun post. Sometimes truncated towers had been built into the roofs of the larger houses. It was said that one could enter these villages with safety only in daytime, and some of them, not even then, unless in convoy. The surface of the road here had been ruined by the habit of Viet-Minh sympathizers of digging trenches across it. For miles on end convoy speed had to be reduced to a walking pace as we bumped across the endless corrugations produced by this rustic sabotage. The landscape on the village outskirts was peaceful enough, with the ancestral tombs scattered about and taking up, incidentally, a great deal of cultivatable space. The more imposing tombs had been built on what slight eminence could be found and great attention had been paid, for the benefit of the ancestral shades, to the view they afforded. It was evident that a certain amount of landscape gardening had occasionally been attempted in the vicinity. The tombs themselves were of pleasantly weathered stone, sometimes charmingly tiled. Often it looked as though a group of villas had been engulfed by some terrestrial convulsion, leaving only the flat roofs with their ornamental balustrades above the ground.

Our first stop was Bien Hoa, where all the passengers got out and bought food. I had not yet reached the stage when I was able to fall in with the scheme of things and buy myself a bowl of Chinese soup or a dried and salted fish, so I went hungry. I was soon to be cured of this reluctance of self-adaptation to a new environment, for I never remember any subsequent journey during the whole of my travels in the country when the hour of departure was late enough to permit me to get breakfast, or rather *petit déjeuner*. It would not, in any case, have been easy to eat in comfort at Bien Hoa as a whole tribe of beggars came out of the village and performed a mournful pilgrimage down the convoy displaying their ghastly sores. Among these were many cases of elephantiasis. The presence of these beggars seemed, by the way, to disprove the French allegation that the Vietnamese never give alms.

It was here too that I noticed that the telephone wires had been colonized by innumerable spiders, which had woven their strands about the wires in such a way as to incorporate them in an enormous, elongated web. At evenly spaced intervals a four-inch spider watched over the territory allotted to it in this vast co-operative enterprise, but as no flies were caught within my sight during the half-hour we waited at Bien-Hoa, I was unable to draw any Bruce-like inspiration in support of collective effort.

Soon after Bien Hoa we plunged into the forest. For many miles it had been cleared for perhaps a hundred yards on each side of the road. Then suddenly the jungle returned, pressing about us so close that the slender, bowed-over bamboos stroked the bus's roof as we passed beneath them. When faced with the tropical forest the problem of the writer and painter is alike. The forest is fussy in detail, lacking in any unifying motive and tends to be flatly monochromatic. There is a baroque superabundance of forms, which, unfortunately, do not add up to a Churrigueresque altar-piece. In the depths of our jungle there may have been superb orchids and even certain flowers indigenous to this part of the world whose blooms are several feet across. But all we could see was a dusty confusion of leaves like one of those dense and often grimy thickets cultivated by people in England to safeguard their privacy.

There was a single moment of excitement, when a colossal boa-constrictor slithered across the road ahead of us. It was a serpent of the kind one has always seen coiled motionless in the corner of its cage at the zoo. Now it was quite extraordinary to see one in such purposeful motion. Somehow the driver missed it, stopped, reversed and was just too late to run over its tail, which was withdrawn with a mighty flexing of the muscles. Behind us the following Chinese lorry went charging into the fernery to avoid us. There were none of the bellowing recriminations one comes to expect at such times. The Chinese lorry was driven out under its own power and on we went.

The midday stop was at a village rather romantically named, I thought, Kilometre 113. There was a ring of the frontier outpost about this that stirred the imagination. We were still in the forest, which had thinned out a little, and we were perhaps a thousand feet above sea-level. Strewn about all over the place were huge, smooth, mysterious looking boulders. Some of them had huts built on the top with ladders leading up to them, and others even small forts. It was here that I saw for the first time a sight imagined by many Westerners to be extremely typical of South-Eastern Asia — the uncovered female breast. There was a Moï village somewhere close by and several Moï girls were hanging about the garrison's sleeping quarters. They were thin and under-nourished looking, with, however, the invulnerable torso of the Polynesian, wreathed in this case only by garlands of small violet-coloured flowers. Several groups of Moïs of both sexes padded past down the road while we were there. They looked dirty, degenerate and miserable, the inevitable fate, as I later learned, of these tribes when they come into contact with civilization. Several of them, with grotesque effect, wore British battledress tops but had bare posteriors.

There was an eating place in the village that was serving pork and peas — take it or leave it — and where you could buy weak beer at the equivalent of five shillings a bottle. Here, too, the frontier atmosphere was very marked and obviously enjoyed by the soldiers who waved aside the eating utensils and preferred to manipulate their victuals with a clasp knife and a chunk of bread. However, the French are poor hands at licentious soldiering, being, perhaps, a little too close to the polished sources of our civilization for this. The restaurant with all its faults and at its toughest would probably have been like the salon of a Hapsburg Pretender compared with any pub in Gibraltar with a Yankee warship in port.

Setting out again we found that we had acquired an escort – a Vietnamese soldier with a tommy gun, who was followed into the bus so closely by a white butterfly that it might have been his familiar spirit. He sat down beside the driver and went to sleep with the butterfly flapping in his face. We were now entering the most dangerous phase of the journey, where a year before most of the vehicles had been burned in an attack and there had been several hundred casualties. A couple of spotting planes circled overhead ready, if necessary, to radio the alarm. After attacks, parachutists are usually dropped but it takes an hour or two for them to get to the scene and by that time it is all over. The Viet-Minh who usually attack in strength have their will with the convoy, and by the time the relieving force arrives they have disappeared.

The road mounted slowly and the vehicles lumbered painfully round the hillsides, so that seen from a bend, the convoy looked like the severed segments of a caterpillar. Gradually we freed ourselves from the dense vegetation, emerging finally into a savannah of coarse grass with occasional clumps of deciduous trees that looked like cork-oaks but were sparingly adorned with pale lemon flowers. The heat was terrific. Having been designed for service in some far northern clime, the bus's windows could only be forced down a few inches and as the sun's decline in the sky began, the bus was flooded with an incandescent glare, from which there was no escape. Slowly we ground our way on towards Dalat. Our passage out of the Valley of the Shadow was marked by our escort's waking up, uncocking his gun and stopping the bus to get out. Now I noticed that the trees had rid themselves of their coverings of parasites, that the swathings of creepers were no more and that lianas ceased to drip from the branches. The road widened and began to look like a corniche in embryo. Pines made their appearance. We were driving into Dalat.

Dalat is the playground of Indo-China and has a fair share of the dreariness so often associated with places thus advertised. Taking full advantage of an altitude of 3000 feet and the pine forests, a forlorn attempt has been made to encourage a sub-alpine atmosphere, but it remains nothing more than an uninspired imitation; a not very magnificent failure. Even imitations, if carried to sufficiently daring lengths, sometimes generate a fascination of their own. But the spuriousness of Dalat was cautious and hesitant. It looked like a drab little resort in Haute Savoie, developed by someone who had spent a few years as vice-consul in Shanghai. Of Dalat, though, one thing must be admitted; that life there, even in peacetime, is not entirely divorced from adventure, since there is a chance, one in a thousand perhaps, of knocking into a tiger if one strolls in the streets after dark.

We skirted a sad little lake, with edges cropped like a pond on Hampstead Heath and wound up the main street past the Salon de Thé, the Crillon Grill, a *dancing*, the Chic Shanghai Bar and into the square. We had covered two hundred and fifty miles in thirteen hours. Now a problem arose. I had been told in Saigon to contact a Madame Schneider, who held some important, but undefined, post and was responsible for foreigners. Madame Schneider would be able to find me a room in a town which might be overflowing with visitors and would make all necessary arrangments for the next stage of my journey, to Ban Méthuot. Her address? Well, as far as anybody knew, she didn't have one. If it came to that, no one in Dalat had addresses, certainly not important people like Madame Schneider. The first person one met in the street would be able to point out where she lived.

As a telegram had been sent from Saigon to warn Madame of my arrival, I half hoped to see either her or her representative awaiting me at the bus terminus. But no; one by one the passengers were claimed by their relations, the crowd thinned and melted away. It was after six, the streets were deserted and the daylight was waning. The local taxi-cab service consisted of tiny traps drawn by the Indo-Chinese equivalent of the Shetland pony. Only one of these remained and I approached the small Vietnamese boy in charge of it.

N.L. Est ce que vous connaissez Madame Schneider?

SMALL BOY. Moi connaisse.

N.L. Ou est ce qu'elle habite?

SMALL BOY. Là bas. Moi connaisse. (*A vague sweep of the arm towards the darkening pine-clad slopes.*)

N.L. Mais, elle habite en ville?

SMALL BOY (*impatiently*). Oui, oui. Moi connaisse. Madame Slé-lé.

It seemed pointless to continue the interrogation in face of the child's rather surly assurance. I got in, the pony's head was turned towards the wilds and we set off. We had reached the town's outskirts when the trap stopped outside a small grocer's shop. 'Madame Slé-lé,' said the boy.

It seemed unlikely that this Vietnamese lady could be the object of my search, and indeed, after I had pronounced the name very slowly and, as I thought, distinctly, half a dozen times, the light dawned. Of course, it was not she, Madame Slé-lé, I wanted at all. It was Madame Sné-dé. The important and celebrated Madame Sné-dé. 'Oui, bien-sûr. Moi connaisse! Moi connaisse!'

Having received the most graphic description of the route to be taken, we set off again. It seemed that neither the street Madame Schneider lived in, nor her villa itself, possessed a name. But following the instructions it would be impossible to go wrong. Unfortunately the outer suburbs were hilly and our pony, not much larger than a good-sized St. Bernard dog, was tired. On slight gradients we got out and walked. Up-hill we had to help with the pulling. In the gathering twilight we found an avenue that seemed to fit the description, although all the avenues and villas were practically identical, with unmade dust roads, crazy paths and overhanging eaves, designed to give protection from the snow that could never fall. I worked my way along the avenue going from villa to villa, but no knock was ever answered. Sometimes I caught sight of Vietnamese servants lurking at the house's rear, but the moment they realized I had seen them, they slipped quietly away and disappeared. Eventually I found a French woman, the first I had seen in this outwardly French town. Leaning out of an upstairs window she pointed in the dim direction of the villa where she thought Madame Schneider lived. So once again, I left the trap, cut across a garden coated with pine needles and managed to steal up on an elderly Vietnamese domestic, who seemed to be a cook, as I caught him in the act of scouring out some pots. Placing myself between him and the back door, so as to cut off any attempt to escape, I began an interrogation.

It is necessary at this point to refer to the existence of pidgin-French and to explain its nature, since this was the occasion when I realized the urgency of mastering its essentials. Pidgin-French, or petit-nègre as it is called, lacks the gay fantasy of its English equivalent, but is, by compensation, far less complex. Its vocabulary is limited to perhaps a hundred words. Verbs are used in the infinitive except where this is difficult to pronounce, when a special pidgin form is devised; thus connaître becomes connaisse. There are adaptations in the way of pronunciation too. The Vietnamese will not bother with difficult foreign consonants. They cannot pronounce r, and f in the Vietnamese language contains a strong element of p in its pronunciation. Thus, for example, bière de France becomes bí' de Pla' or bí' de Pa'; or, to take a sentence 'je veux du fromage Roquefort' is translated, 'Moi content po'-mo' Lo'-po'.' It was only as my conversation with the cook progressed that I began to realize the existence of these difficulties.

N.L. Madame Schneider, est ce qu'elle habite ici?
COOK Moi pas connaisse.

N.L. (*with exaggerated distinctness and quite useless emphasis on final* r) Schnaydair-r-e, Madame Schnaydair-r-e.

COOK (*smiling faintly with recognition*) Sé-dé?

N.L. (*after great imaginative effort*) Oui.

COOK Oui.

N.L. Est ce qu'elle est à la maison?

COOK Moi pas connaisse. (I do not understand.)

N.L. (*beginning to learn lesson*) Madame Sé-dé ici?

COOK Madame partir.

N.L. (*refusing to surrender to the finality of the tone*) Madame va venir?

COOK Oui.

N.L. Quand?

COOK (*employing the indefinite future offered in appeasement to foreigners the world over, meaning, in ten minutes, tomorrow, next week*) Maintenant.

N.L. (*unappeased*) Mais où est-elle allée?

COOK Moi pas connaisse. (*This time, either I do not understand, or I do not know.*)

N.L. (*doubtful now whether this is the right lady*) Madame, elle est mariée?

COOK Oui.

N.L. Elle a un mari, donc?

COOK Non.

N.L. Alors, elle est veuve?

COOK (*in a desperate effort to make the whole thing crystal clear*) Monsieur pas mari, Monsieur médicin. Madame venir, Madame partir. Monsieur venir attend Madame venir. Monsieur, Madame manger.

With a few more hours practice I should have readily understood from the lucid account of the Schneider family activities that Madame had already been home and had popped out again, probably for a cocktail with a neighbour, that her husband, who was a doctor, would shortly be arriving and that they would have dinner together at home. As it was the conversation dragged on fatuously. I gathered in quick succession that Madame was in the administration, that she was a doctor, that she was both, that she was on holiday, had returned to France, was shopping in town, and no longer lived there.

My driver, whose attempts to be helpful had only added to the insane confusion, now tired suddenly of the whole business, demanded in pellucid French sixty piastres, the equivalent of one pound, and rattled off, a small asiatic charioteer, into the gloom. Finally the cook, too, retreated inside, leaving me standing there alone, a prey to mosquitoes and to noisy blundering insects like monstrous May-bugs which struck me repeatedly in the face. It was then that a lorry drove up and deposited Madame Schneider and her husband. They were much surprised to find me awaiting them and told me that they had sent a telegram to Saigon to say that a room had been reserved for me at the Baliverne Hotel and fixing an appointment for me at the Mairie next day. Although quite unprepared for my visit they insisted that I should stay to dinner. Asked how long I expected to stay in Dalat, I replied that I wanted to leave as soon as possible. Madame wanted to know when I wished her to try to arrange an audience with the Emperor Bao Dai, whose villa was just down the road. It seemed that I had passed it without paying it any particular attention. To this are come the Emperors of Annam!

Although there had been some hints at Saigon of the possibilities of an Imperial hunting trip, I had never supposed that an official audience was taken so much as a matter of course and I said something to the effect that I hadn't given much thought to the matter. The Schneiders seemed surprised. This was my first experience of the fact that writers and journalists travelling in the Far East are supposed to be anxious to interview any crowned heads that happen to be within reach, and that to neglect to show much anxiety is considered a little oafish — even a breach of good manners. It is really extraordinary that these august persons should be wounded in their self-esteem when some insignificant traveller fails to express a desire to be received by them. In any case, my hostess thought, the matter of an audience could quite well wait for a day or two as there was little likelihood of my being able to leave Dalat in under a week. It was further explained to me that I would have to return along the Saigon road to a point about seventy-five miles south where it joined the main road to Ban Méthuot. There was a convoy due to leave Saigon for Ban Méthuot next morning, but I should almost certainly fail to make the connection. The next convoy would leave in about a week's time. I thought it strange that the people in Saigon should have arranged, in that case, for me to travel to Ban Méthuot via Dalat, and Madame Schneider said that they had probably taken the map too literally. There were two jungle tracks that cut across country from a village called Djiring, about thirty miles away, but one was the Emperor's private hunting track and his permission would have to be obtained to use it, while as for the other, which had only been completed two years previously, it might be months before — but suddenly Madame had an idea; hadn't there been some talk of a Gendarmerie officer going to Ban Méthuot in the next few days? Picking up the telephone she got through to the Gendarmerie, and sure enough, by a really remarkable chance, a Lieutenant Suéry was leaving next morning. He had a seat to spare in his car and would be pleased to call for me at the inevitable hour of 5 a.m.

The doctor ran me over to the Baliverne Hotel. It was a pretentious building, externally a bad example of timid functionalism tempered with would-be Hispanic swagger. My reception was a good example of Vietnamese passive resistance. It started off with the doctor confidently announcing that he had reserved a room for me by telephone. The Vietnamese male receptionist consulted a list and shook his head. The doctor asked him to make sure and the receptionist went carefully through the rooms, one by one, apparently checking the name of each occupant. No, there was no reservation in that name. Much embarrassed the doctor turned to me. 'It's absolutely extraordinary. I telephoned myself.'

'Would you mind making one final check?' he asked. The clerk shook his head. 'No room has been reserved.'

'Well then let me speak to the manager.'

'The manager is not here.'

In desperation the doctor asked, 'and have you no rooms of any kind?'

'Certainly we have rooms.'

'Then why didn't you say so before?'

'You asked if there was a reservation, and I told you there was none.'

Tired but relieved I signed the register. The reception clerk seemed to remember something.

'At what time will you be leaving in the morning?'

'At five o'clock.'

'Will you require breakfast before leaving?'

'Well — if it won't be too early —'

'Yes, it will be too early.'

While waiting for my luggage to be taken up I saw one of the most amazing sartorial sights I have ever seen. An American car drove up and in came a party of wealthy Chinese. The girls were dressed in rolled-up tartan trousers and cardigans. With them was what seemed to be a Vietnamese mandarin in a flowered silk gown, but wearing a flat tweed cap. A foretaste of the mysterious East to come!

My room was furnished with the cheapest of modernistic furniture, there was a smelly lavatory and an empty water bottle. The page-boy refused five piastres (1s. 8d.) and demanded ten. Huge lethargic mosquitoes floated about the room, but they were so slow in flight that I picked them all out of the air in five minutes. I was glad that my stay in Dalat would be limited to one night.

Awaiting sleep I considered the matter of the extraordinary accessibility of the oriental potentates of our times. Having with me Crawford's *Journal of An Embassy to Cochin China*, which gives a fascinating account of the country at the time of his visit, in 1822, I turned up the passage referring to his vain attempts to be received in audience by the Emperor of Annam — an ancestor of the present sovereign. Crawford, who was kept kicking his heels for two months, never achieved his purpose because it was objected that the Embassy was undertaken on behalf of the Governor-General of India and not of the King of England himself. His experiences throughout show a marked similarity to those of envoys sent in various abortive attempts to establish diplomatic relations with the Emperor of China.

Crawford soon found that although the Cochin-Chinese were hospitable, cheerful, scrupulously polite and entirely lacking in the rapacity of the Siamese, they were 'extremely ceremonious and partial to display and parade in little matters to the extent of ostentation'. In his preliminary conference with a deputation of mandarins of Saigon, eight hours were spent in consideration of the wording of the letter he carried from the Governor-General to the Emperor. While agreeing that the intentions were probably respectful, the mandarins pointed out that it would be contrary to the laws of the country to present it in its original, barbarous form.

For example, the sentence, 'His excellency sends certain presents in token of his profound respect and esteem for His Majesty the Emperor of Cochin-China.' 'This was not to be endured, because, as the matter was explained to us, profound respect and esteem must be considered as a matter of course from anyone that addressed His Majesty of Cochin China.'

At the suggestion of the mandarins, the passage was rendered as follows, 'I send your Majesty certain presents because you are a great King.' Exception was also taken to His Majesty being addressed as 'Sovereign of Laos and Cambodia,' in recognition of the fact,' as Crawford says, 'that he had just conquered a great part of these two countries.' 'The mandarins informed me that it was no honour for the King of Cochin China to be styled "a King of slaves".'

At Hué, the capital, the Chinese translation of the amended

document came in for further criticism. The mandarins were horrified by the crudity of the Governor-General's reference to the death of the late Emperor, who, 'ought to have been represented as not dead, but merely gone to Heaven'. 'This tedious matter' (the further alterations) 'occupied from ten in the morning until five in the evening. . . .'

But it was all to no purpose. The Cochin Chinese continued to be infallibly polite and most sympathetic.

' "It is natural enough," said the mandarin with a smile, "that you should employ every expedient in your power to attain the honour of being presented to so great a king." '

A hint was dropped of certain indiscretions committed by a predecessor, a Mr. Roberts, who on the occasion of his mission in 1805 had included in the customary presents 'a series of prints representing the capture of Seringapatam, and the death of Tippoo Sultaun'. A Chinese merchant sent them word that in his belief the Court 'desired no intercourse whatever with them . . . the Cochin Chinese looked upon the men with red hair and white teeth — that is to say Europeans — to be as naturally prone to war and depredations as tigers'.

Crawford struggled on with his losing battle, but there was nothing to be done. He was entertained and banqueted, noting in one instance that they were served with three bowls of eggs on which hens had been put to sit ten to twelve days previously. By way of consolation he was told at the time of his dismissal that five years before a similar mission from the French king had met with the same rebuff and that the Emperor had refused to accept the presents accompanying it.

The comparison with my own subsequent experiences gives some measure of the decline in the prestige of the Indo-Chinese kingdoms.

CHAPTER V

RÉGION INCONNUE

HAVING been warned of the Lieutenant's liking for punctuality I was waiting, shivering slightly, in the hotel's grandiose drive soon after 4.30. The trouble in the *Hauts Plateaux* of Indo-China is that while the temperature may reach 90° in the shade soon after the sun rises, it usually feels like a mild December day in England just before dawn. Above the creaking of cicadas I could hear the occasional bark of a stag. On the stroke of five came the distant rattling of a car and the jerky reflection of headlights among the trees. The Citroen came juddering up the road and Lieutenant Suéry got out and introduced himself. He was in his forties, a Provençal with a fine melancholy face; one of those Southerners who contradict the accepted Mediterranean pattern with their coolness of manner, their reserve and their taciturnity. Suéry had a worried look and I suspected him of suffering from stomach ulcers. Only his rapid, sing-song speech, which I found almost impossible to understand, gave a clue to his origin.

The car rattled badly. No car could stand up for long to these terrible roads. The chauffeur was a Vietnamese corporal called Nha – pronounced nya. He was the first genial member of his race I had met and he smiled continually. Suéry sat beside him in front and criticized his driving and I was in the back seat surrounded by the luggage. It was still quite dark and after a while a short circuit developed causing the lights to bump on and off. Suéry nagged at the chauffeur about this and after a while Nha told him cheerily that he couldn't find the short in the dark and in any case he wasn't an electrician. I could understand every word Nha said but had great difficulty with Suéry's high-pitched, buzzing replies. Suéry asked me if I had a gun in my baggage, and I said, 'No, why?' Suéry said it would be an extraordinary thing if we did not see at least one tiger or leopard on the track. Viet-Minh patrols? — no, not a chance. We were thirty miles from the regular frontier of their territory, and where we were going it was real no-man's land. No-man's land in the sense that, so far as anybody knew, there was no population at all. Two hundred miles of unexplored jungle without a single village, it was believed. You didn't find the Viet-Minh wandering about in that kind of place. They couldn't live on air any more than anybody else. Anyway the corporal had a rifle and if we came across a tiger we would take a pot at it, just for luck. Of course he couldn't countenance hunting on a duty tour, but we would call that self-defence.

We reached Djiring in a chilly dawn. It was nothing more than a line of shacks on each side of the road. This was where I had been hoping to find a place to get some coffee. But it was too early. A few Moïs were wandering about the street pulling on their long, silver pipes. They were wrapped in blankets worn with toga-like dignity, a fold flung over the left shoulder. The blankets were woven at the hems with some fine, intricate pattern.

We were on the jungle track when the sun came up. It showed a path hardly wide enough in most places for two cars to pass, with an earth surface varying in colour from orange to brick-red. We were passing through unexplored country; a succession of low mountain ranges with peaks reaching a maximum of 3500 feet. Our world was clothed in frothy vegetation, which, on the more distant mountains, looked as close-textured as moss. Lit up by the bland morning sun it was a cheerful, spring-like aspect. As we plunged down into the valleys the landscape closed in on us, till at the lowest levels we practically tunnelled through the bamboos, which seemed to have choked to death all other forms of growth. At slightly higher altitudes we passed between evenly spaced ranks of trees. Their absolutely smooth trunks went straight up without any projection to the roof of the forest, where they put out a parasol of branches. From their bases to the height of perhaps twenty feet the trunks were bastioned with thin strengthening-vanes. There was no way that any of the hundred forms of parasitic growth could take hold. Each tree, it seemed, laid claim to a certain area for its growth, and I saw one with its trunk wrapped almost completely round an intruder of a different species.

There were other trees which had not adapted themselves to the social environment of the jungle and they were loaded with parasitic ferns that had established themselves in the crevices of the rough bark, while lianas, orchids and creepers cascaded from their branches. There was a curious regularity of shape to be observed about some of these parasites, particularly in the case of a chaplet of fleshy leaves fastened about vertical branches, from which there spilled, as from an over-filled basket, green, fretted patterns, repetitive in design as the torn newspaper of the cinema-queue busker. At this season, in early February, there were no flowering orchids, but sometimes in the valley-bottoms, half-extinguished among the bamboos, we caught a glimpse of the fiery smoke of flamboyant trees. A flower, too, grew abundantly by the roadside which looked like willow herb, but was lavender in colour. These were visited by butterflies of rather sombre magnificence — typical, I suppose, of dim forest interiors. Usually they were black with splashes of green or blue iridescence. They did not settle, but hovered poised like fruit-sucking birds, probing with proboscies at the blooms. They fluttered in their thousands above the many streams and once, passing through a savannah, we came across what proved on investigation to be the mountainous excretion of an elephant. At first nothing could be seen of it but the glinting of the dark, splendid wings of the butterflies that had settled upon it.

I was intrigued by the process by which some day the jungle would probably re-claim the track — a digestive action which had already begun. Since most of the trees were without low-level branches, there was little lateral pressure; no remorseless closing-in of the walls of vegetation on both sides. What had happened was that plants had seeded themselves in the track itself and had already reached the stage when they could have been potted-out for the embellishment of all the boarding houses of England. There were many aspidistra- and laurel-like varieties, throwing out new leaves that were often curiously veined, hairy, mottled or lacquered. Some bore small, orange-blossom-like flowers and spiders had increased the nuptial illusion by draping them with gauzy, bridal veils. I saw several familiar birds including bee-eaters, kingfishers and shrikes, and we once passed a peregrine falcon perched most uncomfortably on a slender swaying bamboo. The lieutenant was mortified that no tiger had appeared and said that now the sun was well up it was unlikely that we would see one. However, a troop of gibbons dropped from the trees into our path, awaiting our oncoming in petrified astonishment. At the last moment, when the chauffeur was already braking hard, they departed with fine acrobatic flourishes. Jungle-fowl frequently appeared ahead. They were as small as bantams and nearly as sprightly on the wing as blackbirds. It seems that the polygamous habit of the farmyard exists in the wild state — though on a lesser scale — since a cock was never without his two or three hens. The chauffeur Nha groaned in horror at these wasted opportunities but the lieutenant would not relax discipline even when we saw a huge boar in the track, at right angles to us, lethargic and indifferent, its head hanging down and snout practically touching the ground. It remained a perfect, unmissable target, until we were within a few yards of it, when, without looking up or making any preliminary movement it seemed suddenly to vanish, as if de-materialized.

By the afternoon we had left the jungle and entered a region of *forêt-clairière* — patches of woodland alternating with coarse-grass savannahs. This phenomenon might have been caused by extreme variations in the natural fertility of the soil, or by the destructive cultivation of the region in the past by primitive tribes. There would be a few miles of grassland, followed, as the soil improved, by clumps of fern, bushes trimmed sedately with what looked like wild roses, and then, finally, the jungle again, a bulging explosion of verdure. The lieutenant said that these parts swarmed with all

kinds of game, particularly elephants, tigers and gaurs — a large
species of buffalo of legendary ferocity in Indo-China, which provides all local hunters with their most hair-raising escape stories.
We saw none of them.

For several hours, it seemed to me, the lieutenant had been showing signs of irritation. This took the form of constant criticism of
the chauffeur's driving. It was no mean feat to drive a car along
this track, with its ever loose surface, its acute bends, its gradients,
the patches of freshly grown vegetation through which we were
obliged to crash implacably. I thought that Nha was doing very
well. We had had no nasty turns, so far. I was well content to
relax and look at the scenery. Not so the lieutenant. He began to
indulge in the most acute form of back-seat driving, which included
a regular flow of instructions. It went something like this:

'All right now — gently out of the bend. Now accelerate hard —
all you've got. No, don't change up. Why change up when you'll
have to change down again straight away? Keep your foot on the
throttle, now swing her across — bottom gear — there you are, you
left it too late: stall the engine that way. Never change down after
a corner like that, change before. Now give her full throttle — hey,
slow down! What on earth are you doing? My God, you'll have
us over the top before we know where we are. There you go now —
I told you you'd stall the engine.'

It was evident that Nha was getting rattled. After he had followed
Suéry's instructions as best he could, thereby twice stalling the
engine on a hill, Suéry asked him if he was tired and would like a
rest. Nha got out without a word and came round to the other
side and Suéry took the wheel. Suéry's driving was dynamic. We
roared up gradients on full throttle in each gear, snaking gently on
the soft surface. Bends were taken in grand-prix style. It was quite
exciting.

After about ten minutes of this we happened to be coming down
a hill with an easy gradient. There was a drop of about a hundred
feet into a ravine on the left and a bank on the right. The road had

widened out and Suéry thought he could take the bend at forty. I had a glimpse of a flock of small, green parakeets leaving the top of a tree growing in the ravine, but was unable to follow their flight owing to the swinging away of the landscape. One moment I was looking at the birds flying up from the top of the tree, then the landscape shifted round and I saw the road — also slipping away — and a steep bank coming up at us. I heard Suéry say, 'Mon Dieu', three times very quickly and I wedged my feet up against the seat in front and pushed away hard. There was a crash and something hit me on top of the head and we seemed to bounce up into the air and go backwards. We did fifteen yards back-first down the road in the direction we were going, with all the car doors open. I fell out first and I saw Nha and Suery fall out on opposite sides. Nha sat in the road with his head in his hands and Suéry got up and walked backwards a few steps. His face was covered with blood which was already dripping down his shirt. There was a ringing in my ears but I knew that I was not badly hurt. Nha got up and sat on the running board and said, 'Oh malheureux,' as well as something in Vietnamese. He then grinned and we both went over to look after Suéry. Suéry had a deep, ragged wound over his eye and a lot of small cuts on his face and arms. He had broken the steering wheel with his chest. I wiped the worst of the blood off him with a clean handkerchief and got some plastic skin out of my bag and squeezed it over his cuts.

In half an hour everybody was feeling well enough to look at the car. It was a wreck, one of the front wheels folded half underneath the chassis. By the best possible luck we had covered all but about thirty kilometres of the distance to the first military post, but it was going to be dark in two hours time. Suéry seemed to think that it wouldn't be a good thing to spend the night in the car and Nha explained why, later. We had our second piece of good luck when Nha remembered the existence of a hut used by the Moï guard, which, he thought, couldn't be more than a mile or two from where we were. Taking what we could easily carry, we set out and in

about half an hour came to a shallow clearing in the jungle with a
plaited bamboo hut raised on piles. Two young Moïs in army tunics
and loincloths peered out at us through the door-opening. They
seemed as pleased to see us as if we had been disreputable relations.
A brief, dubious scrutiny, and they both turned away, hoping that
by ignoring our existence we might be persuaded to leave them in
peace. Nha called and one of them came and stood at the top of the
step-ladder. Nha beckoned to him and he turned away as if to appeal
to the other. Finally the pair of them with the clearest possible
reluctance came slowly down the ladder. Suéry gave Nha fussy
details of what he was to say to them and Nha, who said he only
knew a few words of the language, started, as best he could, with
the interpreting, while the Moïs stood there, fidgeting and unhappy.
They were gentle, girlish-looking lads of about twenty years of age.
Following local custom they had had their front teeth knocked out
and wore their hair in a bun. They had a few narrow brass bracelets
round their wrists, and a silver churchwarden pipe protruded from
the pocket of each army tunic. Nha first explained that Suéry was
an officer and they must consider themselves under his orders. Did
they realize that? There was a doubtful assent.

'Very well,' Suéry said, 'ask them what arms they have.'

The Moïs said they had two rifles.

'Tell them to go and get them,' Suéry said, looking a trifle relieved.

The Moïs went trotting off and reappeared with the rifles, carried
smartly at the trail. Suéry took each gun, opened the breech
mechanism, inspected it and looked along the barrels. He seemed
pleased.

'Ask them how many rounds of ammunition they have between
them.'

Nha translated this and the Moïs shook their heads. They had
none.

'My God,' Suéry said, 'well what have they got to defend themselves with?' The Moïs said they had a cross-bow apiece. 'Any
arrows?' Suéry wanted to know, with sarcasm. The Moïs said,

yes, they had arrows and also *coupe-coupes*. 'Very well,' Suéry said. 'Tell them to go and bring the *coupe-coupes*.' The Moïs came trooping back with the *coupe-coupes* over their shoulders. They had heavy, curved blades, as sharp as razors, about eighteen inches long and could be used as knives or axes. 'Good,' Suéry said. 'Now tell them they are to set out for Dak-Song immediately; get there as quickly as they can and bring help. I'll give them a note for the *Chef de la Poste*.'

While Nha was trying to put this into their language you could see the Moïs' faces cloud over. They just said they didn't understand. This was the line they took and they stuck to it. The simple, polished bronze faces, until now good-natured and rather bewildered, suddenly emptied of expression. The light of comprehension went out, or rather, was switched off.

Suéry accepted defeat. He knew that nothing in the world would get those Moïs to walk along that jungle track in the dark. He asked Nha if he would go with one of the Moïs and Nha, looking slightly sick, said yes. But when the proposition was put to the Moïs they prepared a second line of retreat by saying that their sergeant had ordered them to stay there until he came back. And where was the sergeant? He was wounded and had gone away, where, they didn't know. It was days, perhaps weeks since it happened, but he had told them to stay where they were, and stay they would. Did they not realize, said Nha becoming indignant, that a lieutenant was more important than a sergeant and that his orders would over-ride any they had received? Once again the Moïs did not understand.

The lieutenant got up and said he would sleep in the hut.

The idea of spending the night in a Moï hut filled Nha with revulsion, as he told me as soon as the lieutenant was out of hearing. A hut that had been occupied by savages – imagine the smell. Well – I would soon see for myself. And there was another angle that had to be considered. Supposing bandits – or pirates as they were invariably called – happened to find the wrecked car. This would be the first place they would think of to look for us.

Didn't I realize that the lieutenant had been thinking of pirates when he decided against sleeping in the car? Only a few hours away there were several villages and the junction of various cross-country routes. Just the kind of place, in fact, where pirates could always be expected to hang about. He wasn't thinking so much of the Viet-Minh as of *pirates vulgaires* mixed up with Japanese deserters. That's what the Moï guards were there for. Naturally the pirates didn't bother about such small fry; but if they knew we were here — *oh malheureux!* These dolorous exclamations of Nha's were always accompanied by a bright smile. I'm sure that he wasn't particularly impressed by the hazards to which we were exposed, but enjoyed, as people do, making the most of them. The next peril he produced was tigers, remarking with a gay conviction that, 'les tigres vont causer avec nous ce soir'. I pointed out that the Moïs were still alive. He said that although the Moïs were disgusting savages they knew how to deal with tigers and we didn't. Nha had all the distaste of the conservative, plains-dwelling Vietnamese for everything that had to do with forests or mountains and their inhabitants. The Vietnamese, like the Chinese, prefer their landscapes to possess the comfort of the familiar rather than the mystery of the unknown. Nha was already sickening for the ditches and rice-fields of Cochin-China.

Nha's prejudices were, of course, unjustified. The Moï hut was spotless and contained no odours of any kind. It had been made in sections of plaited-bamboo, tied with lianas over a framework. Inside it felt very insecure. At every pace you felt as though your foot were going through the floor. The whole structure creaked and swayed. A large, circular, earthenware tray on the floor served as a hearth and Suéry wanted to light a fire to keep off the mosquitoes. Nha asked him if he thought we should advertise our presence. Suéry said it was either that or being eaten alive by the mosquitoes, and this was a bad area for malaria. They had a rare kind of mosquito up here that bred in running water, the *anopheles minimus*. There was none deadlier.

When we lit the fire we nearly choked ourselves with the smoke, but the Moïs re-arranged the logs and the smoke died down leaving a faint odour of incense in the room. I went out and stood by the door. It was not quite dark. There was a huge owl flapping backwards and forwards across the clearing and nearby, in the undergrowth, a bird sang with a powerful nightingale-like song. I pulled the door across the opening, tied it in position with a length of liana and went to lie down.

Suéry had told Nha to have the Moïs take turns at a watch; but once again comprehension lapsed. No sooner had we stretched ourselves out by the fire than they stole past us and went into a partitioned-off section of the hut, and we saw them no more. I was sure they were thoroughly miserable at our presence, which was probably most offensive to the tutelary spirit of the hut, whom they lacked the means to placate by sacrifice.

Lying as close as I could get to the fire I was hot down one side and chilly on the other. The cool, night air came up through the bamboo floor and, however I lay, projections in the bamboo stuck into my back. Finally I began to doze lightly but was continually awakened, sometimes by somebody getting up and setting the hut asway; sometimes I was not sure by what. But then as I lay trying to collect my wits I would hear animal sounds, not loud and menacing, but casual, confident and none the less sinister; a cough, a sigh, or a soft, restless whining.

I came to painfully, somewhere about dawn, realizing that I had been listening through increasing degrees of consciousness to what I had dreamily accepted as the noise of a shipyard at work. There was a regular industrial crash, made, as I had supposed, by a pile-driver or a riveting machine. With consciousness fully returned and with it the realization of where I was, it seemed unreasonable that this clamour should not stop. Nha was already awake. It was a bird, he said. I thought of a hornbill with the habits of a woodpecker. But no, Nha said, this was the cry of a bird and not the concussion of a gigantic bill against a hollow tree. It was a mystery

I was never able to solve, as, however the sound was caused, I never heard it again. Familiar, though, from that time on was another form of salutation of the dawn, a huge demoniacal, whistling howl that started in first one and then another corner of the jungle until the air resounded with the rising and falling scream of sirens. These were screaming monkeys. They kept up the lunatic chorus for half an hour each morning.

We washed in some greenish water from a nearby stream. There was nothing to eat or drink; no evidence, in fact, to suggest the Moïs bothered about regular meals. Nha raised the question and one of the Moïs offered to go and shoot a monkey with his cross-bow. We thanked him and prepared to leave. Suéry told Nha to stay with the car while he and I walked to Dak-Song. Owing to Nha's perpetual grin, I could not see that he was not pleased with the prospect of being left behind, but Suéry knew him well enough to be able to tell. He asked Nha if he was afraid to stay by himself and Nha said, no, not if he didn't have to stay the night. If he had to stay the night, well then — *Oh malheureux!* Suéry promised that whatever happened he would see to it that he was relieved by night-fall. Nha then asked Suéry if he would like to take the rifle — 'in case you see any boars'. Suéry refused this very gallant offer and having presented the Moïs with a few cigarettes to cut up for their pipes, we started out.

I was glad of this opportunity to walk to Dak-Song, having felt that I wanted to form a closer contact with this unspoiled and un-explored forest than was possible in a closed-in car. It was like a splendid May morning in England, a little cool at first in the shade of the trees, but I knew that once the sun was high enough to shine on the road it would be very different.

The forest was as full of tender greens as an English woodland in early spring. It was temperate in its forms, placid almost, with occasional exuberances that, unsated by excess, one was able to appreciate. The air resounded with the morning songs of birds which were quite unlike any I had heard before. In the gardens of Saigon one was haunted by a monotonous piping. Here the birds produced more complicated melodies than the warblers of the West, impressing me not so much as in the case of our blackbird or nightingale, by the quality of a limited repertoire of notes, as by the variety and range of the melody, which in some cases could have easily been fitted into a formal, musical composition. It was as though a collection of mocking birds had been taught European music by a Vietnamese artist on a bamboo flute. And besides these musical performers there were many more producing sheer noise; the rattling of a stick along iron railings, the escape of steam from a boiler, the squealing of brakes, a single, muted stroke on a gong. I never heard these bird sounds and songs again. Elsewhere in Indo-China great destruction is done to wild-life by indiscriminate burning of the forests by the tribes, and birds are, of course, hunted for food. It is possible that in this supposedly unpopulated area, marked on French maps as *Région Inconnue*, birds and animals exist which are not to be found elsewhere.

Unfortunately there was little to be seen. A few small honey-sucking birds fluttered about the lavender willow-herb and we frequently saw a species rather smaller than a lark, black in colour and with a tail which looked like a single feather at the end of an eighteen-inch long hair. It was difficult to understand as we watched it threading in and out the thick jungle foliage, how its evolution could have been assisted by this unhandy appendage. Once only we saw a hornbill, sombrely splendid in black and yellow, launch itself from a tree top and go swooping through a glade in a dashing, easy flight. On the wing there was nothing incongruous about its immense bill.

We were about five miles from Dak-Song when we had a very bad moment. For hours under the sun's nearly vertical rays the jungle had become tamed and silent. Plodding through the red, shadeless dust, we were dirty and sweat-soaked. Suéry's shirt was spattered with brown bloodstains. I had a bad thirst but still not bad enough to risk a drink out of a stream. Just ahead the track turned sharply to the left to avoid a small, low hill that was very densely wooded. From this as we approached there suddenly came a huge, shattering, calamitous sound. It seemed in some way incongruous, improper to this tranquil atmosphere of an overgrown corner of an English wood on an afternoon in a heat-wave. I judged the sound to be produced by two tigers quarrelling, perhaps, over a kill. The snarling intake of breath followed by the furious, coughing roars was unmistakable. Suéry looked as if he wanted to pretend that he had heard nothing. That was half the trouble, there was something ridiculous, as well as alarming, about the situation. Either of us alone might have retreated up the road as quickly as we could, but together we were obliged to go on. It would have been no more seemly to show alarm than at the casual approach of a bull while crossing a field in either of our native lands. As we strode on I began to calculate the number of steps (thirty) that it would take us to reach the point of maximum danger and the number (two hundred) before we could start to breathe easily again.

But now a distressing complication awaited us. We reached the corner and turned left, but the track instead of going on straight ahead, curved immediately to the right. The chilling sounds broke out again, very close now, and it was quite evident that my two hundred yards, instead of taking us to safety would be fully employed in skirting the base of the hillock and that during that time we should be at roughly an even distance from the tigers. And this was how it turned out. We walked on round the hairpin bend expecting at every moment to see the animals come bounding down into the road in front of us. Every few seconds there was another outburst of roars. Our preoccupied silence was the only indication that we realized that anything unusual was happening. Glancing from side to side for a possible way of escape, I confirmed what I already knew, that the trees were as un-climbable as the columns of a Gothic cathedral. Perhaps half a mile further on Suéry broke the silence. 'They never attack in daytime,' he said.

This, it seemed, was one of the accepted fallacies of bush-life in Indo-China. The republican guard at Dak-Song when we arrived said the same thing. 'I hardly ever drive along the track without seeing one. Shot some beauties. They never attack you in daylight. Rarely attack human beings at all.'

The latter assertion is probably correct but I was only allowed two days in which to delude myself with the former. At Ban Méthuot one of the first French officials I met had been mauled by a tiger while coming out of his garden in the town at mid-day. The tiger was probably old and decrepit as it only ripped up the man's thigh in a desultory fashion before making off down the main street in the direction of the municipal offices and the church.

Dak-Song was a sun-scorched forest-clearing; a few Polynesian huts, and a pile-raised long-house used by Moï conscripts as a barracks. A strange face in such a place is an extraordinary event and Moï children ran screaming to their parents at our approach. The republican guards in charge of the post lived dismally in the huts. There were no amenities of any kind, no shop, canteen or bar. At more or less weekly intervals the convoy to Ban Méthuot passed through, and the checking of vehicles and passes, occupying perhaps one hour, was their only routine activity. They had endless time to devote to the sad reflections that are the occupational disease of colonial soldiering. The staleness of existence couldn't be imagined the *Chef de la Poste* said. The only thing you could do was to go out and shoot a tiger or a gaur, or something like that. Even then you couldn't call it sport. They were too tame. They came and gave themselves up. Committed suicide. The other day he had seen a herd of gaur in a clearing near-by. He had just driven up to them in his jeep, picked out the biggest one and shot it like that. The *Chef* sighed, thinking perhaps of week-end partridge shooting in France.

Our host apologized for a splendid lunch of wild poultry, the flesh of which was very white and sweet and Suéry said that he would try to let him have some tinned stew next time he came through. The drinks were, of course, warm. It always surprised me that the Frenchman in the tropics lacking ice never made an attempt to cool liquids by keeping them, as the Spanish do, in porous vessels.

There was a sawmill at the post and the manager came over for coffee. He had the gentle, humorous cynicism of a man who, having started out with a fund of ideals, has found them not quite sufficient to cover all life's opportunities. Since heart-burnings were the order at the guard's table the manager contributed to the tale of frustration by a description of some of his difficulties. The forest was full of Sao, a quite remarkable wood, impervious as he put it, to destructive agents, and favoured by the Chinese of old for the manufacture of their war-junks. There the wood was, enough to make one's fortune ten times over and yet there was no way of getting it down to Saigon. 'A hundred logs,' said the manager, 'and I'd leave you fellows to rot where you are and clear off back to France.' One of the guards said that it only meant waiting a short time now, 'till the roads are open again'. After that he could ship all the wood in Dak-Song. But the manager laughed. It would be no good at all if the roads were open. That would bring prices right down, only spoil things. What he wanted to find was some way to get the wood down there with the roads closed — like they did with the rice round Saigon. He'd have to find a smart Chinese that could take care of it for him with the Viet-Minh.

After lunch the *Chef de la Poste* showed us round and we happened to be there when a party of unusually handsome Moïs arrived. Instead of being dressed as those of Dak-Song were, in tattered European shirts, these were splendid in tasselled loin cloths, ear-plugs and necklaces of beads and teeth. They had with them a pretty girl of about sixteen, with small, sharp breasts and the everted top lip of a child. One of the guards made discreet inquiries about her, but on learning that she was married, lost interest. They were members of a local tribe called M'nongs, a mysterious people the *Chef* said, who had only made their submission in 1939 since when they had assassinated eight administrators who had gone to live among them. Why? The *Chef* shrugged his shoulders. Nobody seemed to know. The M'nongs were quiet, well-behaved people but it was easy to upset them in some way or other without realizing it. You did the wrong thing and you disappeared. For an administrator it must have been a bit like living in one of those police-states, except that there was no clue as to what was expected of you. You would be getting on like a house on fire, a tribal blood-brother; you might even, as he had heard some of them did, marry two or three native wives. And then you slipped up in some way and nobody ever saw you again. By the way, the *Chef* added, they had one custom here it might interest us to hear about. The men were considered the property of the women, so that a mother bought a husband for her daughter from a woman who had a son to sell. The price in these days, the *Chef* said, was about 800 piastres, so that in the case of a woman with a dozen sons, 'Elle reçoit du fric — n'est ce pas?'

If the Vietnamese had been indifferent, these M'nongs were oblivious. They did their business, which seemed to consist of paying a tax in rice, through one of the tame Dak-Song Moïs. We walked round them looking at their ornaments but none of them so much as glanced at us. We might have been transparent. It was a coincidence that after this first encounter with the noble savage of Indo-China as he is when practically untouched by Western influence, only ten minutes should pass before I was given the opportunity of seeing the other side of the medal. The native guards brought in a half-crazed creature in rags who had escaped from one of the plantations. After having been severely beaten by one of the overseers he had run away and had made a journey through the jungle of three days and three nights to get here. The Frenchmen treated the man kindly and told the Moïs to give him food and shelter. I gathered that it was part of their duty to see that he was sent back, but they said that they had no intention of doing so.

This was the general attitude of the lesser French officials I met. They had no use whatever for the plantation owners and would not lend their authority, unless they were compelled to, to the support of any abuse.

Sometime in the early evening a break-down truck arrived from Ban Méthuot in response to the radio S.O.S. that had been sent. Suéry went off in it and, as it had been arranged that I should continue my journey on the convoy that was coming through later that evening, we said goodbye. I was sorry to part company with Suéry. He was the only Frenchman I ever saw a Vietnamese treat with affectionate respect, so that there must have been something exceptional about him. Suéry thought more of Nha's comfort than he did of his own and he told me that the thing that upset him most about wrecking the car was that it might maroon them both in Ban Méthuot and thus prevent Nha from going back to Saigon to spend the New Year with his people — a terrible misfortune for any Vietnamese. He was most anxious to relieve Nha before nightfall and to be able to take him a good meal.

The *Chef de la Poste* had been on tenterhooks ever since the night before about the convoy's non-appearance. It was now twenty hours late and, as the telephone lines had been cut, they had no news. Soon after Suéry left a message came through to say that it had been attacked. The first few trucks that arrived knew that there had been an attack but could give no account of what had taken place. The drivers sat stiffly in their seats, dazed with fatigue and mantled with yellow dust. The *Chef* said he would put me on the first of them that had a seat to spare, but in each case the passengers were crammed so tightly in the driver's cabin that it was difficult to see how he could twist the steering wheel or change gear. The backs of the lorries were jammed with merchandise.

After five or six of them had passed through the check-point in this way the *Chef* decided that he had found a lorry with a hole in the cargo large enough for a human being to crawl into. He made one of the cabin passengers get down from the front and climb into this crevice, telling me to take his place. I did not like the idea of doing this, and said so, but the *Chef* waved aside such objections saying that I had better take the chance while I could, because if the convoy had been badly shot-up there wouldn't be many more lorries to come. I therefore swallowed my scruples, put my bag in the back and climbed in, although feeling most uncomfortable about the whole affair. The lorry started off, bucking and crashing over the most appalling road I have ever travelled on. It was extremely difficult to stay in one's seat. The vehicles in front had raised a pall of yellow dust which, as it grew dark, the headlights were quite unable to penetrate. Shutting the windows hardly reduced the density of the cloud that swirled into the cabin but was quite effective to hold in the terrible heat generated by the engine roaring in low gear. I felt my presence keenly resented. So much so that I spoke to the driver intending to offer to change places with the man who had been sent to ride in the back, but I got no reply. He looked in fact so grim that I began to feel a little nervous, catching, incidentally, several venomous, sidelong glances from my fellow passengers. After a while the driver took to muttering to the man who was sitting next to him, crushed in between him and the door. A suggestion seemed to have been made and the man nodded in agreement. He opened the door and swung outside, peering back, evidently to see if another vehicle was in sight. Looking, as I thought, intently in my direction he made a sign to the driver who put the gear lever in neutral and pulled the lorry up. I thought that the chances were no better than one in four that they were going to throw me out. However, the driver's friend jumped down and went to the back of the lorry, after which he came back, got in and we went on as before.

At about 11 p.m. we got into Ban Méthuot. The driver suddenly asked me in good French where I wanted to go. I told him the Mairie. He said: 'We've passed it. I'll go back.' I told him not to trouble, that I could easily walk, but he put the lorry in reverse and backed down the street till we came to the Mairie. I asked him how much I owed him, getting out a 100-piastre note; he said 'nothing' and pushed the money away. Thanking him I held my hand out and felt much relieved when he took it, smiled and said, 'au revoir'.

I stood there for a moment looking after the lorry as it lurched away up the street. There were one or two street lamps and as it passed under them the curved canopy painted over with Chinese characters reminded me of an old-fashioned Chinese lantern.

CHAPTER VI

BAN MÉTHUOT

ONSIEUR DOUSTIN, chief representative, in the temporary absence of the Resident, of the French civil authority in the province, accepted the time and manner of my arrival with the imperturbability of a true diplomat. To judge from his manner nothing could have been more normal than my appearance at his door filthy and dishevelled, about thirty hours after I had been expected. When, shortly afterwards, seated before a meal of great complication, my plans were discussed and I mentioned my hope of getting across country to Paksé, there was no exasperated raising of the eyes. In the presence of such lunatic hopes Monsieur Doustin allowed himself only the faintest of sardonic smiles. The trouble with the people at Saigon, of course, was that they just didn't know what was happening; which, said Doustin severely, was a little surprising considering that they were the official source of information. Ban Méthuot to Paksé! The sardonic smile deepened a little. No one had done the trip for a year or two. It wasn't even known whether the track was practicable, or whether it had vanished into the jungle by now. In any case, nothing whatever was known about the state of security of the region. These people that stuck to their offices in Saigon were carried away by their imaginations. There wasn't much traffic leaving Ban Méthuot in any direction, and unless one had a positive mission it was just as well to be philosophical and go wherever the first *moyen de fortune* happened to be going. Even that might mean quite a few days cooling one's heels. And why not? There were few more interesting areas in Indo-China, or the Far East, if it came to that. An anthropologist's paradise, Doustin said. And one that was passing away before your very eyes. I had arrived, in fact, just in time.

86

There was another important point to remember, the *Chef de cabinet* said. In the Darlac province, he personally would guarantee my safety; but once I passed beyond the frontiers of his jurisdiction, ah, that was another matter. Pirates everywhere. People who called themselves nationalists, or freedom fighters, but who really took to piracy just as their ancestors before them had done, because it was the easiest way of making a living. This brought up the convoy attack and Doustin said that he had heard that eight vehicles had been destroyed out of the thirty-odd that made up the convoy. The conversation turned to the tranquillity of life in our respective home countries. Doustin had memories of service in England with the Free French, spent in what I had always thought of as drab provincial towns, but where, according to him, all the problems of existence had been solved. I was continually being invited by French officials to share a nostalgia for such unlikely places as Birkenhead or Dover — Peterborough was Doustin's choice — seen now across the years of fierce, sunny exile as congeries of quaint pubs, full of tenderly acquiescent maidens and wrapped in a Turner sunset. It is extraordinary, too, the experiences that people can succeed in remembering with affection. Doustin had even come to believe that he had liked Naafi tea.

A room had been prepared for me in the *Résidence*. It was not a large building, but conceived in the grand manner, with a wide ambassadorial entrance and a flight of steps worthy of an Italian customs house. Sentries ensconced in the bougainvillaea woke up and slapped their rifle-stocks furiously at our approach. As soon as we entered the house white-clad Moï domestics with tamed, empty faces flitted at our heels.

'Tomorrow morning,' announced Doustin with the voice of decision, 'you will be tired. Very well, breakfast at eight o'clock. An English breakfast, naturally, with an omelette. You don't take beer before eleven, do you? Ah, the English light ale!'

And now came the moment of efficient unbending — efficient, because Doustin could not be otherwise. 'If you want anything don't stand on ceremony. Just stand at the window and holler. *Poussez un grand coup de gueule.*' A light, saloon-bar slap on the back and I was dismissed for the night. The quick, confident footsteps receding down the marble corridor. The yelp of the guard-commander. The sharp acceleration of a car being driven competently, dashingly, away. I put out the light and opened the windows. My cheeks, ears, chin were brushed by soft, disgusting contacts. Hundreds of moths were coming in.

As I was not to see Doustin before ten in the morning, I spent an hour or two before that looking round the town. There was not much to see. Before 1946 there had been a native town, but it had been burned down in the trouble with the Viet-Minh. Now there were a few French villas on each side of a dust road, a sluttish-looking hotel built of wood and green-painted, and a Vietnamese market with a few shack-lined alleys leading off it.

The Vietnamese shops sold a great collection of improbable rubbish; celluloid dolls and soap-boxes, plastic belts, calendars with pictures of Chinese girls playing hockey, spurious rhinoceros horn used as an aphrodisiac and fake tigers' teeth as a medicine. There were dried and salted flat-fish no bigger than five-shilling pieces. Thousands of them. They were strewn about on counters mixed up with haberdashery and bottles of blood-coloured lemonade. There were innumerable hideous Ali-Baba jars, brown and green and with a glaze like toffee. These are made by the Vietnamese and sold to the Moïs for use in their drinking ceremonies. The most popular personal ornament on sale was an enamel brooch depicting a Flying Fortress. For the house one could buy a picture of Sun-Yat-Sen in a mother-of-pearl studded frame, a landscape decorated with artificial flowers and grass, or a mirror painted with planets with aeroplanes encircling them. The most popular utensil, and undoubtedly the one of greatest utility in the East, was the jerrycan. Bicycle repairing was the most popular industry represented in the market. After that came portrait photography; particularly booths which offered a large number of different poses – photomaton style — for a fixed sum. The Vietnamese trotted in and out of them continually. Few Moïs were to be seen but I saw one ultra-civilized Moï woman, probably a convert of some kind, wearing nothing above the waist but a ridiculously inadequate brassière, and carrying a blue plastic handbag.

Frangipani trees grew in the market place. They were leafless with polished, swollen-looking branches, and bore sprays of white, thick-petalled flowers. Hundreds of house-sparrows perched in them.

At exactly ten o'clock I was shown into Monsieur Doustin's office. He awaited me poised beneath a wall map, ready to organize my movements in the period immediately ahead. I was harangued briefly on the military situation, which was presented, as far as I could see, with complete frankness. Doustin was too subtle to indulge in crude propaganda. He would have considered this inefficient, preferring to expose some of the weaknesses as well as all the strength of his side. The Viet-Minh were devils incarnate and the French, well, sometimes they lost patience — went a bit too far. What could you expect with men fighting in these terrible conditions. A couple of years out in the bush and always seeing the same half a dozen faces. How would you like it yourself? Doustin also thought that there was far too much loose, anti-colonial talk about. In this part of the world France had nothing to be ashamed of. They were doing good work and he wanted me to see some of it for myself. So, as there was not much chance of being able to get away from Ban Méthuot for a week or two, he was going to arrange a side-trip for me through the most interesting part of the Moï country. It was all arranged. I was to start tomorrow, and a young administrator and an inspector of schools would be going with me.

Although there was an ominous suggestion of the conducted tour in this, it did not, in fact, work out that way. Whether at heart Doustin was really as confident of being on the side of the powers of light as he seemed, I don't know. My opinion is that whatever his doubts he cast them out, counting them as weakness. He was almost the last of his kind that I met among the French. The rule thereafter was an ability to see two sides to any question, leading to a Hamlet-like infirmity of purpose and sometimes to the darkest of pessimism.

Doustin produced a final suggestion. Before visiting the Moï country he thought I should see a Doctor Jouin, who had lived among the tribes for many years and was considered the leading living authority on their customs. Doctor Jouin was the head of the medical services of that nebulous enclave in Vietnam of undiluted French authority: Les Populations Montagnardes du Sud Indo-chinois, and the author of several weighty anthropological works, published under the dignified auspices of the Musée de L'Homme.

I found him at a table cluttered with the charts and mathematical figures that seem to enter so much these days into what one would have thought the least mathematical of sciences. He was white-haired and gentle, his face permanently illuminated with the Budd-histic peace generated by complete absorption in an urgent and valuable task. From the inside information available to him in his official position, the doctor informed me, he had decided ten years ago that this engaging race was doomed in quite a short time to disappear from the earth. He had therefore set to work to learn what he could of their attractive if primitive civilization before it was too late. In the beginning the task had seemed simple enough and, in any case, he had not intended to probe too deeply. But then he had made exciting discoveries and had been lured on into an un-known country where the horizons constantly receded. Every attempt to clear up some limited aspect of his subject had uncovered endless others. And now he found himself in a trap. He had com-mitted himself to labours which could never be finished. And time and the conditions of the country were against him. It needed a dozen workers like himself to occupy themselves with the still enormous volume of material available which, however, was melting away and which in a few years would be lost for ever.

We started talking about the Moïs in the early afternoon and it was evening before I left the doctor's villa, carrying with me various monographs as well as the manuscript of a work in progress. From these and from our conversation much of the following information has been extracted.

CHAPTER VII

THE MOÏS

IN the early part of the last century the Moïs seem to have been regarded as articulate animals rather than human beings. European traders did their best, but without success, to acquire specimens for zoological collections in Europe. In 1819, Captain Rey of Bordeaux, who carried a cargo of fire-arms to the Emperor of Annam, was assured by no less a dignitary than the Mandarin of the Strangers, of the existence of 'Moys, or wild men'. The Mandarin had seen many of them when commanding a corps of elephants in the interior. They had tails, he said, and he had managed to capture one and bring it back with him to the capital as a present for the Emperor. Rey was interested enough to take this up with the French mandarins at the court, when he visited them, and they confirmed all he had been told, beyond possibility of doubt. 'My respectable friends . . . had never seen these extraordinary creatures; but they had so often heard their existence affirmed by men of character and probity, that they knew not how to disbelieve the report. The tail was said to be in length about eight inches and a half. Although endowed with speech as well as with the human figure, the mandarins seemed, I thought, to conceive them to be only irrational animals.' With the foregoing exception, Rey said, concluding his report of the fauna of Cochin-China, all its abundant variety of animals could be found in the adjoining countries.

Before the end of the century, these opinions had to be modified. The explorer Mouhot — discoverer of Angkor Vat — had published an account of his visit to the Stieng tribe. The Moïs were officially conceded souls and some theorists even began to raise the matter of the lost tribes of Israel. However, until the Colonial era with its census-taking, and head-taxes, these newly promoted human beings remained inaccessible, and still fairly mysterious, in their forests.

The Moïs, it seems, are well aware of the unsatisfactory state of the technical side of their civilization and usually seek to excuse themselves to strangers who allude to it by citing one of their self-deprecatory legends. A favourite one describes the tactical disadvantages suffered at the creation, when the Moïs were last to crawl out of the holes in the ground and found everything worth having already appropriated. Then again, the matter of illiteracy, they say. What could you expect? When the Great Spirit told all the nations to bring writing materials, on which their alphabets would be inscribed, the Moïs with typical improvidence, instead of providing tablets of stone or even wood, turned up with a piece of deer-skin, which later, complete with alphabet, was eaten by the dogs.

There are supposed to be about a million Moïs distributed over the mountainous areas of Indo-China. The exact number is unknown, as a few remote valleys have not even made their official submission. But whatever it is, it is dwindling rapidly, as in the districts most affected by Western penetration some villages have lost half their number in a single generation. They are a handsome, bronze-skinned people, of Malayo-Polynesian stock, related to the Dyaks of Borneo, the Igoroths and Aétas of the Philippines and to the various tribes inhabiting the hinterlands of such widely separated parts as Madagascar and Hainan Island, off the coast of China. They hunt with the cross-bow, being particularly noted for their skill in the capture and taming of elephants, which they sell as far afield as Burma. A clue to the extent of their culture's diffusion is given by their use of the sap of the Ipoh tree for poisoning their arrow-tips. The utilization of this poison, although the Ipoh tree grows in many other areas, is limited to Malaysia, Indo-China, a small easterly strip of Thailand and Burma, Borneo and Timor. The poison's effect is intensified, as necessary, according to the size of the game, by adding to it a strychnine-containing decoction from broial root and extracts of the fangs of snakes and scorpions' stings. A scratch from a weapon dipped in this appalling concoction — the use of which is hedged about with many semi-religious prohibitions — produces death in the case of human beings in a few minutes.

The Moïs cultivate rice by the 'dry' method, which is to say that they burn down parts of the forest just before the beginning of the rainy season, drop their rice seed into the holes in the ground and leave the rains to do the rest. The name Moï is Vietnamese for 'savage'. The Moïs have been enslaved by all the technically superior races, Siamese, Laotians and Cambodians, among others, who have come into contact with them. Far from having derived any benefit from this association with their superiors, the greater the degree of external influence the more deplorable the condition of the Moïs who have suffered it.

The free survivors seem to the casual observer to lead gay and sociable existences, much occupied with gluttonous feasting and the consumption of rice-spirit. This hearty manner of living is said to depend upon and be proportionate to the tribe's inaccessibility. Unless compelled to, Moïs do not work for wages and their civilized neighbours are shocked by what they consider their incurable sloth. Village labours, however, such as the erection of houses or the clearing of the forest, are undertaken communally and with great zest. The Moïs are art-collectors, and wealth consists in the possession of gongs, drums and jars, some of which are of ancient Chinese or Cham origin and therefore of great value, even in the West. Occasionally such museum pieces are wheedled out of them by Europeans who tend to remain in ignorance of the treasure they have stumbled upon, under the impression that they have acquired nothing more than an interesting example of Moï artisanship.

Apart from being used to store rice-wine, jars are accumulated in the hope that spirits will take up their residence in them. When a spirit moves into a jar, the fact is revealed to the owner in a dream, but official recognition is only accorded after an examination by experts for certain external signs. The jar thus honoured is not necessarily an antique, although the spirits usually show artistic discrimination. In any case the jar becomes a valuable piece of property and may be sold, complete with spirit, for a large number of buffaloes. As the spirit, or talismanic virtue, is thought of in some way as being divisible, a handle is frequently broken off when a jar is sold, and worshipped in the same way the complete jar was before. A considerable inter-tribal trade exists in such jars, and expert appraisers and negotiators carry out the transactions. They are said to exact large profits.

According to scientific investigators, such as Doctor Jouin, the most extraordinary thing about the Moïs is their unique racial memory. It is even suggested that a concerted study of their sagas (which are on the point of perishing), might throw an unprecedented light on man's existence in prehistoric times. The Rhadés, one of the least degenerate of the tribes, possess, according to the doctor, a name for and a description of the mammoth and the megatherium as well as the hippopotamus — which has been extinct in the Far East in the historic epoch.

The unique value, it would appear, of the Moï saga resides in the fact that it is ritual and sacrosanct. It may be recited only in certain specified circumstances, and without the slightest modification. Even if words and phrases have lost their meaning, are mutilated or incomplete, no attempt, under powerful religious sanction, must be made at restoration. The sagas, therefore, although involving great interpretational difficulties, have remained a treasure-house of information relating to the remote past. Events of the last thousand years or so seem to have made little impression on the Moï imagination. The brilliant Indianized civilizations of the Khmers and the Chams are hardly referred to. Angkor Thom is the work of 'strangers recently arrived in the country'. The sagas describe the Moïs own establishment in Indo-China after leaving their island homes at an unknown period, which must antedate the fifth century B.C., since at that time they are already referred to in the annals of the kingdom of Fu-Nan.

The non-scientific visitor appears to be most impressed by the innumerable rituals with which the Moïs surround their existence. The most onerous of these are concerned with death. Those which are associated with good health are the least important and tend to be quite perfunctory because to die of sickness is a sign of the spirits' favour and ensures a comfortable hereafter in the bowels of the earth. Doctor Jouin had the greatest difficulty in persuading the Moïs to accept any kind of medical treatment, as they pointed out to him that he wanted to deprive them of the chance of a 'good' death, exposing them therefore, when cured, to the possibility of a 'bad' death by accident or violence. Such a 'bad' death condemns the ghost to wander in eternal wretchedness in the heavens.

Lepers are regarded as having been born under a lucky star, as they do no work, are fed by the tribe and are certain of an exemplary end.

The death rites, on the contrary, are prolonged over two years and are so costly that a single death may exhaust the equivalent of the village income for one month, whereas an epidemic, by causing it to use up in sacrifices the whole of its reserves, is certain to bring starvation in its train.

In arranging their ceremonies the Moïs pay great attention to the type of death the defunct has suffered. There are specially complicated and expensive rites for those who have died from various kinds of violence, who have died in a foreign country, have disappeared and are presumed dead, for young children, lunatics and, of course, for women dead in childbirth who are believed to turn into revengeful demons. The village is surrounded by open tombs, the occupants of which are 'fed' daily and kept informed of all family affairs.

From the sheer multiplicity of the rites, all of which require alcoholic consumption, the intriguing side-issue emerges that respectability and drunkenness are allied. The upright man gives evidence of his ritual adequacy by being drunk as often as possible, he is respected by all for his piety, a pattern held up to youth. The words *nam lu* uttered in grave welcome to the stranger in a Moï

facing: THE WIFE OF THE M'NONG CHIEF IGNORES THE CAMERA

village, and meaning let us get drunk together, have all the exhortatory value of an invitation to common prayer. Moï villages are said to be one of the few places in the world where the domestic animals, dogs, pigs and hens, having fed in the fermented mash from the sacred jars, are to be seen in a state of helpless intoxication. Conviviality is the rule; a norm of polite conduct. Passers-by are begged to join in Moï orgies of eating and drinking and it is bad taste — that is offensive to the spirits — to eat or drink less than is provided by the fearsome liberality of the hosts. To prevent any possibility of the visitor's unwittingly committing this kind of discourtesy, or remaining in a state of disreputable sobriety, an attendant squats at his side keeping a careful check on his consumption and ensuring that he drinks at least the minimum measure of three cow's horns.

The other aspect of the Moï way of life that seems to have created the greatest impression upon those who have studied them is that, although, by occidental standards, crimes are few, the conceptions of right and wrong seem to be quite incomprehensible to them. In their place, and incidentally governing conduct by the most rigid standards, are the notions of what is expedient and what is inexpedient. The Moï is concerned rather with policy than justice. Piety and fervour have no place in his ritual observations. Contrition is meaningless. There is no moral condemnation in Moï folklore of those who commit anti-social acts.

All this as well as the elaborate ceremonials accompanied by their ritual drunkenness is explained by the Moï conception of a universe dominated by a number of powerful spirits who, together with the manes of their own ancestors, control their destinies. The relationship is a contractual one; the spirits and the manes appearing rather in the light of strict and exacting creditors. Broadly speaking there is nothing either particularly benevolent or hostile in the attitude of these ghostly autocrats towards their human feudatories. All they claim are their just debts — the ceremonies. No more and no less than these. As long as they are scrupulously paid, all goes well

97

with the individual, the family and the tribe. Drought or deluge, 'the bad death', epidemics – in fact, misfortunes of all kinds are merely indications that the rites have been violated, and the only remedy lies in finding the offender, and compelling him to put the matter right by providing the prescribed reparation.

The view taken of human conduct and its effects is totally opposed to the religious teachings of the West, which accept that the wicked man prospers and that the moral debts of those who break all but the eleventh commandment are settled in another existence. Among the Moïs retribution is swift and terrestrial. The wicked – that is, the ritually negligent man – is quickly ruined. If he continues to pile up spiritual debts he is certain of a sudden death – the invariable sign that the ghostly creditors, becoming impatient, have claimed his soul for non-payment.

The thing works out in practice much better than one might expect. Crimes against the individual, such as theft or violence, are viewed as contravening the rites due to the plaintiff's ancestral manes. The aggressor, however, is seen as no more than the instrument of one of the spirits who has chosen this way to punish the victim for some ritual inadequacy. The judge, therefore, reciting in verse the appropriate passage of common law, abstains from stern moralization. Both sides are in the wrong, and rather illogically, it seems, the aggressor is sentenced to make material reparation and also – what is regarded as far more important – to provide the animals and liquor necessary for the ritual reparation to be paid to the offended spirits. The ritual reparation, of course, takes priority, and in cases of hardship may be paid for in instalments. The offender is compelled by law to take part in this feast which provides as a secondary function the means of reconciliation of the two parties.

There is no distinction among the Moïs between civil and criminal law and no difference is made between intentional and unintentional injury. If a man strikes another in a fit of temper or shoots him accidentally while out hunting, it is all the work of the spirits and the payment to be made has already been laid down. No eyebrows are lifted. It is just another human misfortune to be settled by a drinking bout at which the whole village gets tipsy. The Moïs do not apply the death penalty, since otherwise the community would expose itself to the vengeance of the ghost of the executed man. Two of the greatest crimes are the theft of water and of rice, which are under the protection of powerful spirits. Owing to the sacrilegious nature of such an offence, which exposes the community to the resentment of the spirits involved, the offender in this case is banished for life.

The white colonist, in his treatment of the Moïs, has been at once both sentimental and predatory. The smaller administrators, disinterested -- since they have nothing to lose whether the Moïs work or not -- tend to regard them as delightful children. An outstanding example of this attitude was the celebrated Sabatier who refused to allow missionaries in his territory, had the bridges demolished when he heard that a high official was on his way to investigate the labour problem, and is said to have married three Moï wives. After seeing the first effects of white encroachment in the Moï country, he went even further than this, advocating complete withdrawal and allowing the Moïs to live their lives in their own way. But the government found it impossible to refrain from meddling, from suppressing tribal warfare, judging, counting, taxing and above all -- and fatally -- making labour compulsory for the requirements of Europeans. It was the action of the planters who were determined to have labour for their plantations that defeated Sabatier.

The planters are a very small group of men; a few families who possess Indo-China's richest fortunes. Their attitude towards the Moïs is probably identical with that of any of the old slave-owning aristocracies towards the producers of their wealth. It is one of utter contempt; without which effective exploitation would probably be impossible. In the past they have employed labour recruiters, paying high premiums for each man who could be induced or tricked into signing on for three or five years — a period of indenture which the labourer rarely survived. Coolies were kept under armed guard and thrashings were liberally administered. Sometimes they were re-sold and transported to the Pacific Islands. Recent attempts to temper these conditions have met with the most resolute opposition, the planters asking, pertinently as they believe, what after all is the purpose of a colony?

Thus the conflict between administrator and planter continues, and whatever mitigations of the Moïs' lot may have taken place, the principle of compulsion persists. For the privilege of having the white newcomers in his country each adult male pays a tax in rice and must give up a number of days annually for labour on the plantations or roads. It is the infringement of the Moï's liberty which is the fundamental vexation. For fifty days he is prevented from performing the rites, therefore compromising him heavily with the spirits, who demand to be repaid. There enters also the factor that in a finely balanced economy the loss to him and his family of this amount of time may make the difference between sufficiency and ruin. Moï society recalls that of Islam or the pre-Columbian civilization of America in that every action of the individual from birth to death is rigidly controlled. It is a tightly unified system which has shown itself fairly successful in dealing with the internal life of the tribe, but brittle and without resistance to external shock. Moï customary law and the rites deal with every eventuality, and take into account every situation but one. The Moï has not been permitted the initiative to meet an attack from an unexpected quarter. If someone offends the village's tutelary spirit, the thing can be put right without much trouble. But if a timber-cutting company with a concession comes along and cuts down the banyan tree that contains the spirit, and takes it away, what is to be done? It is the end of the world.

CHAPTER VIII

DARLAC

THE whole district of the Dak Lac is seen as if through dark glasses. There is not a great deal of colour. It is a study in smoky blues, greens and white. The light has a cool Nordic quality and the lake itself is an Icelandic *vatyn* with the mountain reflections blurred in the dim sparkle of the frosted surface. The islands seemed edged with ice, but this edging is a packed fringe of egrets and when an eagle drops among them the ice dissolves as the egrets rise, to reform again as they settle. One's views of the lake seem always to be obtained through the spare branches of the frangipani or the *lilas de Japon* — negligent brush-strokes on silk, with a sparse adornment of white blossom.

In the morning the mountains float above a cauldron of mist in which islands slowly materialize, and along the near shore, below the administrator's bungalow, the topmost branches of the trees are elegantly supported upon layers of vapour. Later the scene solidifies and the lake is seen to be encircled by mountains, covered to their peaks by a tight webbing of jungle. The water's-edge is feathered by bamboos. As the sun drops in the sky, its light is no longer reflected from the moss-like sheath of vegetation on the distant highlands, which, instead of glowing with yellow light, as they would in Northern climes, turn to the darkest of smoky blue. Fishing eagles turning against this dark background show their white underparts and the end of their dive is marked by a fountain rising from the water. At this hour the butterflies appear and fly down to the lake. They are black, slashed with lemon and as big as bats. Egrets pass in drifts on their way to roost. The last movement is a curved line of cranes, with black, heraldic silhouettes against the darkening sky. All day and all through the night the cool sound of gongs comes over the water from unseen Moï villages.

The administrator's bungalow was built on a prominence by the lake's verge. Standing on the balcony you could look down at the groups of white herons mincing through the shallows beneath, and flapping their wings in a sudden flurry of panic to free themselves from the entangling weeds just below the surface. The bungalow was surrounded by a defensive pallisade and there was an inner belt planted with sharpened staves, their foot-long protruding points hidden in the grass. Below was a military post with a few Moï conscripts. The post stands at the head of a pass guarding the way to Ban Méthuot. At the other — the eastern end — of the winding, marshy valley is the coastal town of Nha Trang. But long before Nha Trang, and not very far, in fact, from the post at Dak Lac, are the first outposts of the Viet-Minh. Up to the present the Viet-Minh have not troubled to come up into the mountains. But one day my friends supposed they would and when they did it would certainly be up that valley, where every morning we could hear the schools of monkeys howling at the dawn.

Apart from the huts the Moï guards and their families lived in, there was only one other human habitation in sight. This was the Emperor's new shooting box, in the process of completion, which crowned a pinnacle still higher than that of the administrator's bungalow. It was less than Imperial in style; a cubic structure of vaguely Germanic inspiration. There was more of the pill-box than the pleasure-dome about it, an unconscious reflection, perhaps, of the unhappy times. A steam-roller — a truly amazing apparition in such an environment — was flattening the surface of a well-laid asphalt road leading to the summit when I visited the site. It had been chosen, they said, so that His Majesty, when not actually hunting could have the satisfaction of watching herds of wild elephants from his windows. On the occasion when I made free with the Imperial view-point, it goes without saying that there were no elephants to be seen.

My friends at the post were Ribo, the administrator, and Cacot, an inspector of schools, who was spending a short holiday with him. Ribo had 118 Moï villages, with a population of about 20,000, under his jurisdiction. Both of these young men were well under thirty, genial, expansive, optimistic by temperament and pessimistic by conviction. The post turned out to be not only an outpost of French Colonial domination but of Existentialism. On my first evening there, after a full-scale French dinner, with two wines and a liqueur, I was expected to make an intelligent contribution to a discussion on Marcel Aymé's *Le Confort intellectuel* which had just arrived from Le Club Français du Livre.

Before this, however, we went out shooting on the lake in a Moï pirogue. The pirogue was very long and narrow. To avoid upsetting it, it was necessary to sit or crouch perfectly still in whatever position one elected to adopt. Cacot, whose intellectual pessimism never extended to such matters as hunting, proposed to return with the pirogue's bottom covered with duck, but I was beginning to realize by this time that this kind of luck was not to be expected when I formed one of a hunting party.

The pirogue slid over the water, its rounded bottom stroking the matted aquatic plants that lay just below the surface. The mountains had now put on their featureless mantle of dusky blue and brilliant white clouds bulged up from behind them. Swallows kept us company, zigzagging around us, and eagles wheeled in the sky. Large fish jumped occasionally and brought fishing hawks swooping over their position. A village somewhere was playing the gongs — two slow and four fast beats repeated over and over again.

The Moï spotted a large number of duck, lying like a heavy pencil-line, drawn near the lake's horizon. Cacot became very enthusiastic and suggested that we should go crocodile hunting after dinner. He thought we might get a few deer, too, while we were about it. The Moï was manœuvring the pirogue towards the duck, taking advantage of the cover provided by the islands and the reeds. We cut lanes through the lotus-beds spreading from the islands and this slowed us up. Cacot could not see the necessity for this, as he said that no one ever went shooting on the lake, so the birds would be tame. We were within about a hundred yards of them when they took off, with a twittering noise, like a flock of frightened finches. They were ferruginous ducks, which I only knew from illustrations. There were about two hundred of them and curiosity was their undoing because the whole flight suddenly turned towards us and passed over our heads, with Ribo and Cacot blazing away at them. Several of them dropped like stones into the lake, but the weeds were so thick that we only picked up one that fell by the pirogue. It was a handsome reddish-brown bird, a little smaller than a mallard, with slate-blue bill and legs. We nosed about the lake for another hour but the ducks would never let us get anywhere near them again. Cacot said that he thought that the Emperor had been shooting there.

Determined to go home with some sort of a bag he now concentrated on the only other birds on the lake which he thought might be edible. These were isolated black-winged stilts, elegant and fragile-looking, which, seeming never to have come under fire before, let us get within a few yards of them. Cacot shot several. They were very tenacious of life and, although severely damaged at close range, dived and remained below the surface for so long a time that it seemed as if they were determined to drown rather than be captured. They were found with great difficulty by the Moï, groping about among the under-water weeds. In flavour they were much inferior to duck.

After supper we went out hunting in Ribo's jeep. Fortunately Cacot had been talked out of the crocodile shooting expedition on the grounds that we should all get malaria in the swamps. Cacot had a powerful light, like a miner's lamp, attached to his forehead, carrying the battery in a haversack. We drove along one of the Emperor's private hunting tracks and Cacot turned his head from side to side trying to pick up a reflection from the eyes of game. Finally this happened. Five pairs of luminous pin-pricks shone in the depths of a clearing, belonging, Cacot whispered hoarsely, to deer. Jumping down from the jeep he plunged into the long grass, the beam of light jerking and wavering in front of him. At the end of the glade the deer could finally be made out, awaiting his coming, heads and necks above the grass, immobile as dummies in a shooting gallery. The light steadied, there was a red flash and charging echoes. The deer's going was not to be seen. The clearing was suddenly emptied. Cacot came back and got into the jeep, saying that he was feeling tired. On the way home he brought down a small skunk-like animal with a long difficult shot. It had coarse, bristly fur, which Cacot seemed to think was of some value. After it had lain in the garage under the bungalow for a day it began to stink and the driver was told to bury it.

That night I was awakened by a prolonged slithering sound in the room, followed by a click. It was not a loud sound by any means but there was a suggestion of danger about it, which evidently impressed the subconscious mind. There was no electric light and it did not seem a very good idea to me to get up and look for the matches, because although I could not account for the click the slithering sound corresponded in my imagination to the noise a large snake would make in crossing the floor. I, therefore, lay quietly under the mosquito net, which I hoped would prove a deterrent to any exploratory reptile. The sound was repeated several times and then stopped. I went to sleep.

Almost immediately, it seemed, I was awakened by a truly hideous outcry, very definitely in the room and coming from a point not more than six feet from where I lay. This was a gurgling peal of ghastly hilarity, ending in the cry, *jeck-o* repeated several times. Although in the stillness of the night I ascribed this to some kind of predatory monster, it turned out next morning to be no more than the house's tutelary jecko lizard, a large and repulsive monster of its kind which liked to lurk during the daytime in an angle of the bookcase, switching its tail angrily over the volumes of Jean-Paul Sartre. The jecko, it seems, is only dangerous to the extent that it defends itself vigorously when attacked and is regarded as fateful

by the Vietnamese who draw auguries from the number of times
it repeats the concluding bi-syllable of its call.

I was never able to account for the slither and the click.

The sun was well up when we drove out next morning. Out of
respect for the conventions of the country there had been some
talk of making a dawn start, but many civilized delays had spun out
the time. It was a genial morning. We dropped down the spiral
road past the shore of the lake, which was still peeling off its layers
of mist. There were a few Moïs out fishing in their pirogues,
floating, it seemed, in suspension. Moïs were pottering about in
the streams running down to the lake, setting fish-traps or washing
out their kitchen pots — a job they were very particular about.

Our path was beaten across fairly open country. There were rice-
fields on both sides, but the rice had been harvested a month or two
before and now they were deserted except for buffaloes mooching
about looking for mud-holes, and a few storks. The Moïs, who had
nothing much to occupy themselves with at this season, were wandering about trying to find some way of using up the time between
one drinking bout and the next. There were families sauntering
along the path who looked as if they intended to walk a mile or
two until they found a suitable spot for a picnic. The mother would
be carrying a fat section of bamboo, with the food packed inside,
while the father had a jar of rice alcohol slung on his back. The
children ran about loosing off their cross-bows unsuccessfully at
any small birds they happened to see.

We passed fishing parties, organized *pour le sport*, more than with
serious intent, since a little effort was diluted with much horseplay.
The method in favour was for a number of persons to stir up the
water of a stream or pool until it became thoroughly muddy
and presumably confusing to the fish. Then they stabbed into it
at random with a kind of harpoon shaped like a bottle but much
larger and made of wicker, with a sharp circular edge at its open
bottom. Both sexes took part and the fishing provided an excuse

for endless practical jokes, involving duckings. These people were M'nongs, belonging to the same tribal group as those I had seen at Dak-Song, and one of the main divisions of the Moïs, who occupy a large, vague area to the south of Ban Méthuot. They are supposed to be slightly less advanced than the Rhadés whose territory begins a few miles away to the north and who are the strongest and most numerous of the Moï tribes. You could always distinguish the M'nongs by the large ivory cylinders they wore in their earlobes. The ones who still lived by hunting and, occasionally, raiding were supposed to carry poison for their arrows in one of these hollow cylinders and the antidote in the other.

We stopped at the village of Buon Dieo where there was a new school to be inspected, one of the five in the territory. At a distance Buon Dieo looked like an anthropologist's scale model in an exhibition, a perfect example of a village in some remote and unspoilt South-Seas civilization. It was all so well-ordered that one expected to find litter baskets, and notices saying 'a place for everything and everything in its place'. There was not a scrap of refuse nor a bad smell in the village. If the long-houses had been a tenth part of their size you could have described them as arty and crafty, with their technical-institute pattern of woven bamboo walls. And the clean, new images at the head of the step-ladders up to the houses, the geometrical patterns on the well-scrubbed sacrificial posts and the strings of dangling figures cut out of paper. It was all so much of an exhibit — rather too clean and lifeless — the ideal M'nong village arranged for the benefit of visiting students. But the scale of the thing saved it and made it real. That and the 7000-foot peaks of the Annamite Chain that formed the background. Some of the best *cases* were a good sixty yards long. The village was lifeless because the people were keeping out of sight until the chief could be brought, and the chief was hastily putting on the European sports-shirt he wore as a badge of authority.

The chief of Buon Dieo had the sad, old, wizened face of a highly successful Levantine shopkeeper with a tendency to stomach-ulcers. Besides his sports-shirt he wore a dark-blue turban, a loin-cloth beautifully woven with a fine design of stylized flowers, and an ornament in the form of a pair of tweezers suspended from a chain worn round his neck. Ribo had visited the chief only a few days before, so that it was hoped that the ceremonial forms to be gone through would be much less involved than usual. We first visited the school which the whole village had combined to build in ten days. Ribo said that you only had to appeal to the Moïs' imagination to get them enthusiastic over a project, to make them believe that it had their spirits' approval, for them to be filled with this kind of Stakhanovite fervour. One of the villagers, who had been in the army and was therefore considered a man of culture, would give three days a week as a teacher. The school had just been inaugurated with the sacrifice of a buffalo and there were a few gnawed bones lying about on the floor. Ribo's severe criticism of this seemed to me unfair in this model village from a colonial exhibition. In embellishment of the otherwise bare class-rooms were several posters of Monte Carlo.

The common-room of the chief's house was furnished with impressive simplicity. There were benches round the walls, carved out of some ebony-like wood, and clean rush matting on the floor. There was such a complete absence of household odds and ends that one had the impression of his wife going round tidying up after each visit. The principal objects were a battery of gongs of various sizes together with several drums, the largest of which, a massive affair hung with bells, the chief said was worth at least ten buffaloes. Not, of course, that he would ever think of selling it, in view of its sentimental associations. It had been in his wife's family for several generations, and was only struck on occasions of great solemnity such as the appearance of a comet. The main beams of the house were sparingly decorated with what upon inspection proved to be advertisements and cartoons cut from French and American illustrated journals.

There were seven jars attached to a framework in the centre of the room and as soon as the chief's sons-in-law had arrived and hung up their cross-bows on the beam over the adventures of Dick Tracy, they were sent off with bamboo containers to the nearest ditch for water. In the meanwhile the seals of mud were removed from the necks of the jars and rice-straw and leaves were forced down inside them over the fermented rice-mash to prevent solid particles from rising when the water was added. The thing began to look serious and Ribo asked the chief, through his interpreter, for the very minimum ceremony to be performed as we had other villages to visit that day. The chief said that he had already understood that, and that was why only seven jars had been provided. It was such a poor affair that he hardly liked to have the gongs beaten to invite the household god's presence. He hoped that by way of compensation he would be given sufficient notice of a visit next time to enable him to arrange a reception on a proper scale. He would guarantee to lay us all out for twenty-four hours.

This being the first of what I was told would be an endless succession of such encounters in the Moï country I was careful to study the details of the ceremony. Although these varied in detail from village to village, the essentials remained the same. The gong-orchestra starts up a deafening rhythm. You seat yourself on a stool before the principal jar, in the centre, take the bamboo tube in your mouth and do your best to consume the correct measure of three cow-horn's full of spirit. Your attendant, who squats, facing you, on the other side of the jar, has no difficulty in keeping a check on the amount drunk, since the level is never allowed to drop below the top of the jar, water being constantly added from a small hole in the side of the horn, on which he keeps his thumb until the drinking begins. After you have finished with the principal jar, you move to the right of the line and work your way down. There is no obligatory minimum consumption from the secondary jars. At frequent intervals you suck up the spirit to the mouth of the tube and then, your thumb held over the end, you present it to one of the dignitaries present, who, beaming his thanks, takes a short suck and hands it back to you. In performing these courtesies you are warned to give priority to those whose loin-cloths are the most splendid, but if, in this case, the apparel oft proclaims the man, age is a more certain criterion with the women.

The M'nongs are matriarchal and it is to the relatively aged and powerful mothers-in-law that all property really belongs. Although the women hold back for a while and it is left to the men to initiate the ceremonies, the rice-alcohol, the jars, the gongs, the drums and the house itself are all theirs. It is therefore, not only a mark of exquisite courtesy but a tactful recognition of economic realities to gesture as soon as possible with one's tube in the direction of the most elderly of the ladies standing on the threshold of the common-room. With surprising alacrity the next stool is vacated by its occupying notable to allow the true power in the house with a gracious and impeccably toothless smile to take her place. This toothlessness, of course, has no relation to the lady's great age and arises from the fact that the incisors are regarded by the Moïs as unbearably canine in their effect and are, therefore, broken out of the jaws at the age of puberty.

The chief's wife at Buon Dieo possessed, in spite of her years, a firm and splendid figure. She wore a gay sarong, probably obtained from a Cambodian trader, and in the intervals of drinking smoked a silver-mounted pipe. Her ceremonial demeanor was slow and deliberate as befitting her station and it was some time before the wife of another dignitary could be invited with propriety to join the party. A small group of these awaited their turn and at their backs hovered a row of solemn, Gauguinesque beauties, the chief's daughters, whose husbands, if any, being of no account in the social hierarchy of the tribe had been sent about their business while such important matters were being treated. No more than seven or eight leaders of Buon Dieo society separated us from these bronze Venuses, but each one would have to be entertained with protracted urbanity.

With a great effort, the two or three dowagers were disposed of, and we were down to the nursing-mothers, who, removing their babies from the breast and passing them to onlookers, tripped lightly towards us. Although the rice-alcohol, with its queer burnt-cereal taste, was weaker than usual, my friends said, it was beginning to take effect. The Moïs had slipped into an easy-going joviality and the nursing-mothers received some mild familiarities, for which they exchanged good-natured slaps. Their capacity for alcohol, though, was greater than that of the elder ladies, and they were not to be deceived by a mere pretence of drinking on our part. Calling for beakers they sucked up the alcohol, spat libations, syphoned off liquor until the beakers were filled, and presented them to us. Taking stock of the situation we saw that we had drunk our way to within two nursing-mothers of those perfect young representatives of the Polynesian race, the chief's daughters, who flung us occasional glances from between sweeping lashes. But we were all flagging, dizzy with the alcohol and the stunning reverberation of the gongs. And the morning was wearing on. It would have been difficult to imagine our condition by the time we had drunk our way down to an interesting social level. The Moïs encouraged us with smiles and gestures, but we could do no more.

It was at a village in the vicinity of Buon Dieo, where two years previously an extraordinary affair had taken place. A family of eight persons were suspected of magic practices to the detriment of the village. According to local custom a representative was chosen as accuser and a trial by ordeal arranged. This consisted of the villagers' champion and the head of the accused family plunging their heads under water, the first to withdraw his head, in this case the accused, being held to have lost the day. According to the rulings of customary law governing this rather unusual case the charged persons were found to be possessed by certain minor demons, located in each case in a bodily organ. The general attitude thus was a sympathetic one. The prisoners were regarded as dangerously sick and only curable by the removal of the affected organ. After this was done they would be once more regarded as entirely normal members of society. The fact that death quickly followed the operations was entirely incidental and most sincerely regretted by all concerned. This was all the more so since the eight were regarded as having, quite accidentally, died the 'bad' death and therefore certain to be converted into revengeful ghouls unless propitiated by the most costly sacrifices, spread over a period of two years. In conformity with this obligation every animal in the village was soon slaughtered and the rice reserves converted into alcohol. The villagers then borrowed from neighbouring communities until their credit was completely exhausted, after which they settled down to starve.

It was at this point that the affair reached the administrator's ears. As a result eight of the principals in the case were tried in the French court and received thirty years apiece. No Moï, of course, could ever understand the justice of this, and it would be impossible to convince him that the appalling fate of the prisoners, all praiseworthy men in their eyes, is anything more than the revenge of the spirits of the eight who died. It is because their sacrifices were insufficient. If only their resources hadn't given out, all would have been well. And there is something in the last suggestion, because it was only the exhaustion of the food supplies that caused the administrator to hear about the affair.

Beyond the model villages of the M'nong R'lams lay the country of the less evolved M'nong Gars. The villages of the M'nong Gars were built along the banks of the Krong Kno in the shallows of which the villagers seemed to spend most of their day bathing or inspecting and re-setting their fish-traps. The Krong Kno was a swift, yellow current, divided by sandbanks on which unconcerned M'nong Circes sat in groups arranging their tresses.

Buon Ročai, where Ribo had business, had been the headquarters of a well-known French anthropologist, who had been determined

facing: A LONG-HOUSE AT BUON DIBO

to live as a M'nong, eschewing all the aids of Western civilization. Some time before our visit he had been reduced by various maladies, including beri-beri, to a condition when he could no longer walk, and the M'nongs, foreseeing the possibility of having to arrange the expensive burial ceremonies prescribed when a stranger dies in the village, got a message through to Ban Méthuot, asking for him to be taken away. He seemed to have been well liked. The hut in which he had lived for a number of months had been declared taboo and everything in it was exactly as he had left it. The table was still littered with the papers he had been working on, with his fountain pen lying among them. There was an uncorked bottle of French gin, a miniature camera and several films. Ribo said that he used to exchange legends with the M'nongs and that their favourite was the story of Ulysses and the Syrens which much resembled one of their own, dating from the days when their ancestors, contemporaries perhaps of the Homeric Greeks, had been a seafaring people. In this village there were several sufferers from *tukalau*, a fungoid disease of the skin only found in Polynesia and among certain South American tribes. The M'nong Gar long-houses were not raised on posts like all those we had seen until now.

At Buon Ročai we were joined by the chief of a canton of M'nong Gar villages. He was importantly dressed in a thick black coat, a vest and carpet slippers, worn over several pairs of woollen socks. A Turkish towel was wound, boating-style, round his neck, and to complete this ensemble — which did not include trousers — he wore a ten-gallon cowboy hat with a chin-strap. The chief's face was stamped with the rodent expression of an Oriental who has had too much to do with Europeans. He smiled frequently showing a row of gums that had been badly damaged in a too-conscientious effort to remove all the evidence of teeth. The chief was evidently not a man to be afraid of ghosts, as according to Ribo he had committed two murders, but was too valuable for administrative purposes to be put out of circulation — an unusual concession to expediency in so stern a moralist as Ribo.

113

facing: BUON ROCAI, SHOWING JARS HOUSING TUTELARY SPIRITS

It was decided to stop next at Buon Lê Bang, where the anthropologist's fiancée lived, so that Cacot, who would shortly be passing through Saigon on his way back to France, could call at the hospital with news of her. When we arrived the village was in the middle of a ceremony. A buffalo had been sacrificed that morning and now bleeding collops of flesh, complete with hide and hair, were hanging up all over the village. Brillat Savarins were industriously engaged in chopping up meat and compounding it with various herbs, according to their secret recipes. Frameworks had been put up outside all the houses on which brilliant red strips, attached at regular intervals, were drying like chilli peppers in the sun. Scintillating, metallic looking flies spiralled about them.

The villagers were in a hilarious state. They had already been at the alcohol for four or five hours and there was a deafening clamour of gongs from the principal house. The ceremonial stiffness had long since worn off and we were assailed on all sides with offerings of raw meat and alcohol in bakelite cups. We went into the common house, in which, until they had outgrown it numerically, the whole village had lived. There was none of the strict division here of the M'nong R'lams, with the partitioned-off family apartments which it was incorrect to enter, and the common-room, with its neatly arranged ceremonial objects, where the visitors were received. This, instead, was a low, single chamber, perhaps fifty yards in length, lit by the two entrance apertures at each end, and a certain amount of light that filtered through the woven bamboo walls. The space occupied by each family was marked off by the formal arrangement of the family's possessions. This was applied even to the cooking pots, suspended from the wall, each in its place and exactly level with the neighbour's identical cooking pot. The jars, too, formed unbroken ranks from one end of the house to the other. It was an astonishing display of a passion for order, which had arisen, apparently, from the exigencies of sharing the limited available space. One imagined some senior personality, in the role of orderly officer, running his eye along the line of pots on his daily tour of inspection, with a critical frown for the occasional improperly folded blanket.

Cacot asked to see the anthropologist's fiancée and she was instantly produced along with a couple of young relations. She was a splendid creature with large black eyes and a deep yellow, but by no means unpleasing, complexion. The removal of her teeth had been clumsily done, resulting in permanently swollen gums and a slight displacement of the top lip. Although slightly tipsy she managed to retain a pleasantly demure manner and many bakelite cups had to pass from hand to hand before she could be persuaded to raise her eyes. The two younger Gauguin models sat twisting their hands, heads averted, and faces, as far as one could see, masked with fright, having quite sobered up under the effect of our terrifying presence. It appeared that the all-powerful old women of the tribe were sufficiently drunk by now not to require propitiation, so Cacot asked without more formality if any of the girls were available for marriage. The fathers immediately appeared, clearly delighted. Both the younger girls were ready at any time, and their mothers would pay a high price in jars and gongs for approved sons-in-law. Unfortunately the older girl was already promised. In the case of a good-looking girl like that the competition was bound to be strenuous, and no wonder a European had fallen for her. Being a divorcee, the father pointed out, she was exceptionally well off, as, according to law, she had kept all her husband's property when he had left her home. Cacot said he would decide on the younger of the remaining pair and marry her, with a holocaust of buffaloes, when he came back from France. He gave the girl a few promissory pats about the torso, and she did a painful best to look pleased. Whether this was taken seriously or not, I don't know. Probably not. The Moïs enjoy leg-pulling as much as anybody else.

After leaving Buon Lê Bang we were on the Emperor's new hunting track. Moïs were hacking this out of the virgin forest with implements that looked like garden hoes. They were paid six piastres a day, the piastre being worth fourpence officially, or about three-halfpence on the blackmarket, and they were lucky to be able to work off their fifty days compulsory labour in this way and not on a plantation. When this road was finished, the Emperor would be able to drive in his specially fitted-up jeep, with a wooden platform built up, throne-like, in the back, right into the heart of what is supposed to be the richest hunting country in the world.

It was a mysterious landscape with mountains like thunder-clouds threatening from the horizon. Clumps of bamboo spurted up from low, boiling vegetation. For the first time I saw the miracle of a peacock in flight, that Cacot fired at hopelessly, soaring with trailing plumage to the very top of a fern-swathed tree. The country was over-run with tigers and all the M'nongs' stories were of them. Local wizards were reputed to specialize in tiger-taming and obtained their hold upon the villagers by allowing themselves to be seen riding upon the back of a muzzled tiger. Ribo was quite convinced that this took place; but even the most unimaginative European becomes infected with local credences in such places as this. There were a thousand inadvertent ways, too, of calling up a tiger, always ready, it seemed, to appear, like an uncomplaisant genie at the rubbing of ring or lamp. Most solecisms and lapses of table manners were reputed to have this unfortunate effect. It was particularly disastrous to scrape rice from a pot with a knife. Ribo said that the prestige of the tiger and their supposed human accomplices had risen so high that the M'nongs were becoming afraid to hunt them. After a recent hunt in which the tiger was killed, all the dogs who had taken part were found dead next day. Poisoned by a sorcerer, he thought. It was two of these tiger-men that the *Chef de Canton* had done away with. There was something curiously symbolical about the victory of this puny creature in his collection of cast-off Western clothes against the men in the tiger-skins.

The last village reached that day was Buon Choah, belonging to a small and exceptionally interesting tribe called the Bihs. When

Doctor Jouin had visited the valley, two years before, they still retained their ancient burial customs which, he said, were identical with those of the Hovas of Madagascar. For two years the dead were exposed in open coffins in the trees. After that the bones were taken down and thoroughly cleaned, and before final burial. the skull was carried round the fields by an old woman of the family, and offerings were made to it. Doctor Jouin's photograph of the elevated coffin, which he needed for a book on Moï funeral customs, had been destroyed during the Japanese occupation and I promised to take another for him. But I was too late. In the two years since Jouin had been there American evangelical missionaries had been to the village, persuaded the Bihs to give up such customs, and by way of giving something in exchange had taught one of the village boys to play the harmonium.

We had been spotted on the outskirts of Buon Choah and by the time we walked into the village an extraordinary spectacle was taking place. Women were scrambling in lines down the step-ladders of the long-houses, like cadets coming down the rigging of a training ship. They then formed up in two rows — one on each side of the path, standing fairly smartly to attention. They wore white turbans and navy-blue calico blouses and skirts. The chief came hurrying to meet us, carrying under his arm a copy in English of the Gospel of St. Mark and the usual diploma awarded for meritorious service to the Japanese.

Ribo and Cacot seemed faintly displeased and said something to the chief, nodding in the direction of the women. The chief snapped out a word of command and the blouses began to come off. When the women weren't being quick enough, the chief and the heads of families shouted at them in stern reproof. In a few seconds the reception parade was ready and we made our way to the chief's house between two score or so of freely displayed Balinese torsos. I believe that Ribo and Cacot thought that the blouses, too, were the work of the pastor, and felt that the moment had come to draw the line.

At Cêo-Rêo, not far from Buon Choah, are located the villages of those enigmatic personages, the Sadets, of Fire and Water, whose fearsome reputation is widespread throughout Indo-China. It is astonishing to realize that from the remotest antiquity the Kings of Champa, Laos and Cambodia — that is, the temporal powers between which Indo-China was divided — all paid tribute to the formidable spiritual authority of these two poor Jarai tribesmen.

The Sadet of Fire is the guardian of a fabulous sword; a primitive, crudely hewn blade, according to report, which is kept wrapped in cotton rags. The mere act of half-drawing this weapon — to which the aforementioned kingdoms all lay claim — would be sufficient to plunge the whole of living creation into a profound slumber; while to draw it completely would cause the world to be devoured by fire. Until the reign of the present king of Cambodia's grandfather, a caravan of elephants bearing rich presents was sent annually to the Sadet of Water.

Both the Sadets seem to be regarded as the incarnation of supernatural beings, possessing involuntary and apparently uncontrollable powers, which are malefic rather than benevolent. The Sadet of Water is associated, in some obscure way, with epidemics, and is a kind of spiritual leper, surrounded with the most awesome taboos. When he travels through the country, shelters are specially erected for him outside the villages, and offerings are placed in them. Neither Sadet is allowed to die a natural death. As soon as one is considered to be mortally ill, he is dispatched by lance-thrusts, and a successor is chosen by divination from the members of his family. The mantle of this relinquished authority is said to be assumed with much reluctance by the person designated.

CHAPTER IX

THE RHADÉS

NEXT morning we reached the country of the Rhadés, who are said to be the most advanced of the Moï tribes. Like all the others they are great talkers and topers and have the familiar self-depreciatory humour ('our women are the ugliest in the world'), but they have not yet been infected with that sense of doom, that listlessness in the face of threatened extinction that seems to beset most members of the animal species after they have passed a certain stage on the downhill path. It has also been found that the Rhadés will accept slight modifications in their way of living if such innovations can be represented to them as approved by the spirits.

Ribo had sent word calling the personalities of the village of Buon Plum to a palaver. Their village had been selected as the guinea-pig for the social experiment that was his pet project. The idea was to introduce agricultural innovations and anti-malarial measures. Buon Plum was to become a model village; an object lesson to all its neighbours, who, it was hoped, would be anxious to follow suit. That was how it went in theory. But it was clear that Ribo could not convince himself that it would really work out that way. There were so many factors to be taken into account; some, I thought, that as a French official he felt unable to specify. However, Ribo had gone so far as to persuade the people of Buon Plum to put in a great deal of work, clearing an area of forest and planting a communal orchard and vegetable garden. They were to plant maize and manioc, which they wouldn't know how to turn into alcohol. As a result, he hoped (but doubted), they would eat more and drink less. This time he was going to talk to them about anti-malarial measures.

We were met, outside the village, by the chief accompanied by the heads of families, each carrying leaves of tobacco and a small bowl containing cooked rice and an egg. It was correct to take a leaf of tobacco from each, and to symbolize acceptance of the food by touching the egg. The chief had the fine, pensive face and the curving nostrils and lips of the best type of Yemeni Arab. (Do anthropologists still go about taking cranial measurements and if so, what could they make of the diversity of the Moïs?)

The chief and his notables were all turned out in their best turbans, jackets and loin-cloths. Every man held ready for inspection a Japanese diploma or a certificate of service with the French-raised militia. Ribo, alarmed by the formal atmosphere, decided to ask the chief, at this stage, for the ceremonies preceding the palaver to be cut to a strict minimum. The chief bowed gravely in agreement but pointed out that as a newcomer — myself — was present, a brief rite inviting the protection of the various spirits could not be avoided. Ribo shrugged his resignation and we accordingly went up into the common-room of the chief's long-house, where my friend's pessimism deepened at the sight of the lined-up alcohol jars. The arrangement of the room was almost identical with that of the M'nong R'lams; the benches running round the walls, the battery of gongs and the great buffalo-hide drums. On the beams, hung with leather shields, cross-bows and drinking-horns, were the art-treasures I was coming to expect; a daringly sporting Vietnamese calendar showing a bathing beauty, a car-chassis oiling chart, a Tarzan cartoon.

At a sign from the chief I took up position on a stool opposite the principal jar but with my back to it. The gongs struck up but I could see nothing of what was happening, as all the activity was going on behind me. I was alone in the middle of the room facing a blank wall awaiting my formal presentation to the spirits before I could be allowed to join the ceremony. Someone came and stood behind me and began a low-voiced incantation, barely audible above the clangour of the gongs. I was told afterwards that this was the sorcerer, who had come in with a white cock, had bathed its feet in water and was now waving it over my head. As soon as the incantation was complete the sorcerer turned me round on the stool and handed me the bamboo tube from the tall jar. At the same time the chief's wife, the only woman in the room, took a thin, open-ended copper bracelet from one of the jar handles and fastened it round my left wrist. This conferring on the welcome stranger of the copper bracelet must be a custom of extreme antiquity, since it is practised by Moï tribes all over Indo-China, most of which have lived in separation in historical times. It carries with it temporary tribal protection and a number of minor privileges, which vary in detail from village to village, such as the right to touch certain of the sacred drums. There is a fuller degree of initiation which is undertaken by some Europeans wishing to take part in the more closely guarded ceremonies such as those accompanying the removal of the front teeth at puberty. In this case the initiate pays for the sacrifice of a pig, and a little blood drawn from his foot is mixed in alcohol with that of the pig and drunk by all present. On such occasions a thicker bracelet is con-ferred, on which is engraved a secret mark. Further sacrifices are indicated by additional marks, the bracelet serving thus to record, for all to see, its wearer's services to the community, and is the equivalent on the spiritual level of the Japanese diploma or the French certificate of military service. Many Europeans are to be seen wearing half a dozen or so of the thinner bracelets. They are one of those mild affectations, like tying on the spare wheel of one's car with liana, which mark the old Indo-China hand.

Having by this time taken part in several Moï ceremonies, I was beginning to appreciate some of the fine points which at first I had overlooked. Thus, I had noticed that when beginning to drink from each fresh jar a polished ritualist like Ribo spat a libation through the loosely woven bamboo floor, doing so in a most grave and deliberate manner. Following this practice for the first time, I noticed that although the spiritual essence of the libation may have been accepted by the tutelary spirits, the physical presence was received with acclamation by eagerly guzzling ducks, which, attracted by the sound of the gongs, had marshalled themselves under the floor, directly beneath the jars. The row of notables seated opposite nodded benignly at this gracious performance. Their spirits were beginning to pick up, under the belief, probably, that a full-blown ceremony was going to develop after all. Attendants were hovering hopefully in the background with titbits of raw meat on bamboo skewers, and others who had been surreptitiously sent down to the river were now arriving with tubes full of water and waited in expectation of the order to top up fresh jars. The boys seated at the gongs were beating out a frenzied rhythm. But Ribo was looking at his watch, and as soon as the minimum three cows' horns had been accounted for, he asked the chief for the palaver to begin.

The Moïs, in the way of most so-called primitive peoples, put themselves to great efforts to be polite to strangers. Although there was no doubt about the general disappointment at this breaking up of what had looked like being a good party, there was a great show of understanding of the importance of the occasion, and every village male able to attend was immediately sent for. Within a few minutes they were all lined up like a photographer's group along one wall of the common-room; as earnest-looking as theological students in the presence of a Cardinal. Not an eye strayed in the direction of the jars from which the neglected drinking-tubes curved despondently. There was a dead silence and as soon as Ribo began to speak every man and boy was clearly straining his ears, although no one understood a word of French. It was curious that none of the matriarchs was present.

Ribo began with a familiar gambit. 'Tell them Tuón,' he told the interpreter, 'that the spirits are angry with the Moï people. Tell them that when the people of Buon Plum were counted, twenty years ago, there were eighty-six adult males. Now there are forty.' Tuón put this into Rhadés and Ribo said that, although unable to speak the language, he understood it enough to know that the plain facts were being clothed in the poetic eloquence which the Rhadés, with their reverence for the spoken word, would expect of their administrator.

'The Rhadés will vanish from the Earth,' said Ribo, warming to his subject. 'The Annamites will come to Ban Méthuot as they came to Dalat. They will cultivate the rice-fields of the Rhadés and their dogs will scratch up the bones of the Rhadés' ancestors.' In a lugubrious voice Tuón rearranged this Jeremiad for local taste. The Arab-looking chief seemed depressed. Ribo belaboured his hearers shrewdly with threats of post-mortuary horrors unless they helped themselves before it was too late. 'Do you want to keep out the Annamites?' he asked. 'Do you want to keep the country for your children and grandchildren to be able to perform the rites for your spirits?' There was a brief roar of assent. Ribo explained that the only way this could be done was to increase their numbers by combating the malaria that was killing them off. This could be done by buying medicine and mosquito nets with the money earned by the sale of surplus fruit and vegetables. Was that agreed? It was. And would the chief see to it that the new wealth wouldn't be turned, as usual, into jars and gongs. The chief gave his word.

With this the palaver was at an end and we were about to go when the interpreter told us that a meal had been prepared for us. Among the Moïs it is disgracefully rude, and offensive to several powerful spirits, to refuse an offer of food. Such an offence would in theory be compoundable only with a sacrifice of alcohol. A great effort should also be made to eat all that is offered. Ribo was alarmed again. The Moïs are the most omnivorous race in the world, and he warned us that a delicate situation might arise if, for instance, we found ourselves served with a dish of the highly prized variety of maggots that are cultivated by some tribes for the table.

However, we underestimated the sophistication of the chief of Buon Plum. A rickety table and three chairs were carried into the common-room. The first bowl arrived and we saw, with relief, that it contained only plain rice. There followed a dish of roasted wild poultry, and — a culinary surprise about the equal of being served an elaborate French sauce with one's fried fish in an English café — a saucer of *nước mắm*, the extract of fermented fish whose truly appalling odour is so strangely divorced from its flavour. There were ivory chopsticks provided and dainty Chinese bowls. The whole village in its undissolved photographer's group looked on in entranced silence. As we picked up our chopsticks the chief made a sign and one of their number came forward and began to play on a flute.

The interpreter Tuón was an *évolué*. This in Indo-China is the usual designation for one who has forsaken the customs of his or her race, dresses in European cast-offs, wears an habitually subservient expression and is sometimes privileged, by way of compensation, to ride a bicycle. True to type, the evolved Tuón looked like a beachcomber, but perhaps his evolution was not complete, since he had not yet acquired a fawning smile. Ribo had noticed that some of the people of Buon Plum had been taking him aside, as it seemed, to discuss some private matter, and he asked what they had been saying. Tuón said evasively that they weren't pleased about something. Weren't pleased about what? Ribo insisted. About the people who had been sent to the plantation and hadn't come back, Tuón said. And what was to stop them? Ribo asked. If they had wanted to come back, they would have done so.

But Tuón grumbled in a most un-evolved manner. I was beginning to see him in a loin-cloth again. He was tactless enough to tell Ribo that the men were being kept by force on the plantation, and the villagers had told him that not only could they not carry on with the orchard and the vegetable garden, they would have to reduce the area of their rice-field if these men were not released. Ribo said that we would go to the plantation and look into the matter for ourselves.

Two days later, when on our way back to Ban Méthuot, the investigatory visit was paid. The plantation was one of a number in the country supplying rubber to manufacturers of motor-car tyres. It continues to prosper because of its location, where it is temporarily out of reach of the Viet-Minh, although the administrative buildings were burned down in an attack in 1946. Most of its competitors in the south have been put out of business by the desertion of their labour, or by their too-close proximity to the fighting zones.

There was something feudal in the spaciousness of these great Romanic buildings of the plantation, a contemptuous patrician setting of extremes of grandeur and wretchedness. Crouching peons squatted in their rags at the foot of splendid stairways and humped bales of rubber in its various stages beneath colonnaded arches. The *colonus* was fetched from some central domestic lair, emerging to meet us through the kitchens. It was difficult to place his origin with any certainty although he was undoubtedly a European. He looked younger than he was and moved fussily in a perpetual effort to use up some of his too great store of vitality. He was dressed like a townsman, wore a talisman against the evil-eye on his wrist-strap, and a religious medal, which he sometimes fumbled with, suspended from a fine, gold chain round his neck. I imagine that he lived in patriarchal intimacy with his family and his servants. He was probably abstemious, experienced intense, narrow loyalties, and was quite implacable. He smiled a great deal.

We were shown into a huge room, which the director probably disliked, and seated round a most elaborate cocktail cabinet. With the technique of a cabaret tart the director poured out large shots of whisky for us, serving himself with what was probably a little coloured water. Two henchmen came in and sat down; enormous, pink-faced fellows who mopped their faces, and, in imitation of their chief, smiled incessantly. They were like the pictures one has seen of trusties in an American penitentiary, and there was something about their inarticulate and rather sinister good humour that provided a perfect foil for the dapper geniality of the director.

Ribo asked if that month's renewal contracts had been prepared

for the men who would be working another year. The director
said they had. Good, Ribo said, in that case they could now be
signed in his presence. The Italian said they had been signed already.
How was that? Ribo asked, when he had made it most clear that he
wanted to be present at the signing. The director was charming,
repentant, conciliatory. How really extraordinary! He had quite
misunderstood. Still there would be plenty of future occasions.
Monsieur the administrator must realize perfectly well that all he
wanted was to co-operate. This was just a little more convincing
than the patently insincere regrets of the receptionist in a high-class
hotel. The director bathed us in his smile. Very well, said Ribo,
coolly, we would go and talk to the signatories, now,

The director was delighted. With a flood of protestations he asked
that it should be remembered that he never demanded better than
to be given the chance to show any of his good friends round. The
whole of the plantation was wide open to them at any time. He
had nothing to hide. He turned to his trusties for moral support,
and they grinned back gleefully at him. There you are, the director
seemed to say, by his look. He waved the bottle of whisky at us.
He was never happier than in company. And now we were here he
was going to take the opportunity to show us over his model
establishment, the fine, up-to-date workers' huts, the infirmary. . . .
After that he insisted that we come back to dinner.

It was a good two hours before Ribo, battling against the tide,
got what he had come for. We were taken into a yard where about
fifty Moïs were lined up awaiting us. These were the coolies whose
contracts had been due for renewal, and of them only three had
refused to sign and were being sent back to their villages. They
were as miserable looking a collection of human scarecrows as one
could have seen anywhere, and suddenly I realized that in the
villages I had never seen a poverty-stricken Moï. Ribo checked
their names off against a list he had, while the director, as if to forestall the possibility of any criticism, launched an offensive of his
own. Calling Tuón, he told him to ask this ragged assemblage if

they were satisfied with the treatment they had received. There was no reply to the question and the director seemed much surprised. Ribo now took a hand. 'Tell them to speak up,' he said. 'If they are dissatisfied with their contracts, let them say so. There is absolutely nothing to be afraid of.' The two bodyguards looked on cheerfully with folded arms. The director went up to one of the dejected figures and prodded him cautiously with his finger. 'Ask this man if he is satisfied.' Tuón spoke to him and, with averted eyes, the man mumbled a reply. 'Well,' said the director confidently, 'and what does he say?' 'He says that he is satisfied,' Tuón told him.

The director turned with a spreading of the hands. Only a moment's respite was allowed for this to sink in before he was pressing his advantage. 'Now ask them all — I say all of them, if they have not received the premium of 150 piastres. You, you and you,' said the director, permitting his fingertip to approach to within an inch of the rags, 'have you or have you not received your premium? If not, you have only to tell me now and I myself will give you the money.' There was a prestidigitatory flourish and a wad of clean notes appeared in the director's hand, and were waved under a line of apathetic noses. 'They have all received the premium,' Tuón said.

A sunny smile broke easily in the director's face and the bundle of notes described a last, graceful arc before disappearing into his pocket. 'What did I tell you? They have all received the premium. A generous advance on their wages. Money to send to their necessitous families.' The thing was clearly concluded. The director was afraid that he was being victimized by certain invidious persons he preferred not to name who put themselves to a lot of trouble to spread silly reports about him. There was one way only to deal with that kind of thing and that was to expose it to the light of day, and, foo! — some imaginary object was blown away with a light puff of the director's breath, and the director's palms were brushed quickly together in brisk gestures of exorcism. He turned now, awaiting the visitors' pleasure. Had they seen enough yet? If so . . . The Frenchmen, dour, almost stolid beside this Etruscan mime, were reluctant to be persuaded. Tuón was more depressed than ever. The Rhadés had let him down. He drooped in his convict's garb. The fifty solemn coolies stared at their feet. The director and his men were on good terms with all the world.

Ribo made a last attempt, while the director arched his eyebrows and rolled his eyes in humorous tolerance. 'Tell them we came to see them because we heard that they were dissatisfied. Now we know that this was not true. They have chosen of their own free will to work for the Company. We shall go back and tell their people that they are happy.' A voice in the rear rank mumbled something and Tuón went towards it. The two strong-arm men, still smiling, although now incredulously, moved forward. Two Moïs were blotted out in the towering bulk of each of them. The director was looking at his watch again. Ribo asked what the man had said. 'He says he was forced to sign,' Tuón told him. There was no sign of triumph in the colourless voice.

How was he forced to sign? Ribo asked. The big men were making for the dissenter who was looking from side to side, as if for a way of escape. Ribo followed them. 'Tell him to speak the truth,' Ribo said, 'and I promise no harm shall come to him.' Tuón spoke to the man again. He had the rather womanly good looks one finds so often among the Jarai tribes to the north, and it was hard to believe that he came of the same stock as the semitic-looking chief of Buon Plum. His legs and arms were covered with scars which showed up a pale, ugly pink against the dark bronze of the skin. He said that he had been kept a prisoner until he agreed to put his thumb-mark on the paper. The two trusties stood over him as he mumbled out this revelation, barrel chests thrust out, grinning down at him. Their attention was only distracted when another voice was heard. A second man had found the courage to tell the administrator that he had been taken and his thumb forced on to the contract. There was a growing murmur as this extraordinary rebellion spread. Others joined in to say that they had only found out at the end of their fifty days' obligatory service that they had been tricked into putting their thumb-mark on a contract for a year. They were always having to put their thumb-mark on something or other, like receipts for the tools they were given to work with. Tuón was going from man to man up and down the lines. He came back to say that only three of the coolies would stay of their own free will.

But now Ribo was faced with a new problem. It was one thing to badger the Company into releasing a few workers who might be held there by force or trickery, but quite another, as it seemed clear would happen, if this were followed up, to attempt to deprive a powerful and wealthy concern like this of the whole of its labour. Ribo knew that, traditionally, administrators were broken for attempts of this kind. The thing was too big. It had got out of control. The genie he had summoned up could not be appeased by a trifling reform. Either the Company must be allowed to continue to get its labour by fraud or force — since it was evident that this was the only way it could be got — or it would go out of business. It was as drastic as that. And then, with the Company no more, and the untended plantations reverting to the jungle, where would the tyre companies get their rubber, and ultimately the French motorist his tyres? It seems, in fact, since there is no reason to suppose that other rubber plantations in Indo-China are run on Christian principles, that this commodity which is regarded as essential to the conduct of our civilization is often only to be obtained by turning a blind eye to illegalities and oppression, and that there is little difference in practice between the secret gangsterism of these days and the open slavery officially abolished in the last century.

There was only one course open to Ribo; to withdraw as gracefully as he could after promising the Rhadés that the whole matter would be investigated. The director was not in the slightest degree shaken. He would probably have preferred to avoid this unpleasant incident, because he was affable and expansive by nature, liked to get on with people and did not enjoy scenes. But he knew perfectly well that Ribo could do nothing to him, that is to say, nothing serious, without challenging the purpose of the colony itself. A Resident himself, whose power was far greater than Ribo's, told me later that all he could do was to put a brake on the activities of the planters. 'We snap at their heels, like curs — that's all it amounts to. If it wasn't for us they'd go into the villages after the labour and bring the men back at the point of the gun.'

And now I knew why Ribo, Doctor Jouin and all the rest of them were so sure that there was no hope for the Moïs. They always told you that it was the malaria, although it didn't make sense that it was only in our time, after all those centuries of resistance to malaria, that it should begin to finish them off. Ribo might succeed, with his model villages, in checking that downhill plunge, in holding the level of the population of Buon Plum or even in setting it on the uphill climb again. But while, beneath the show of solicitude on the part of men of science and low-level officials, the real purpose of the Moï village as seen from above was to provide forced labour, there could be no real recovery.

CHAPTER X

THE VANISHING TRIBES

BAN MÉTHUOT was dull enough after the Dak Lac. I was promptly re-installed by Doustin among the silent splendours of the Residence, and told, once again, to 'pousser un grand coup de gueule' out of the window if I wanted anything. Doustin thought that there was little hope of leaving Ban Méthuot yet awhile, in any direction, and mentioned that the convoy which had left Ban Méthuot, following mine, had been badly shot up. However, one would see — one would see, and smiling secretly he withdrew, to the crashing of the sentries' salute. I felt that he had something up his sleeve.

In the cool of the later afternoon I visited the local missionaries. Having heard something of their activities in the Dak Lac area, I was curious to see these people who taught their Moï converts to sing in harmony from Sankey and Moody and distributed woollen berets, as a sign of grace, to their children.

Mr. Jones, the missionary, was a spare, bearded American, who looked like a New England farmer out of a picture by Grant Wood. His expression was one of severe beatitude, and his wife, too, gave the impression of being the happy possessor of a simple formula which had relieved her from doubts and misgivings of any kind. I do not believe that either of the Joneses had ever wrestled with an angel, nor would they have seen any point in the pessimistic attitude of most of the prophets. The practice and propagation of their religion was to them a pleasant and satisfying activity, offering, moreover, plenty of scope for self-expression. They lived in the best villa in Ban Méthuot, and were aided in their tasks by two cars and a plane.

The pastors of the American Evangelical Mission do not agree

with a diet of locusts and wild honey. It is normal for them to arrive in a country, I was told, with several tons of canned foodstuffs,
calculated to last the length of the stay. Referring to the luxurious
appointments of his villa, Mr. Jones went out of his way to assure
me that they were normal by French Colonial standards. Moreover, he said, he and his wife often slept in the bush. He went on
to say that they both liked and admired the French immensely and
did their best to co-operate with them in every possible way. They
were in better odour, in fact, than the French Roman Catholic
Mission, which had been banned from some areas for its political
activities. By this the pastor supposed they had taken some sort of
interest in the natives apart from their spiritual welfare — a thing the
American Evangelical Mission never did. I waited in vain for the
quotation beginning, 'Render unto Caesar', and refrained from
telling the pastor that the missionaries are universally thought by
the French authorities (I believe them to be wrong) to be political
agents of Washington. In this the French show a lack of understanding of the American mind, arguing with Latin simplicity
that as the missionaries make few converts — in the Buddhist
parts of the country, none at all — why, otherwise, keep them
there?

In reply to my inquiry after the progress of his labours the pastor
said that they were making some headway against unbelievable
difficulties. To take the language problem alone. Like most of these
Far-Eastern languages, it was barren in abstractions, which provided
the most appalling difficulties when it came to translating the Holy
Writ. To give just one example, he cited the text, 'God is Love'.
In Rhadés there was no word for God. In fact these people didn't
get the idea at all without a great deal of explanation. Also there
was no word for love. So the text came out in translation, 'The
Great Spirit is not angry'. It got over that way, he supposed, but
not as he would have liked it.

You could imagine, he said, the kind of effort that went into the
preparation of his address when he visited a new village for the first

time. 'Before starting in on them, we had to build a prayer-house of our own. We told them that we wouldn't go into any of their houses that had been tainted with the blood of heathen sacrifices. After we got the place built, and it cost us plenty — in commodities like salt, I mean — we went right in there and endeavoured to preach the Christ crucified and risen, to all that attended.' The pastor said that they always took pictures of the crucifixion to give away, having learned that the natives were interested in the technique of any new blood-sacrifice. Some of the natives used to turn up expecting a ceremony with what the pastor called 'that damnable alcohol of theirs', and when they didn't see any jars about the place they went away again. 'However we didn't give up the fight. There was nothing so sweet to my ears as to have one of these poor, ignorant, deluded souls we had struggled and prayed for, come to us and say, "When I die you will plant a cross on my grave and not a buffalo skull." That was victory indeed,' said the pastor, and for a moment there was a true pioneering gleam in his eyes.

I asked if he had ever found the tribes intolerant of his preaching, and the pastor said, no, on the contrary. The trouble was that the natives were only too ready to accept any message but wanted to be allowed to fit in the new revelation among their own idolatries. He just couldn't make them understand that God was a jealous god. That was another term that they didn't have in their language, and he had to spend hours explaining to them. A typical attitude after hearing the gospel was to offer to include the new spirit in their Pantheon along with the spirits of earth, water, thunder and rice. This usually went with the suggestion of a big ceremony, to be provided by the pastor, at which a number of buffaloes and jars would be sacrificed and the new spirit would be invited to be present. 'We just can't get them to see how foolish and wicked these sacrifices are. Why only today we saw some natives drinking in a field and when they saw us in the car they came running over to offer us alcohol. Can you imagine that? We actually recognized people we had already given instruction in their own language out of a little manual we produced.' The pastor put a book in my hand. It contained, said the title-page, thirty hymns, a section on prayer, an explanation of twenty-six religious terms, a short summary of the Old and New Testaments and a Church manual, with duties of preachers, elders, baptism, the Lord's Supper, dedication, the marriage service and the Apostle's Creed. And all this was written in the Rhadés language with its lack of such words as God, love, hate, jealousy. A formidable accomplishment indeed!

Bringing up the matter of the plantations and their effect upon his endeavours — since coolies working thirteen hours a day and seven days a week would obviously be unable to attend Divine Worship — the pastor drew in his horns immediately. He was concerned only with the natives' spiritual welfare, and their material conditions were no interest of his whatever. One thing could be said in favour of the plantations, in fact, and that was that a man working there was at least put out of the way of temptation. His view was that it didn't really matter what happened to a man in this world so long as he had acquired the priceless treasure of Faith. When Jesus said that 'He that believeth in me shall be saved' he was not referring to this life. Naturally, if one of his Christians got into trouble he would try to come through for him, so long as it didn't annoy the French. I realized quite sharply that the pastor was totally uninterested in the natives as a whole, but only in 'our Christians (we love them like children)'. He collected souls with the not very fierce pleasure that others collect stamps.

It is curious that a twentieth-century evangelist should join hands in this belief in the unique and exclusive value of faith with his first missionary predecessor, the seventeenth-century Jesuit, Borri. Borri was scandalized and depressed at a display of most of the Christian virtues on the part of a people who had not benefited by conversion. '. . . others profess Poverty, living upon Alms; others exercise the Works of Mercy, minist'ring to the Sick . . . without receiving any Reward, others undertaking some pious Work, as building of Bridges, or other such thing for the Publick Good, or erecting of Temples . . . There are also some Omsaiis (priests) who profess the Farrier's Trade, and compassionately cure Elephants, Oxen and Horses, without asking any Reward, being satisfy'd with anything that is freely given them . . . insomuch that if any Man came newly into that Country, he might easily be persuaded that there had been Christians there in former times; so near has the Devil endeavour'd to imitate us.'

There was, however, a remedy for this distressing state of affairs, for '. . . This is that part of the Earth call'd Cochin-China, which wants nothing to make it a part of Heaven, but that God should send thither a great many of His Angels, so S. John Chrysostom calls Apostolical Men, and Preachers of the Gospel. How easily would the Faith be spread abroad in this Kingdom . . . for there is no need here of being disguis'd or conceal'd, these People admitting of all Strangers in their Kingdom, and being well pleas'd that every one should live in his own Religion . . . nor do they shun Strangers, as is practis'd in other Eastern Nations, but make much of them, affect their Persons, prize their Commodities, and commend their Doctrine.'

Borri had his wish. The Angels, Apostolical Men and Preachers of the Gospel arrived in great numbers, and it was under the pretext of protecting them from Annamese oppression that the French conquest of the country was undertaken.

That evening I went mistakenly to a restaurant that masqueraded under a European name. I believe it was the Restaurant something or other. In this part of the world one is always at the mercy of the Far-Eastern peoples' broadmindedness and ingenuity in matters of food, and consequently there sometimes arises a craving for something simple, definite and nameable. The Restaurant fell badly between two stools. Although a juke-box groaned gustily in a corner, the screen that only partially excluded the kitchen details was ominously decorated with dragons, and the remnants of a meal that had been eaten with chopsticks were snatched from my table as I sat down. Without my being given a chance to express my preference, a moody Vietnamese waiter now arrived with a plate of eggs, which might have been laid by thrushes. They looked like highly coloured and greatly magnified frog spawn and were bathed in green oil. This was followed by the *plat du jour* for Europeans, described as a *Chateaubriand maison*, a huge slab of blueish-grey meat, undoubtedly cut from the haunches of some rare, ass-like animal that had been shot in the local forest. '. . . Et des pommes Lyonnaises,' said the sombre-faced waiter arriving again, and releasing over the plate a scoop-ful of fried, sliced manioc. This was accompanied by a bottle of perfumed beer.

Since it was an odd day of the month, and therefore lucky, my neighbour, a French soldier, following the example of several other patrons, decided to play for his dinner. The system favoured was *Tai-Xiu*, in which three dice are used and the house wins when the score is under ten, besides taking as its percentage any bet when triple threes come up. None of the players seemed to realize that the luck of odd days is universal and not one-sided. Chanting most dolefully, the waiter shook the dice in the bowl and threw them on the table. My neighbour lost and paid double his bill. The house sooth-sayer now arrived and took his hand, informing him after a brief study of its lines and for a small payment, that he had offended a minor demon and that the time was unpropitious for him to travel by elephant, to build a house or begin clearing a rice field.

For the further diversion of its patrons this restaurant had fixed to its wall a large, glass-fronted box, housing white rats. A brain sharpened by a study of the problem of perpetual motion had devised a system of miniature treadmills which kept the rats continually on the move. Only rarely was one allowed to perch for a few seconds on a narrow ledge before being dislodged and plunged into hectic activity again by the arrival of one of its companions. It was an hypnotic spectacle and one felt sure, especially in the throes of digestion of one's ass-steak, that somewhere arising out of this was to be drawn a cruelly Buddhist moral.

I strolled back to the Residence in the failing light, hoping that it was not too dark to see a tiger before it saw me. Green fire-flies were pulsating in the shrubberies. Owls had taken up positions on garden gateposts, not so much as budging as I passed them, and occasionally as a breeze stirred I caught the fine-drawn wailing of a distant gramophone or the brief spate of notes of some strong-throated Eastern nightingale. As I turned into the garden of the Residence a Moï guard materialized, like Herne the Hunter, against a tree-trunk, pushed a bayonet towards me and shouted a challenge; a whiplash of monosyllables in some unknown language. This was a recurrent embarrassment. There was nothing to be done but to stand there, with occasional blossoms drifting between us, and say anything in English that came into my head. After a few moments, embarrassment touched the Moï, too, the bayonet drooped, there was a slurred-over drill movement and he sank back; his face screened in aerial roots.

Within a few minutes of my return Doustin was tapping at my door, smiling his controlled smile, and mildly triumphant. It appeared that an important politician, a French Deputy, had just arrived and would be leaving at three o'clock in the morning for Pleiku, which was about two hundred miles to the north. Did I want to go? I did.

The Deputy, who was an ex-Governor of Cochin-China, was travelling with his secretary and a chauffeur, and the whole party, as usual, was armed to the teeth. Outside the towns in the central plateaux of Annam it is really no man's land, and Viet-Minh patrols probably use the roads as much as isolated French cars. It was always assumed that the Viet-Minh were regular in their habits and did not travel at night. The Deputy was going to make the best of this night journey by shooting game, if he saw any. He had a splendid new gun, a five-shot repeater, and both the Deputy and his secretary said that they would be very surprised if they didn't get at least one leopard.

We were held up for some time on the outskirts of Ban Méthuot through taking the wrong track. The big, soft American car nosed its way through the bamboo thickets, its headlight beams trapped, as if in a thick fog, a few yards ahead of the car. At night the sameness of the forest was immeasurably intensified. In the end the driver found the right track and we plunged forward confidently into the tunnel of bleached vegetation. The Deputy and his secretary, wrapped as if for grouse-shooting on the moors, sat with tense gun-barrels poking through the windows on each side. There was a single moment of excitement when we saw, swinging before us, a cluster of pale lamps. The driver braked and doors were half-opened but it was only the tossing eyes of a herd of domestic buffalo, which now, fully revealed in the headlights, turned their hindquarters to charge from us, plunging noisily through the solid walls of bamboo.

In the early dawn we had still shot nothing and the Deputy with failing eyesight, but unimpaired enthusiasm, had to be restrained from opening fire on more buffaloes, a group of Moïs on the horizon, and finally upon piles of elephant droppings in the road. Our final and profitless exploit was a great advance through thorny bush after the will-o'-the-wisp sound of screaming peacocks, which could always be heard in the trees fifty yards ahead. After this rifles were put aside and the shooting members of the party relapsed into a gloomy coma as we climbed out of the hunting country into the pleasant, sunlit plateau of Pleiku.

It was a wide, Mexican-looking landscape, a great, rolling panorama of whitened elephant grass with the worn-down and partly wooded craters of ancient volcanoes in the middle distance, and a blue ribbon of peaks curled along the horizon. Elegant white hawks with black wing-tips circled above us. Occasionally we saw a few Moïs of the handsome Jarai tribe, marching in single file and in correct family order; the young men first, carrying their lances, then the women and finally an old man — the head of the family. Before reaching a village this little procession would halt to allow the old man to take his ceremonial place at its head. The Jarais carried their household goods in wicker baskets of excellent workmanship, slung on their backs. They smoked silver-ornamented churchwarden pipes and wore necklaces of linked silver spirals.

Pleiku was an authentic frontier town, with military notices on all sides. Pine trees grew in the bright red earth, but there was no grass — only the red soil and the pines. The smart, Mediterranean-looking villas were set back from the road and surrounded by spiked pallisades. A few cars with armoured wind-shields were running about, and civilians as well as the soldiers carried rifles. We passed a strong-point at the cross-roads and I was charmed to see that warning was given by beating a gong. Hairy, long-snouted pigs, indistinguishable from wild boars, dashed about the streets. I noticed that the urbanized Jarais had discarded their fine wicker baskets and jars, replacing them with jerry-cans. All Pleiku resounded with the same powerful nightingale song which I had heard, only in rare bursts, in Ban Méthuot.

The cross-country journey into Laos, which at Saigon had sounded so simple and reasonable, and at Ban Méthuot had taken on a more problematical colour, was now at Pleiku beginning to look like a hopeless proposition. Laos, as one approached it, seemed to exert a powerful anti-magnetic repulsion. At Saigon there were vague memories of many cross-country trips, dating perhaps from pre-war days. In Ban Méthuot professional hunters were thought to have sometimes made the journey. But in Pleiku the information was uncompromisingly definite. No one went there at all, said Monsieur Préau, the Resident, and the most he could promise to do, in the most favourable circumstances, would be to get me to Bo-Kheo, about half way to Stung Treng, in Laos, and after that it would be up to me.

But even the Pleiku — Bo-Kheo section of the journey would call for careful organizing, because it was a year or two since anyone had done it, and therefore the bridges might be down. From Bo-Kheo to Stung Treng, Préau said, there used to be a regular lorry service run by the Chinese. Regular, but on what days? It was important to be in possession of all the facts, because there were no Europeans in Bo-Kheo, and nowhere to stay; therefore one's arrival had more or less to coincide with the lorry's departure. And, said Monsieur Préau, he would have to see me quite definitely on the lorry and the lorry in motion, before turning back, because Chinese lorries had a habit of breaking down and sometimes it took several weeks to get spare parts — several months in Bo-Kheo perhaps, since how were they to get there?

Then again there was the question of the security of the Bo-Kheo — Stung Treng area. By that, he meant, whether or not there were bandits about, and if so what kind, and how many. All this information would take a few days to get and Préau suggested that I might like to fill in the time visiting some of the outlying military posts in his territory. He was sending a man next day for a report to Mang-Yang, their furthermost outpost in the East, and I was welcome to go with him.

Doustin had sent an official telegram to Préau, advising him of my arrival, but in addition to this I carried a personal letter from Ribo and Cacot, from whom I had parted on the best of terms. The three men had been in the Colonial Service together in Mauretania. Préau evidently wanted to do all he could, but had I known at the time what he was up against in Pleiku, I should have hesitated to trouble him with my presence. A few days before, Viet-Minh groups had visited most of the villages in the zone and had requisitioned rice. They had also set up their own posts, some of which the French were still trying to find. At this moment when it was thought necessary to press every available Moï into the militia, the planters had suddenly brought pressure to bear for the increase of the supply of labour to the plantations. Préau was between the devil and the deep, but I only learned this, a little at a time, in the days that followed.

Next morning we set out for Mang-Yang. Among the Resident's many troubles was a chronic shortage of transport. That morning the jeep we were to use broke down as soon as it was started up, and the driver spent the time, until Préau arrived to find out what had happened, shooting at pigeons with a cross-bow. In the end we had to go off in the Resident's Citroen, leaving him only a lorry for use in emergency. Mang-Yang was about eighty miles away, nearly half way to Qui-Nhon, on the coast, which, with a belt of territory of uncertain width, was solidly in Viet-Minh hands.

My companion, Préau's secretary, was an excessively peaceful-looking young man. He sat beside me in the back of the car, with a sporting gun on one side and a Sten on the other. Our road wound around the great eroded stumps of volcanoes, and it was in these bare surroundings, quite out of their normal element, that we suddenly saw ahead of us a group of seven or eight peacocks. They were sauntering in the road and paid no attention whatever to us. It would have been possible to run them down. My friend fired and the birds, without signs of alarm, trooped away into the grass, all but one, which fell sprawling in a ditch. The driver went to pick it up. There was something that was rather shocking about the ungainly posture of this bird in its shattered dignity. It was slightly indecent. Searching in the stiff screens of plumage, the driver could find no injury, there was no dappling of blood, the muscular legs struck out, and when released the wings beat down strongly. Which ever way the bird was held, its head curved up towards us fixing us reproachfully with its eyes. The secretary told the driver to kill it, and the man looked embarrassed. He made some incomprehensible excuse, speaking in Jarai. Nobody, it seemed, cared to kill the bird and it was stowed away in the back of the car. I felt uncomfortable about this and the secretary probably did so too, as he talked about taking the bird back and keeping it as a pet. When later in the day we opened the back of the car to inspect it, the

secretary was horrified to find that all the bird's fine feathers had
been quietly plucked out at some time when we had left the car
unattended.

At Dak Ayun a yellow fortress bristled in the plain; a log-built
affair with bamboo pallisades in place of barbed-wire entangle-
ments. Patrols would have to walk round it, and it could hold off
an attack by a company of not too resolute infantry, but the first
field-gun would blow it to matchwood in a few minutes. The
machine-guns of Dak Ayun protected the survivors of four Bahnar
villages which had been concentrated beneath its walls. The
Bahnars, a somewhat lowlier tribe than the Jarais or the Rhadés,
had suffered Viet-Minh reprisals for giving information to the
French. A party of Viet-Minh tommy-gunners had arrived, judged
the notables concerned, and executed twelve of them on the spot
with their own lances. The secretary had to report on the condition
of the refugees.

The senior N.C.O. in charge of the fort took us to see them. He
was as pale as if he had come from watching an execution, and had a
black Landru beard. The Bahnars were living in wretched shelters
of leaves and branches. They were filthy, diseased, ragged — and
probably starving, since they had lost their animals. The tigers
were attacking them, the N.C.O. said. Tigers were so bad in these
parts that his men had orders never to leave the fort unless in pairs
and carrying their arms. Among this stench and misery I noticed
a woman weaving cloth strikingly patterned with stylized monkeys.
Her weaving frame was carved with almost Persian intricacy. This
was the fate of Moïs who defied the Viet-Minh by giving information to the French. Later I learned that even severer punish-
ments awaited those who offended the French from fear of the
Viet-Minh.

Leaving these tragic people, we started off for Mang-Yang. The
pale-faced N.C.O. asked to come with us. It was a great treat for
him, he said, to be able to leave the confinement of his stronghold,
and he added that as mortar-fire had been reported that morning

in the Mang-Yang sector, we might just possibly run into a Viet-Minh fighting patrol, in which case an extra Sten in the car might make all the difference. It was true that from that point the road showed more signs of border affrays. We passed a burned-out car with a grave beside it, a deserted and partially demolished Moï village and a wrecked bridge, now being rebuilt under the eye of a crouching machine-gunner.

At Mang-Yang we had come to the extreme limit of the territory held, however tenuously, by the French. This ultimate outpost, temporary or otherwise, of the Colonial possessions in Central Annam was held for France by a slap-happy sergeant from Perpignan, a cabaret-Provençal, who roared with laughter at the thought of his isolation, and poured us out half-tumblers of Chartreuse, which was all he could get to drink. Every morning, with teutonic regularity, the Viet-Minh fired five or seven mortar-bombs at them from over the crest of the nearest hill. They replied with their trench-mortar and that was the end of hostilities for the day. There was nothing to stop you going out if you wanted to, and he himself used to make short expeditions to collect butterflies. The only other excitement was produced by the occasional passage of a herd of elephants. He used to fire at them with the Bren, but so far without results.

Laughing loudly, the sergeant made us climb to the top of a tower where he kept his butterflies, his Bren, a row of French pin-ups and his store of Chartreuse. His view was superb. A patch of the forest was still smouldering where the morning's mortar shells had fallen. The sergeant said it was a pity we hadn't come earlier and suggested we stayed the night, when we could be sure to see some action in the morning. We asked him how he got on with the Moïs, and he said that he was lucky to be where he was and not down in Cochin-China in command of Bao-Dai Vietnamese. Down there it was nothing for a fort to be sold out to the Viet-Minh, but the Moïs had never done anything like that so far. They didn't seem to know the value of money. That reminded him, he said, his men had caught a tiger-cub the day before, and we must see it before we went. He called one of the guards and told him to fetch the cub, but the man said something and shook his head. The sergeant burst out laughing again. 'Well, what do you think of that? *Ah, mince alors* . . . they've eaten it.'

. . . That ubiquitous tiger! I never saw one, except for a single specimen at Dalat, hanging, as large as a pony, from a tree, to be skinned, while a brace of Vietnamese doctors bid excitedly against each other for the teeth and the valuable medicinal portions of the intestines. Even the evangelical pastor at Pleiku, with whom I dined that night, had only to go for an hour's moonlight drive in order to see one, and had actually found one in his front garden a few evenings before.

It was from the pastor that I learned, quite accidentally of course — although this was boldly confirmed later by a French official — what happens to Moïs who fail to advise the French of the presence of the Viet-Minh in their neighbourhood. He told me that he had just come back from Kontum where he had been visiting one of 'our Christians' who had been put in prison for this omission. Quite casually the pastor mentioned that this Christian, who had been three months in the prison, couldn't use his arms yet. I asked why, and the pastor said, as if it followed as a matter of course, that they had been disjointed at the interrogation. Were there any more than his Christian involved? Why, yes, about eighty had been arrested, of which he guessed that no more than twenty had been strung up. And who had done this? The pastor mentioned the name of a military commandant I had already met. Both he, and his wife, he said, found him in their personal relations a very charming man. In fact, he treated them so well they found it hard to believe that he could be, well — kind of rugged, when it came to such disciplinary matters.

There was a well-known tea plantation not far away, and the French officials, as usual, had not been afraid to let me know, in a roundabout way, what they thought of it, and of the methods of the

facing: MANG-YANG: THE LAST FRENCH POST

planter. But the missionaries had nothing but praise for the Algerian that ran the place, and it turned out that he had given them their furniture. There was something quite extraordinary in this situation that, while French Colonial officials privately condemned what was ultimately the Colony's *raison d'être*, and if admitting the use of torture, turned their backs in distaste upon the torturer, these men of God shut their eyes to abuse, and would even accept gifts evidently designed to ensure their goodwill and perhaps co-operation. It should be emphasized that in the small conventional details of conduct, they were, like Brutus, honourable men; patterns of American small-town society, clean looking and clean living, hospitable, friendly and married to wives who might have been voted second most likely to succeed in whatever had been their particular collegiate class-year.

But one began to wonder whether a whole catalogue of easy, short-range virtues had not been outweighed by some gigantic, fundamental shortcoming — which might have been that they had added respectability to the three original virtues of Faith, Hope and Charity, and had made it greatest of the four. If unpleasant things like lynchings at home and torturings abroad happened, it was best to ignore them; most respectable to pretend they didn't exist. To do otherwise would be to 'meddle with politics', a form of activity much disapproved of by Pontius Pilate. I repeat that the American evangelical missionaries were the happiest looking people I have seen in my life.

It so happened that I soon found myself visiting the plantation whose director the missionaries had found so generous. Strangers in Indo-China soon find out that the great plantations are thought of by the colonists as the principal show-places the country has to offer; only slightly less spectacular, perhaps, than Mount Fuji from one of its accepted viewpoints, Niagara Falls, or the Grand Canyon. In actual fact I cannot conceive of anything less exciting, since in the ends of efficiency a plantation is governed by an order that is

facing: PLEIKU: THE SACRIFICE

wearisome in the extreme. Usually only one type of bush or tree is cultivated and the fact that there may be hundreds of thousands or even millions of them does nothing in my opinion to lessen the tedium.

The plantation we visited had roads along which we did 50 m.p.h. for mile after mile in a jeep, seeing nothing but dull, little bushes of absolutely uniform size and spacing. We were taken to a height from which there spread out beneath one a peerless landscape, across miles and miles of which it was as if a fine-tooth comb had been drawn, producing a monotonous warp of close-drawn lines. The director scorched along in his car through this vast and boring domain, showing us with pride the barrage he was building, designed to produce some fantastic kilowattage, and with sorrow the ruins of splendid, seignorial buildings that had been gutted by the Viet-Minh. There were three million tea plants and only a thousand coolies, which was a desperate state of affairs, the director said. They suffered, too, from the chronic idleness of the natives' disposition. The government saw to it that they handled them with kid-gloves — they were paid a fixed rate of five piastres for a working day of twelve hours, plus 800 grammes of rice and an allowance of salt — but whatever was done for them they showed no signs of realizing how well off they were.

At the plantation house we found why the official who took me to the plantation had been sent for. The Deputy with whom I had travelled up from Ban Méthuot awaited him. There had been a little luncheon party in the Deputy's honour, and the Deputy and the planters now got my friend in a corner and formed a ring round him, faintly menacing beneath the post-prandial geniality. In the meanwhile the lady of the house discussed literature. She had just been reading, in translation, Mr. Graham Greene's *The Heart of the Matter*, and found it too terribly depressing — quite the most depressing book she had ever read. Did British colonials really lead those awful existences? And, besides that, as ardent Catholics, both she and her husband did not know whether they approved of the theme. She sighed and looked round her, doubtless reassured, after

Greene's harrowing account of the bungaloid crudities of West Africa, by the infallible heritage of Latin civilization in her surroundings.

Meanwhile voices at the other end of the room were raised. The Deputy was laying down the law. The plantation had to have more labour, and he had come up from Saigon to see that it got it. The local authority said that there was absolutely nothing to be done. Every available man had already been drained from the villages in the neighbourhood. If the villages were to survive an irreducible minimum of able-bodied men had to be left in them. The Deputy told him that three hundred more men were needed, and they were going to have them by hook or by crook. My friend pointed out that between military service and labour in the plantations they had practically exhausted the man-power of the Jarai tribe. This gave the Deputy an idea. Military commitments up here in the plateaux were unimportant, he said. If necessary the three hundred men could be transferred from the *Garde Montagnarde*. It was at this point that the administrator gave up. Three hundred soldiers would be withdrawn from the forts and set to work picking tea-leaves at a time when enemy infiltrations were more frequent than ever before. Thus, assuming that it was in France's interests to keep its hold in Indo-China, were the nation's interests sacrificed to the short-term ambitions of a small, powerful group of its citizens.

Putting down the book which depressed her so much, the direc-tor's wife had an idea. The perfect solution, she thought, would be if the government would allow them to employ the Chinese nationalist internees, who were being held in the Tonkinese camps, instead of leaving them there to eat their heads off in idleness. She was sure that the Chinese would be only too pleased to have the chance to work. All those present agreed with her, and the Deputy said that he would raise the matter in Saigon.

'The plantation,' said the administrator, on our way back, 'will burn — and they know it. It is only a question of time. But before that happens they are determined to squeeze out the very last drop of blood.'

CHAPTER XI

CENTRAL ANNAM

THERE is a school at Pleiku for the children of the Jarai and Bahnar tribes in the neighbourhood. With some difficulty, and by putting pressure on the chiefs, the children are persuaded to come and sit in its class-rooms, where they learn a few words of French and acquire higher education embracing a nodding acquaintance with Napoleon's campaigns and the names of the principal rivers of France. As it happens, the European idea of education as a process quite separate from other aspects of living and occupying most of a child's energies until, say, at least the age of fourteen, is quite incomprehensible in its wastefulness, from the Moï's point of view. A Moï cannot be persuaded that there is any virtue in knowledge which cannot be applied. At six years of age the Moï child is introduced as a matter of rigid tribal custom to certain light tasks in the rice-field; he learns a little carpentry and receives preliminary instruction in the arts of gathering food. He is usefully employed, for his labours are integrated with the village economy, and they increase in usefulness in proportion to his growing older. These serious activities are, no doubt, far more enjoyable than learning lessons in a class-room. However it has been decided that if the Moïs are to be turned into valuable colonial citizens they must be educated according to Western standards. So to the school-room they go.

The recruiting campaign for scholars having gone well at Pleiku, it had been found necessary to build an annexe. But at this stage tribal custom was too strong to be ignored. The children's parents would not allow them to occupy the new building unless it had first been consecrated for use; that is, put under protection of the tribal spirits by an appropriate sacrifice.

A sacrifice of this kind must be made as soon as possible after

sunrise, as it takes several hours to prepare the flesh for the subsequent feast. At seven o'clock, then, in the cool morning, when the
pines threw long shadows over the red earth, a young buffalo was
dragged into the school-yard and tied to the sacrificial stake.

The buffalo is regarded by the Moïs as spiritually more than an
animal, and hardly less than a human being. It is therefore entitled
— unlike other animals, which are simply knocked on the head — to
a slow and highly ceremonial death. This is always accorded it.
As a further sign of respect, the animal is presented before the
sacrifice, as in this case, with a generous drink of rice-alcohol from
one of the sacred jars.

It was held by a rope of rice-straw round the neck and was
terrified by some mysterious animal premonition. In the background had been set up ritual masts, their stems ornamented with
stylized geometrical designs; suns, moons, toucans' beaks, flies'
wings, buffaloes' teeth, and their tops sprouting artificial branches of
frayed bamboo, from which hung streamers and carved plaquettes.
These masts are the Moïs' equivalent of flagpoles. They are highly
artistic and their intention is to attract the visual attention of the
spirits to be invited to the ceremony, just as they are summoned
audibly by gongs. After the sacrifice the masts are planted about the
villages as a permanent decoration, providing thus a perpetual gala
effect. The sacrificial stake, too, often subordinates solidity to
art. It sometimes breaks, allowing the buffalo to escape. However
lamentable its condition, no attempt is made to recapture it, since
this would conflict with the spirit's evident wish.

As soon as the buffalo had been attached, a group of pupils,
carrying gongs and dressed in sombre, handsome blankets, appeared.
With a slow, mournful beating of the gongs they began to circle
about the buffalo which, more alarmed than ever at these sinister
preliminaries, made panic-stricken efforts to break free. Four more
pupils joined the death procession. They carried a huge drum
supported on a framework of poles, which had been borrowed from
a local chief. This drum, I learned, was valued at fifteen buffaloes

and there had been a great deal of fussy admonition on the chief's part before he could be persuaded to let it go. A few minutes later, the chief himself, who had been worrying about his property, turned up, and, wearing a military medal on the breast of a new, white sports-shirt, took his stand in the front row of the audience to make sure that there was no culpable negligence. When beaten, the drum gave out a most important sound, a muffled growling, agreed by those present to be irresistible to the spirits, however aloof.

What followed was a most distressing spectacle. Two of the fathers stood out. Carrying *coup-coupes* (the Moï weapon which is half knife and half axe), they approached the animal from behind. They succeeded after several false attempts, when the heavy knife struck home with a hideous chopping sound, in hamstringing first one leg, causing the animal to hop about on a single back leg in a frantic effort to avoid the blows, and then the second leg, when it collapsed on its hocks, its rear legs bent uselessly under it. This frightful disablement failed to prevent it from shuffling with desperate energy round the post, while, like minor bull-fighters that have fulfilled the role assigned to them, the men with the *coupe-coupes* retired, and two others, armed with lances, stepped forward. The subsequent tragedy was long drawn-out and incomparably bloodier than a bull-fight, when until the last moments of its life the bull is majestic and incalculable. About this grotesquely shuffling bulk there was squalor and humiliation in which we were all involved. No particular technique, it seemed, was demanded of the killers, and they had a good half-hour in which to pursue their prey with desultory proddings and stabbings. Finally, with a frightful shuddering groan — the first sound that it had uttered — the animal expired, was immediately dragged away and thrown on a brushwood fire, where it was left to scorch superficially for about fifteen minutes. No attempt has ever been made to reform or modify cruel sacrifices of this kind, and this is the end which awaits every buffalo in the Moï country. One is told by the French that it is part of their policy to respect the religious customs of the natives. In such matters as this there is much official susceptibility where the natives' freedom of action is concerned.

In the early afternoon we came back. There were thirty-seven jars of alcohol lined up with a number of bamboo tubes protruding from each, and every Moï in Pleiku, including all the pupils, was exceedingly tight. Politely, following the Resident's example, we took our place for a few seconds before each jar, rejected the baskets of chopped, raw meat, and nibbled with slight nausea at skewers with tit-bits grilled *à la kebab*. This token participation was obligatory, otherwise the Resident risked having the heads of the families declare the ceremony null and void and refuse to allow the children to attend school. After a few minutes we arose to go, but the Jarai school master spotted our intention and came reeling towards us to beg the Resident to wait a moment. There was a surprise arranged for us and, raising his arm, he shouted a command. The thirty-seven pupils rose unsteadily from their jars and, leaning upon each other for support, formed a swaying line. There while we faced them rather sheepishly across the blood-splashed earth and beneath the buffalo skull, now scraped clean and shining and impaled on a spruce ritual post, they burst into Auld Lang Syne, rendered to the words, 'Faut-il nous quitter sans espoir — sans espoir de retour?' They wanted to show us that their school years had not been spent for nothing.

The remainder of the day was spent in an official visit to the Vietnamese community of Pleiku. To guard against any fifth column activities on behalf of the Viet-Minh, all the Vietnamese in the district had been concentrated in the single village of Phu-Tho, which was guarded by a French fort. The purpose of the Resident's visit was to offer official congratulations on the eve of the feast of Têt, the Chinese and Vietnamese New Year; orginally celebrated with the abandonment of all endeavour for the first three months of the year — a period which it has now been found convenient to reduce to a week.

The attitude of the Resident towards his Vietnamese minority was one of uneasy tolerance. I had now, in unbroken succession, met four French administrators who were all highly intelligent, broadminded and well-intentioned. They recognized evil, and as far as they could without risking their positions, they fought it where they saw it. At least one of them, although he would not openly admit it, was a fervent anti-colonialist. Yet none of them could ever find a good word for the Vietnamese. They conceded that there was a special charm in the way of living of the Laotians and the Cambodians. The Moïs, of course, were children, lazy and improvident but delightful. But the Vietnamese — well, you never knew where you were with them, they suffered from an inferiority complex, concealed their true thoughts or feelings, were cruel and had no religion to speak about, were 'not like us'. It is unsafe to discuss the Vietnamese in a French audience, because a reproving voice will always be raised to tell you to wait until you have lived thirty years in the country before you talk of fathoming this muddy psychological pool. The most intelligent Frenchman seems to be influenced subconsciously in this matter by the sheer dead-weight of prejudice of his uncritical compatriots. I am reminded of the British interpretation of the Chinese character as portrayed in the popular magazines of the period following the Boxer rebellion, when for a generation the Chinese supplied us with villains of fiction who were obnoxious in a two-faced and totally un-English way.

To me this suggests that the French like the Laotians and the rest of them because they do not fear them. They can relax their defences in the comfortable knowledge that these are harmless and declining peoples, and with this their good qualities become, rather nostalgically, apparent. They are like the Spanish conquerors of the West Indies who delayed official recognition that the Caribs had souls until their extermination was almost complete, or like the Americans who are sentimental about their vanishing Indians, forgetting the massacres of the last century when the only 'good injun' was a dead one. The Vietnamese are a subject people who refuse to go into a graceful decline. There are 17 millions of these 'bad injuns' and nothing is too bad for them.

The manner of my friends, therefore, when we were received by the notables of Phu-Tho, was courteous but not genial. It seemed that we had arrived a little sooner than expected because a dignitary, meeting us with clasped hands and low bows at the flower decorated arch of entry, begged us to wait until the official drum was fetched. This arrived a few minutes later, carried on poles by a scampering group of notables, who gravely lined up before us and, hoisting their pennants, conducted us with slow and solemn pomp to the pagoda.

There is more poetry in a Vietnamese village but less art than in a Moï one. Under magic compulsion the Moïs carve the objects dedicated to the spirits with designs which have come to have a secondary, artistic value. There is little of this kind of art about poor Vietnamese villages. Unlike the Moï who is non-specialized and self-sufficient, the Vietnamese belongs to a money society and is a market for manufactured products, most of them shoddy; although he may have one or two good pieces of pre-war Chinese porcelain about the house. He does not object to living in a hovel provided that it contains a vase of flowers, and the essence of the perfect household represented by the bright and blossom-decked niche dedicated to the ancestral spirits. The Vietnamese is fortunate in that his household lares do not suffer from the fussy obsession for order of their Moï counterparts.

The pagoda of Phu-Tho, then, was nothing more than a wooden shack, with a corrugated-iron roof — the most valuable part of its construction — which would have disgraced any Moï village. For all that, it was gay with jonquils, narcissus and chrysanthemums, coaxed into choice and grotesque shapes by the devoted cunning of these serene-faced patriarchs. One wall of the pagoda could be opened-up completely, and before this opening we sat on a row of chairs, while joss-sticks were lighted and gongs reverently thumped. An official presented us with a rectangle of vermilion paper apiece, excellently painted with Chinese ideograms for conventional New Year's greetings. Mine read 'five felicities under the same door'. These Chinese New Year's greetings are much prized throughout Indo-China, particularly in remote districts of Cambodia and Laos where there are no Chinese. Here the meanings of the ideograms are unknown and the consequent element of mystery enhances their magic virtues. One sees them pasted on most door posts in some villages, where they are carefully preserved the year round.

Our visit to the pagoda was in deference to a principle no different from that followed in Moï villages. We were being presented to the tutelary spirit. The pagoda of a tutelary spirit is to be found in every Vietnamese village, and sometimes there are two or more. In the past the ancient cult has been modified by the system of Confucius and by Buddhism, but now the driving force in the two great philosophies has faltered and waned, and the cult still survives. The tutelary spirit was once some outstanding village personality, or even its founder, for whom, in return for services rendered, has been created a sort of spiritual baronetcy. In Phu-Tho there was nothing particularly colourful related of the character of this semi-divine distinguished citizen, but at another village I visited he had been a thief of quite extraordinary prowess. For the annual feast some meritorious person was granted the privilege of representing him in a ceremony which consisted in the representative's breaking into the pagoda at night and carrying off the sacred tablets. He was then chased, caught, pelted with mud and refuse by the indignant villagers, and received a ritual beating to which every tax-paying male was allowed to contribute his blow. Having recovered from this treatment, he became the guest of honour at the subsequent feast.

It was inevitable that the presentation of the pagoda should be followed by the Vietnamese equivalent of the alcohol jar. Unfortunately the civilities of the morning had provoked in the case of each of us a severe attack of the kind of indigestion that follows an excess of rice-alcohol. We were alarmed then, when, cramped with heart-burn, we were led into the Spanish-type patio of the *chef du conseil's* house, and observed a table laden with bottles of sweet, heavy, French aperitifs. We took our seats at the table eyeing the bottles dully, while the notables filed slowly in, and stood in a circle facing us, round the walls. They were dressed in black coats and turbans and white trousers. There was a moment of confusion when it was realized that someone had usurped the Resident's. chair of honour, distinguished by a towel that had been hung over the back, but this was soon put right, and the *chef du conseil* standing forward, with head bent slightly and clasped hands, delivered a fairly long speech of welcome in Vietnamese. As soon as this was over the notables advanced implacably with cakes of rice, honey and nuts, stamped into the shapes appropriate to the season, others arriving with cups of tea, while yet others resolutely uncorked the bottles — chosen I was certain for their colour, as they were all red — and poured out a white bakelite mugful of Cap Corse, Suze or Campari — whichever happened to be nearest. Our attendants then took a respectful pace back to allow us to drink. There was a moment of hesitation while the notables looked on anxiously, then the Resident, abstemious by nature, but conscientious in his duties raised his glass. Murmurs of approval came from the onlookers. and now, to our consternation, we saw that bottles of champagne were being uncorked. But the notables were all smiles and highly delighted with the miniature explosions of the popping corks, reminding them, no doubt, of celebratory firecrackers, and therefore highly suitable to the occasion. For the champagne the white bakelite mugs were removed and replaced in the interests of colour-harmony with pale blue ones.

At last, although from a glance at a side-table it was clear that more colour-combinations of liquors and mugs had been intended, the Resident seized an opportunity to rise. The ceremonial drum was rushed into position, the banners elevated and off we went, at a rapid if unsteady shuffle. But it was not back to the Resident's Citroen that we were led. Instead the procession stopped before another house, a replica of the first, with the Spanish patio, the towel-draped chair, the felicitous cakes, the encircling notables and a startling vision of a liquor called Eau de Violette in lemon-coloured containers. This, we found, was the house of the religious head of the community, who was, if anything, more important than the mayor, and we should have been taken there first but for the fact that our host had been caught unprepared by our premature arrival.

Next day the awaited news had come from Stung Treng, and it was discouraging. Cambodian bandits, displaced as I learned later by operations against them in Central Cambodia, had arrived in the area. It was a good spot for bandits, removed as far as possible from the centres of authority and yet populated by many prosperous fishing villages along the Sré-Pok and Sé-San rivers; tributaries of the Mékong, between which the road to Stung Treng ran. The Resident said that he had business with the chief of the Jarai village of Ču-Ty, which was a good way along my road. This man was also chief of a *secteur* of villages and his jurisdiction ran as far as Bo-Kheo, being in this direction, at the native level, co-extensive with that of the Resident himself. The Resident said we should be able to get up-to-date information from him of the situation on the borders of Cambodia and Laos.

Accordingly we set out in the Resident's lorry, accompanied by a schools inspector from Pleiku who wanted to visit the school at Ču-Ty, and an entirely Europeanized Jarai interpreter, who wore handsome French clothes and the latest fashion in plastic belts and wrist-straps. This young man, who was in his early twenties, was the first successfully Westernized Moï I had seen. He looked like a minor French film star and was indistinguishable from a Southern European, except, perhaps, that he smiled more. The Resident happened to mention that he was a young man of exceptional intelligence, adding that it was a further testimony to the inherent mental capabilities of primitive peoples, that he knew of another Jarai boy who had left his village for the first time when nine years old had just been commissioned in the army after having passed out of the officer's school with the highest marks of his class.

It was clear that the road westwards to Ču-Ty was regarded as of strategic value, because Jarai labourers were hard at work clearing the forest to a depth of about a hundred yards on each side. The vast bonfires they had started gave rise to a strange phenomenon. Millions of winged insects fleeing the conflagration were being chased by certainly thousands of birds; offering a wonderful opportunity for a naturalist interested in the ornithology and the insect-life of South-East Asia. Some of the birds were trim and tight-looking; flycatchers, perhaps, successfully engaged in a normal routine. Others, managing with difficulty their spectacular plumage, extracted less profit from the holocaust. Sometimes, absorbed in the chase, birds came floundering into the lorry and disgorged a half-swallowed butterfly before taking off. There were other predators, too, that benefited. The elegant hawks of the plateau of Kontum had gathered to feast upon those whose caution had been dulled by excess.

The village of Ču-Ty was built imposingly on a hill-top, and its chief awaited us at the head of the steps leading to the veranda of his long-house. He was a huge, grinning villain; a Jarai Henry the Eighth, whose name, Prak, meant money. He possessed five elephants, three wives, several rice-fields and a jeep, given to him by the planter of Pleiku, who was reported to pay him ten piastres for each man supplied to the plantations, in addition to the half-piastre paid by the government. Prak was one of those energetic, scheming rascals, who could have been in other times a king among his people, but had sold himself for a trifling sum.

There were none of the elaborate Moï courtesies forthcoming where Prak was concerned. He had learned Western forthrightness in such matters, and awaited us on his veranda, dressed in a single-breasted jacket, while a servitor stood at his elbow with a quart of brandy and a breakfast cup to serve it in. Prak was not the man, either, to worry about ritual offerings of eggs and rice or tobacco leaves. He made a sign and a member of his retinue picked up a piece of wood, dropped from the veranda and fell upon a passing piglet. There was a light-seeming but practised blow, the pig fell shuddering and the man set fire to a nearby pile of brushwood and threw the corpse in the flames. The whole thing was done in perhaps two minutes. The sow wandered up and sniffed nostalgically at the gout of blood left by her offspring on the scene of the tragedy. We went into the long-house whilst Prak snapped out a few orders, sending his minions scurrying in all directions to line up alcohol jars and fetch water.

While the sacrifice was in preparation we strolled over with the inspector to visit the school. It seemed very large for the size of the village. There were about thirty children in a class-room, decorated with their own drawings of jeeps and man-faced tigers. As we entered the room the children stood and began to sing what was perhaps the school song, consisting of a repetition of the words, 'Bonjour Monsieur, merci Monsieur'. The inspector praised the Jarai master for the attendance and the master told him that when any child failed to attend regularly Prak sent for the father and beat him.

The school master was petrified by the importance of the occasion. When the inspector told him to let us see the physical culture class in action, the only thing he could think of getting them to demonstrate for our benefit was breathing exercises. We stood there watching the small chests inflating and deflating hundreds of times, as it seemed, before realizing that the school master intended the repertoire to go no further than this. Finally the inspector, whose eyes were beginning to bulge, could stand it no longer, 'Surely that's not all they've been taught?' The school master explained that he had thought best to perfect one thing at a time and that they had tended to concentrate, until now, on rhythmical breathing. His scared voice could hardly be heard above the busy intake and expulsion of breath. The inspector went over to tell them to stop but although the children showed the whites of their eyes at the approach of the fierce, pale face, they could not be made to understand. 'Well, for God's sake get them to do something,' the inspector said. 'Don't have them stand about like this. Get them on the move. They have got legs, haven't they?' Prak looked on, wiping the palms of his hands together and leering ferociously at the school master who, in desperation, managed another order, and the boys formed a line and began to run round in a circle. When asked by the inspector what they called that, the school master said, correct running. The inspector swore and we walked away, leaving the pupils and future citizens of Ču-Ty to their correct running, which they continued until we were out of sight.

In spite of the informality of Prak's reception his conduct of the ensuing ceremony was exemplary, and it was an interesting one, preserving possibly more of its ancient character than any I had previously seen. The Resident was seated before the jars with his right foot placed on the customary copper bracelet, which itself rested on an axehead and contained some cotton and pieces of pork cut from the recently slain pig. A bowl containing the pig's heart and its four feet was placed on the ground so that the Resident faced it while the sorcerer went through the familiar manipulations with a white cock. Prak's wealth was, of course, displayed in an impressive battery of gongs, and when these struck up they raised a din which brought the domestic animals scurrying from far and near for their share in the libations. Prak's alcohol, too, was stronger than I had tasted, the principal jar being hardly weaker than proof whisky. None of the members of the harem appeared, but it was soon evident that they were conducting a ceremony of their own, for a strange sound was heard from the interior apartments. It was a gramophone, playing sambas and rumbas; the favourite, Maria de Bahia, being played some half-dozen times while we were there. The interpreter who had been sitting apart, his face graven with a

smile of resolute tolerance, told me that such Latin-American popular recording was the only type of Western music popular with the
Moïs.

The afternoon's entertainment was concluded when Ču-Ty's
leading elephant hunter gave a demonstration of his skill with the
cross-bow. Having heard much of Moï aptitude with this weapon
(for example, they kill even elephants with an enormous bow
loaded by two men), I was ready to be shown marvels. With
suitable reverence we stood by while the great man was handed his
bow, selected from a quiver a two-foot length of untipped bamboo,
and slipped it, with professional unconcern, into the notch. One
half expected a cruel piece of eccentricity of the William Tell order,
which would have to be sternly discountenanced by the Resident,
or, failing that, the splitting of a wand at thirty paces after the
manner of Sherwood forest. Our marksman, however, requested
from Prak, and was granted, permission to aim at a fairly stout sacrificial mast from about half this distance. The bolt was discharged
with such terrific force that I did not see it in the air. However, to
the great satisfaction of the onlooking villagers, it missed the mast.
The second bolt went home and it took two men to pull it out
again.

The Resident now asked Prak for information about the road to
Stung Treng and Prak told him that there were bandits in and
around Bo-Kheo itself, and that shooting had been heard in this
village on the previous day. Further conversation followed in private;
it probably had to do with the demand for three hundred more men
for the plantations. When this subject happened to come up I
asked one of the Resident's staff what would happen to a man who
ran away from the plantation and went back to his village. The
answer was that the chief, who had received a premium for him,
would undoubtedly send him back again. If, on the other hand, the
man left his village to avoid labour or military conscription, he
would be breaking customary law, since it was an offence for a
man to leave his village without the chief's sanction. One could

facing: PLEIKU: A DRINK FROM THE SACRED JAR

imagine the fate of any fugitive who threw himself on Prak's mercy.

When we left Prak escorted us part of our way in his jeep. With great difficulty he was levered into the seat next to the driver, half-tipsy and humming through his nose, 'The Lady in Red'. Behind him sat the elephant hunter, having substituted a Sten-gun for his bow. Thus the cortège set out for Pleiku. As we passed the school the pupils were lined up at the roadside waving tricolors and chanting, 'Bonjour Monsieur, merci Monsieur', which, as it sounded extremely like something by Ketelby, seems to suggest that this composer's inspiration was sometimes more truly oriental in feeling than most of us have supposed.

Back at Pleiku we discussed over a dinner of roast peacock — which was rather like tough veal — the possibility of my getting through to Stung Treng. Once again the Resident told me that he would willingly take me to Bo-Kheo, but thought that it would be extremely ill-advised to make the journey. I formed the opinion that he was secretly worried at the idea of my going so far, even as Bo-Kheo, because, as he later confessed, apart from any responsibility he felt over me, he frankly didn't want to lose an almost irreplaceable car. This being a very reasonable and understandable attitude, I felt that I could not trespass any further on the Resident's kindness. The original intention, as suggested by Monsieur de la Fournière at Saigon, had been to take advantage of any lifts I could get with people who in the ordinary course of their duties were travelling across country. But the people didn't exist, and it had never been any part of my intention to inveigle administrators, hard pushed as they were, into making special journeys, involving risk to their personnel and vehicles, on my behalf. I therefore told Monsieur Préau that I had decided against attempting to make the cross-country journey to Laos and would return, as soon as an opportunity offered, to Saigon.

The Resident then suggested as an alternative that I might go

facing: PRAK, WHOSE NAME MEANT 'MONEY'

further north to Kontum, the ultimate town in French occupation. Kontum is the centre of the Bahnar country, where Bahnar villages are still to be seen, not as I had seen them in wretched degeneration at Mang-Yang, but unspoilt, with their amazing communal houses with steepled roofs and their primitive communism which is carried to such lengths that a single chicken will, if necessary, be divided into fifty parts. It was an attractive idea, but I felt that this delay might endanger the visit to Laos, which might be cut off by the rains before I could get there. When opportunities of this kind turned up one always had to think, not so much about the time expended in the actual journey, as the time one might have to waste, stranded somewhere, awaiting some means of getting back. The Resident then made another suggestion. He was obliged to make a routine visit to the village of Plei-Kli, which was one hundred miles on the road to Ban Méthuot. If I wanted to take this opportunity to get back to Ban Méthuot, he would come with me, as it would provide him with a good excuse to get away for a couple of days. This suggestion I naturally fell in with, only too relieved to find that I should not have to lose a week or two in Pleiku before an opportunity arose of getting away.

Our arrival at Ban Méthuot coincided with the first day of the feast of Têt. All activity in the town was paralysed. The shops were shut and there was nobody about. For the Vietnamese this was the combination of all the religious feasts of the Western world, and, since there is no Sabbath in the East, it was the only holiday of the year. Just before midnight a ceremony had been staged in each Vietnamese house to take leave of the household spirit of the expiring lunar year, which is believed to return at this time to the Jade Emperor with a detailed report of the family's actions, for good or for evil. The departing spirit had been provided, in addition to a lavish send-off meal, with money for the voyage, mandarins' shoes, a winged bonnet of the kind that only spirits and mandarins are entitled to wear, and the legendary carp on which the spirit would ride to heaven. The feast would serve also to welcome the incoming spirit and to invite the ancestral spirits to participate in the ensuing New Year's festivities. The day of our arrival would be dedicated to visits exchanged by families and friends, the Scottish custom of 'first footing' in reverse, as there is some competition to avoid being the first to cross a threshold at the New Year, since to do so is to carry the responsibility for any misfortunes which may fall on the family during that year.

Monsieur Doustin was, of course, not at all surprised to see me again, but did not know how he was going to get me back to Saigon. The whole country would be in the catalepsy of the Têt for a full week, and, even after that, he had no idea when a convoy would be formed. The recent attacks had thrown the merchants into a panic. Ban Méthuot, it seemed, was effectively sealed off by solemn feasting and by war. Back in my old room at the Residence I resigned myself to a prolonged appreciation of the view from my window, which looked out over a gracious garden with a peach tree in bloom. It seemed that one or two young couples had succeeded in evading the festive confinement and had made a pilgrimage to admire the classic distortions of the branches and to have themselves photographed against a background of blossom.

Perhaps twenty minutes of reflection were allowed to me before Doustin re-appeared. The Emperor Bao-Dai's plane was arriving in half an hour, and if it were to be returning to Dalat or Saigon he saw no reason why he shouldn't ask for a lift for me. We therefore jumped into his car and shot out to the airport, arriving there just as the plane had touched down. It was a Dakota, and I was truly delighted to see that a dragon had been painted on the fuselage.

The Emperor was the first to alight, followed by a young lady in black velvet robes, whom from her carriage, which was even more regal than that of most Vietnamese girls, I stupidly presumed to be the Empress. I was later informed that she had been Miss Hanoi 1949, and had accepted the position of air-hostess on the Emperor's plane. Several French officers and civilians followed but there were no Vietnamese in the Imperial entourage. I was presented to the Emperor who shook hands with reasonable vigour, while I recalled that up to the reign of his grandfather an even accidental physical contact with the Son of Heaven would have involved strangulation, although if the offender had committed the breach of taboo with the intention of protecting the Divine Emperor from some danger, he would have been posthumously promoted to a high rank in the mandarinate and furnished with an expensive tomb.

Although thick-set for a Vietnamese, Bao-Dai was not, as American newspapers have described him, 'pudgy'. In contrast to the experience of some newspaper correspondents who told me that he always seemed bored when interviewed, I found him cheerful enough, possibly at the prospect of a hunting-trip. He asked me if I hunted and I said that I did not. (I had been warned that it was not a good thing to be invited to join a Bao-Dai hunting party.) The reply surprised the Emperor and the well-arched Imperial eyebrows were raised slightly higher. I explained that I lived in England where game was neither plentiful, varied nor spectacular. The Emperor said that I should try elephant shooting and that there was no better place to make a start than Ban Méthuot. Doustin then asked the Emperor if he would be returning to Dalat or Saigon, as if so I would like a lift, and the Emperor told him that he was going hunting for a few days, but that I was welcome to fly back with him after that. In fact he might decide to send the plane back the next day, in which case the pilot could take me.

But not two hours later I was disturbed once again in the contemplation of my peach tree and the strolling Vietnamese beauties. Doustin came to report that two officials from Dalat who had been staying in the town had just been given permission by Bao-Dai to return by way of the Emperor's private hunting road, and I could go with them if I liked. They were leaving immediately and would stay at the Poste du Lac in readiness to make the usual small-hours start in the morning.

We were received with the exuberant melancholy of the true

existentialist. While the two hunters got out their various weapons, fussed happily with them and deluded themselves with a mirage of false hopes for the morrow, I retired to the veranda and thumbed over the latest selection to arrive from Le Club Français du Livre. Whenever I raised my eyes it was over an impeccable landscape. Eagles were shattering the ice-blue mirror of the lake and a flight of white birds, far off against the dim mountains, were no more than particles of glittering metallic dust.

Thus night descended. At dusk we heard the motor of the electric generator start up and my host smiled with cautious satisfaction. Light pulsated in the filaments of the electric bulbs for perhaps thirty seconds before failing. As on every previous evening the engine had immediately broken down. We lit the lamps and settled down to an evening's reading. But there was a sudden alarm. Somewhere below us in the forest, we heard a car accelerating uphill, and peering through the window we could see headlights shining through the trees. The car was coming in our direction. There could be only one explanation of this extraordinary event — the approach of the Imperial hunting party. It seems that taken thus by surprise, our host felt himself ill-prepared to receive a visit from the most august personage in the land. At all events the lights were quickly extinguished — a cautionary measure which was quite successful, for we heard the car stop and depart.

Those who follow the mystery of the hunter know not the lassitudes affecting ordinary mortals. The Emperor's hunting-trips, which last all night, are said by those who have taken part in them to involve the most appalling risks and exertions. Fortunately the Vice-Mayor and the Chief Justice's wish to make a start before dawn was frustrated by our host's civilized horror of such excesses. As a compromise, breakfast was served to the howling of monkeys at daybreak. Ten minutes later we were out on Bao-Dai's hunting track. On all occasions when the Emperor travels by road between Dalat and Ban Méthuot, this is the way he comes and I think that there may be some significance in the strange fact that no escort is required, although the track is far nearer the territory continuously occupied by the Viet-Minh than the main road where attacks are so frequent. This ties up perhaps with the fact that there had never been an attempt on the Viet-Minh's part to assassinate the Emperor, and it is not an original hypothesis that the Emperor's role in relation to the French may be similar to that now claimed for Marshal Pétain, *vis-à-vis* the Germans. Some secret understanding may in fact exist between the Emperor and the extreme nationalists.

The road, narrow and winding, affords many a sickening glimpse of a fern-clad precipice through the screen of lianas and bamboos. On this morning it was bitterly cold and only the heights were free from a thick, clammy mist. Suddenly, without warning, we would emerge from this, while climbing, into the brilliant sunshine, so that the mist lay spread out below us like the surface of a steaming lake, with islands of rock and vegetation. Once a silver pheasant came winging up through the surface like a gorgeous flying-fish, and flew on to settle in one of the tree-top islands. The Vice-Mayor and the Judge shot several wild-cocks that, however maimed, clung to their lives with the frightful tenacity of their kind. Five peacocks, surprised in the deserted Moï rice-field, flew vertically to the topmost branches of a tree, and there were slaughtered — perfect targets sitting silhouetted against the sky. But this was the total bag, and a mighty wild boar absorbed at close range a charge of ball-shot and departed with no sign of inconvenience.

We stopped to collect some orchids for the Vice-Mayor's wife. They were white and orange like tiny jonquil flowers and hung in clusters on waxen stems. While the Vice-Mayor was up the tree, I took an interest in some of the insects. There were huge dragonflies that came darting up and remained stationary at a distance of a foot or so, accompanying me as if inquisitive. Their wings, which were without the usual sheen, moved with such rapidity that their bodies seemed to be unsupported in the air. Another large winged insect was equally happy in at least two of the elements. On alighting, its wings were folded away with great deliberation into a protective case, after which, streamlined, and without impeding projections, it scampered off to forage among the fallen leaves and grass-roots.

At midday we stopped to cook a meal of tiny eggs. This part of the forest was intersected by many small streams and the damp earth sprouted an endless variety of ferns, from all the small recognizable ones of Europe to some as large as palms and others that looked like bracken but were the colour of the brightest beech-leaves in autumn. After the early morning, for some reason or other, one did not expect to see game, but there were plenty of large inedible birds about, and the frequent appearance of a *coq de pagode* which looked like jungle-fowl but had a long tail and could have only been eaten, said my friends, by a starving man, sent them several times scrambling vainly for their guns.

It was near here that we saw, in the distance, the last of the Moï villages, and decided that it would do our digestions good to walk to it. We crossed over a bridge of twisted lianas and walked perhaps half a mile along a path through rice-fields. The village was a M'nong Gar one, with the houses built on the earth itself. In the distance it was a pleasant enough sight, with its yellow, thatched roofs, the sacrificial masts with their streamers, and the children playing in the clean, open spaces. We passed the mounds of several abandoned graves and others which were still open, with miniature houses built over them containing the personal possessions of the defunct; his clothing, blankets, necklaces, jars, drum, the rice bowls that are replenished daily, and the horns of the buffalo sacrificed at the funeral.

By the time we reached the village it was deserted. There was a single woman left alone, sifting herbs outside her hut, but she paid not the slightest attention to us. Three of our party of four were armed, and we wondered whether the sudden appearance of armed men in their midst had caused the villagers to disappear like this. At the other end of the village we found more signs of life. Two men were at work making *coupe-coupes* in a primitive forge, while a boy worked the bellows made from two thick sections of bamboo, filled with wooden pistons. These also ignored us, but one of the men suddenly got up, with face averted, and went away towards the entrance to the village. The Vice-Mayor suspected that he might be going to organize an ambush in case we committed any hostile action. He thought that it was best to act in a natural and unconcerned way, so we picked up various half-finished *coupe-coupes* and put them down again, and wanted to take an interest in the woman's occupation, but she had gone. The Judge rather overdid his nonchalance — much to the alarm of the Rhadés chauffeur — by fingering the ornaments on one of the sacrificial masts. The Rhadés chauffeur who only knew a few words of French, said he could not speak the local dialect. The village he said was forbidden and we must go immediately. He could give no explanation for this opinion and when questioned drained his face of intelligence and took refuge in 'Moi pas connaisse'.

There was something a little sinister about this village that was deserted even by the domestic animals. No sooner had we left the forge than it became silent. The imagination, too, was affected by the framework supporting buffalo skulls, flanked by two Easter-Island figures that had been stained by sacrificial blood. As we reached the outskirts we heard the slapping of naked feet behind us. The man who had stayed behind in the forge was running after us. He stopped a few paces away and bowing his head respectfully took his right elbow in his left palm and came forward to touch hands with each of us in turn. He was the chief, we found, and seeing that we intended no harm he had had an attack of bad conscience at his shocking breach of good manners in letting us go like that. Now, said the chauffeur, who had suddenly recovered his wits, he had come to invite us back to the village to broach a jar of alcohol with him.

CHAPTER XII

CHOLON AND COCHIN-CHINA

AIR-FRANCE planes from Dalat were booked up three weeks ahead. By what I thought at the time was a miracle I got a seat on a plane run by a small company, without any delay. It turned out later that there was not much demand for this plane as the company had had one or two crashes on the run. There was not much hope of a successful forced-landing in those jungles.

While waiting to take off, I chatted with a fellow passenger, a Vietnamese student, who wanted to know what I was doing in the country. I told him, and the conversation immediately took a political turn. Which Vietnamese intellectuals had I met? I confessed that I had met none. The student didn't see how I could form any objective opinion of the conditions of his country when the only opinions I listened to were those of French colonialists. This reasonable point of view had already occurred to me and I said that the chief reason why I had made no contacts among the Vietnamese was that, judging from their manner, they would be difficult to approach. The student said that this was natural enough, as I would be taken for a Frenchman. He persisted so strongly that I should meet certain intellectuals that I was sure that he was about to suggest how this could be done when the plane took off. We were seated on loose camp-stools and as soon as the plane began to lurch in the hot air-currents we were thrown about rather badly. My friend, who was flying for the first time, was violently ill and I did not have the chance of speaking to him again.

Saigon was as rumbustious as ever, with lorries full of Algerians patrolling the streets and the cafés full of German legionnaires. I dined at a Chinese restaurant on the main road to Cholon. This was outside the European quarter and I enjoyed the district because of

the turbulent processes of living that went on all round me. Although I noticed in my newspaper that this restaurant advertised
itself as having an *Emplacement discret*, the walls were much
scarred from a bomb which had been thrown in it the previous
night. Perhaps for this reason it was crowded, in deference to the
theory that two shells do not burst in the same crater. The waiter
said that they hoped to have a wire-grille fitted by the next day,
which would keep the grenades out. Their little incident had only
contributed two casualties to the grand total of seventeen for the
night. But a colleague had been one of the unfortunate pair. His
condition, said my waiter, was very grave, and, curiously enough,
all this had been foretold by the resident fortune-teller, who I now
observed to be approaching my table carrying the tools of his
trade and smiling in anticipation of the grisly predictions he would
unfold for suitable payment.

I had happened to read that a Vietnamese nationalist newspaper had been suppressed and this gave me an idea. Next day I
called at the paper's office and asked to see the Editor. He was not
there. When would he come? Nobody knew. Well, would he
ever come? I was trying to pin down one of the blank-faced
employees to commit himself to a definite statement, but, without
knowing it, I was a beginner engaging in verbal ju-jitsu with
masters of the art, whose forbears for several generations had
schooled themselves to meet force with evasion. Too much
directness on my part only produced a 'pas connaisse', and while
still trying to talk my way out of this fog of non-co-operation I
found myself manœuvred out into the street. A Vietnamese was
walking on either side but in a casual and non-committal manner,
as if they were going somewhere on their own account and they
happened by chance to find themselves walking at the same speed
as myself. Refusing to talk anything but the pidgin French which
allowed for the maximum of misunderstanding, they suggested
that I might like to disclose, without reserve, the full nature of my
business with the Editor. There was nothing for it but to tell them.

Others joined them, friends it seemed, particles broken haphazardly from the great, anonymous crowd, and I was invited to repeat my story. While we strolled thus, separated continually by boys on bicycles, beggars, animals and children playing with toys, the thing was considered and at last — it was hinted at, rather than announced — I gathered that if I called back that afternoon I might, or might not, see someone who would interest me.

I was naturally not surprised when I returned that no one I recognized was there. The faces of that morning were not to be seen, and when I called across the counter to one of the much abstracted clerks, I got the 'pas connaisse' that I expected. There was a flight of stairs at the end of the room and I went up them into a first-floor room. A young man came out from behind a partition, and said in English, with a good accent, 'Are you the Englishman?' He wore thick spectacles and had a grave, studious expression. In starting to introduce myself I spoke French, and he asked me, a trifle sharply, to speak English. I told him the reason for my presence in the country and that as until then I had been exposed solely to French propaganda I thought that I should make some attempt to balance this with propaganda from the other side. This remark was not considered funny. With a sternly reproving glance the young man told me that all Vietnamese patriots were members of the Viet-Minh and that if I really wanted to see Viet-Nam, I should not bother with French-occupied territory but cross the lines to the Democratic Republic. I told him that I should be delighted to do so, if given the opportunity. He then asked to see any documents that might help to establish my bona fides, and I showed him my passport and various letters. The application he said would have to be submitted to the branch of the army of the Viet-Minh which dealt with such matters. He thought that it would take several weeks to get an answer and to make arrangements for 'crossing over'. I asked whether he thought permission would be granted and he said, yes. He regretted being unable to give me his name and told me that I should be unable to get in touch with him again, but he would find means to contact me when the moment came.

This was the first of such political experiences, and that night the second occurred in the most improbable way.

I had been invited to spend the evening with a French journalist and his Vietnamese mistress. It was evident from the start that it would follow the standard pattern: dinner at the Chalet, followed by an excursion to Cholon for a visit to the gambling casino and one or more of the night-clubs. Cholon is a purely Chinese city, about three miles from Saigon, which it overshadows in almost all activities. For some reason or other it is supposed to be more 'typically Chinese' than the great seaports of China itself, and one is told in proof of this that the city shots in some Hollywood epic of life in China were taken in its streets. There is a great, swollen war-time population of perhaps three-quarters of a million, most of whom live wretchedly, and an exceptional proportion of million-aires whose number is continually added to by black-marketeering triumphs arising out of the present war. The Chinese are go-betweens for both sides. They sell food from the rural Viet-Minh areas to the French towns, and the dollars smuggled in from France, which are needed to buy arms, to the Viet-Minh. As they are not affected by causes, either good or evil, they prosper ex-ceedingly.

Cholon capitalizes, to some extent, its exotic attraction for Europeans, but this is offset by the necessity at the same time to provide titillation for the rich Chinese, who form the bulk of the patrons at the places of amusement. The result is an astonishing pastiche. Our first visit on this particular occasion was to the 'Van Canh Nightspot', at which a certain Ramona was billed to appear each evening, 'dans ses danses exotiques'. The band was Philippine and played with great feeling such revived classics as 'September in the Rain'. Ramona, who was stated to be 'direct from Mexico City' but who, I noticed, spoke Italian to her partner, performed a hip-rolling fantasy of her own devising, inspired undoubtedly by the Bosphorus rather than the China Seas. The clientèle was composed in the main of elderly Chinese rice-merchants, who danced with Chinese and Vietnamese taxi-girls.

After this, my friend was lured by his girl into the 'Parc des Attractions', where she, but not he, was frisked at the entrance for concealed weapons. Like most Vietnamese, she was a victim of the passion for gambling, and by limiting herself each day to a certain sum which she placed on well-known exceptionally lucky combinations, her losses were regular but not disastrous. On this occasion, influenced by her interpretation of a dream, she lost in record time. This was one of Cholon's two great gambling dens, and here, in a cheerful fun-fair atmosphere, the wealth of the Vietnamese people, both high and low — since all incomes are catered for — drains steadily away into the coffers of the Chinese, who, of course, are made to pay very dearly by the French authorities for the facilities thus afforded.

We finished up at the 'Paradis', and it was here that the amazing circumstance happened. The 'Paradis' is favoured by the Chinese, who are attracted by the discreet indirect lighting, which is lowered as often as possible during sentimental numbers. Most of the girls — at least, the Chinese ones — who act as hostesses are supposed to have been sold into glittering servitude by their impoverished parents, and it is a polite convention to refer to this as soon as possible over the champagne, and to press one's temporary partner for details of this romantic aspect of her past. A celebrated crooner, Wang Sue, was at the microphone, but it was 'September in the Rain' again, and while the powerful sing-song voice intoned 'the leaves of brown came tumbling down' my friends went off to dance leaving me to the mercy of the 'taxi-manager' who arrived with *une girl* they had secretly ordered for me. (Why has English been chosen as the lingua-franca of such pleasures?) The fourth member of our party had the fragile aristocracy of manner of most Vietnamese dance-hostesses. Her features, powdered chalk-white, wore a kind of death-bed composure. She was sheathed in the traditional costume, in this case of white silk, had incredible finger-nails, and every hair on her head was, I am quite sure, in place. The only human touch in this total of geisha perfections was a man's wrist watch which bulked enormously on that lotus-stem wrist.

The two girls were evidently old friends, probably colleagues. They chatted happily, and once, from the oriental, fan-screened glances I intercepted, it seemed that I was the object of their remarks. When the other two got up again, the girl said, 'You are English aren't you? Do you think that we Vietnamese are as civilized as the French?' Somewhat surprised by this first sample of small-talk in a Saigon night-club, I replied, yes, that I thought they were. From this point on the conversation followed the lines of that with my chance acquaintance on the Dalat plane, although as the circumstances were more favourable, it was carried to a more profitable conclusion. It was through this girl that I was put in touch with the leading Vietnamese revolutionary-nationalists in Saigon.

A message left next day at the hotel invited me to call at a certain address at a certain time. I went there and found that the address given was a luxurious-looking villa. There were several expensive cars outside. A group of Vietnamese, who were at first reluctant to give their names, awaited me. Among them was a prosperous lawyer, a bank director and an ex-member of the Cabinet of the Governor of Cochin-China. All these people were members of the wealthy, land-owning class, and all were whole-hearted supporters of the Viet-Minh, which, if, as it is said to be, under communist control, would supposedly dispossess them as soon as it came to power. One of this group was actually known to be a high-ranking member of the Viet-Minh, but was left unmolested in Saigon by the French as providing an unofficial diplomatic contact, which could be used whenever the occasion necessitated.

It would be tedious to describe the conversation that followed, but it may be summed up by saying that these people made it clear that the Vietnamese would never be satisfied with anything less from France than India had obtained from England. The 'Independence within the French Union' conceded a year before was described as a bad joke, since it left France's control of all the key positions unaltered. The publication by the Viet-Minh of a secret report prepared in 1948 by Monsieur Bollaert, the previous High Commissioner, for submission to the Prime Minister, had not helped. A great deal of publicity had been given to the sentence which might be roughly translated, 'It is my impression that we must make a concession to Viet-Nam of the term, independence; but I am convinced that this word need never be interpreted in any light other than that of a religious verbalism.'

And that was how it worked out in practice, my informants said. To take the example of the police force. A great show had been made of turning over to the Vietnamese of the Sureté headquarters in the Rue Catinat. But all the French had actually done was to leave the incoming officials an empty building and open up themselves again at another address under the title of Sureté Fédérale. As the Sureté Fédérale had kept all the archives, the Vietnamese organization was disabled from the start. Then again, French troops would be withdrawn from Vietnamese soil, but, somewhat vaguely, 'when the opportune moment arrives'. And, of course, extra-territorial rights were retained, by which persons other than Vietnamese nationals were tried in mixed courts presided over by a French judge. This meant that Cambodians and Laotians, as well as French, were not subject in Viet-Nam to Vietnamese law, while all matters relating to security came before a French Military tribunal.

Thus, I was informed, was independence interpreted. But there were other and more sinister French manœuvres which envisaged the possibility of the Vietnamese independence becoming real and took steps accordingly. Certain districts such as the Hauts Plateaux and the areas occupied by various tribal groups in Tonkin had been declared racial minority zones and separated entirely from Viet-Nam. And now, at the assembly of the Union Française the Cambodians, who had never raised their voices before, had been worked upon to demand the return of their old provinces in Cochin-China as well as legal right of access to the port of Saigon. Militant religious sects as Cao-Daïsm and the Hoa-Hao, originally banned by the King of Cambodia and the Emperor of Annam, had been encouraged as potential separatists and aided in the formation of private armies. In this way, Viet-Nam, even fully independent, would be weakened in every possible way.

And now after this revelation of rankling injustices and huge-scale political manipulations, a curious complaint was made, the *cri du coeur* of the Asiatic's injured ego, a single comparatively insignificant fact, but significantly disclosed at the end of the list of oppressions: the French were as insultingly exclusive as ever — 'the *cercle sportif* does not admit Vietnamese'. Perhaps, if the French — and the English — had been gentler with their colonial subjects' *amour-propre* in the matter of such things as club memberships, their position in the Far East might have been a lot less precarious than it is.

Planes to Laos were infrequent and the earliest seat I could get was for a fortnight later. In the meanwhile, a French acquaintance, who was trying to sell British Land-Rover cars to the Cambodian army, mentioned that he was sending a sample car to the army head-quarters at Pnom-Penh and asked if I would like to go with it. I accepted the offer, with great pleasure, especially as my friend would be making the journey by plane and suggested that we might spend a few days together in Cambodia. He had lived for several years in the country and knew it as well as any European could.

There were four days to spare before the car went to Cambodia and I filled in this time by going on one of the more-or-less standard excursions round the re-conquered part of Cochin-China arranged for foreign correspondents by the French army. These trips could be quite exciting if one ran into action, and this made the French a little chary about them, because sometimes correspondents saw more than they were supposed to see, and sent back a batch of un-

favourable telegrams. Bob Miller, of the United Press, for instance, was in an armoured barge going up a canal at ten o'clock one night when three sampans were picked up ahead by the searchlight. Two of them failed to stop and were riddled by machine-gun fire. The third gave up and three peasants — an old couple and their son — were brought aboard. They were carrying rice; travelling by night, probably to avoid the exactions of local officials. Their cargo was tipped into the water. The boy, who tried to escape by jumping over the side, was killed by a hand-grenade thrown in after him. The officer in command was exceedingly young, charming and co-operative. He was convinced that the peasants had not been partisans of the Viet-Minh, but they had broken the curfew regulations, and what followed was the logic of warfare. In a country where they were enormously outnumbered by a hostile populace, it was only by making people understand that breaches of regulations would be punished with extreme severity that they could hope to keep the upper hand. But this kind of logic is apt not to be so apparent to non-combatants, including newspaper men, who sometimes protest that it was the attitude of the Nazis in occupied countries.

The scenes and sensations of the next four days followed each other so thick and fast that the memory of them is a photo-montage, a jumble of hardly separable images; the enemy strong-point seen through the bamboo pallisade — irresponsive to the machine-gunner's provocation; the thump of the armoured barge nosing through the sedges, ibises rising up from its bows; the soldiers in isolated posts, reining-in their minds with spinsterish occupations, mat-making or knitting; the resigned homage of the notables of fifty villages; the cannonading at night heard from the dim, daemonic interior of a mandarin's palace.

Luong Hoa stands out. There was a Catholic church with a statue of an Annamese saint standing before a junk, and a remarkable grandfather clock which might have become a cult-object,

facing: SAIGON: INCENSE SPIRALS IN THE CANTONESE PAGODA

since the priest bowed slightly in passing it. The clock was covered all over with those rather sickly illustrations which usually accompany religious texts, but it was evident that this was local work as a few Chinese lanterns had been fitted in among the roses and angels. Ever since the Jesuits first went to China, the Far East has been bombarded by clocks, and the palaces of most oriental potentates are as cluttered with them as a French municipal pawnshop. But this, if only on account of sheer size — it must have been nine feet tall — was certainly a worthy object of the villagers' pride. Luong Hoa had recently suffered forty casualties in a battle with the Viet-Minh.

The French senior officer commanding in this section who showed me round was a man in his middle fifties who bore an astonishing resemblance to the French film actor Raimu. He was a typical *père de famille*, bluff-natured and mildly eccentric, who liked to have a drink with the sergeant in charge of any post we visited. Dogs took to him wherever we went, and hung about snuffing affectionately at his boots. He carried a tin of condensed milk in his pocket and every now and then would pour out a dollop for them to lick up. It seemed impossible to associate this man with the bloody happenings that must have occurred within the zone of his command, and perhaps by his orders.

We went stumping together through the next village on foot. It was a delightful place, with half the village fishing in a stream by the side of the road and brightly painted houses with good quality coffins displayed for the neighbours' benefit outside most of them. Bougainvillaea exploded streakily across the ceramic-tiled front of a pagoda; a benign dragon writhed across the roof-top, and a dancer, embarrassed by trailing robes of porcelain, waved her cymbals across the gables at a jovial savant facing her. The Commandant patted the heads of Vietnamese children and said that to attempt to drive through the village after dark, let alone walk, would be certain death. He was another of those French officers who remembered with affection some dingy jumping-off point in England for the invasion of Europe, and we were joined from the first moment by the bond of our common experience of Ellesmere Port.

Our road threaded continually through Catholic and Cao-Daïst areas which were said to war incessantly with one another. The local Cao-Daïsts, although in some way schismatic, recognized the Pope at Tay Ninh, even if they did not subject themselves whole-heartedly to his authority. The Commandant said that they specialized in piracy on the waterways with which the province was net-worked. It had always been Cao-Daïst policy to attempt to dupli-cate French administration with their own exact counterpart on the ecclesiastical level, but now, he said, they were trying to extend this principle to their military organization, and only the other day a complete Headquarters' Staff arrived from Tay Ninh to be attached to his own H.Q. at Tanan. He sent them packing.

The Catholics, said the Commandant, with no diminution in cheerfulness, were an even worse menace. Some of them hadn't had an ordained priest since the missionaries were expelled in the early part of the last century and they spent their time raiding other villages, gathering in their church for two hours every evening to howl the canticles, after which they raped their female captives. Every village we passed was surrounded by double or triple stock-ades, and sometimes a moat, and overlooked by *miradors*. Some of these structures, said the Commandant were so rickety through neglect that they would topple over if anyone tried to climb up them.

And this was the state to which the Jesuit Borri's 'near heaven' had come.

That night we dined in the officers' mess at Tanan. On the previous night one of the hand-grenades, which I succeeded always in just missing, had come in through the window and wounded an officer. This time the Commandant had posted sentries so that we should all have a nice quiet evening. But no sooner had we taken our seats than there was a series of explosions. The defence-towers on the outskirts of the town were being attacked by mortar-fire. A few minutes later the French 25-pounders joined in. One after another the officers were called to their posts. By the time the entrée was served the Commandant and I faced a very junior officer across an otherwise deserted table. Soon the light failed and we decided to call it a night.

Of the next day, I remember that we visited the exemplary village of Than Phú, whose state of grace was due to the fact, the French thought, that except for fifteen nominal Catholics the village was a Buddhist one, without Cao-Daïst converts. Than Phú possessed a historic pagoda, the only building, the French said, that had been spared when the Viet-Minh burned the place. It contained a bell in which about 150 years ago Gia-Long, the last of the great Emperors, had hid when fleeing from the rebellious Taysons. To prove that this could be done the bonze crept into the bell. But he was a tiny, wizened old fellow and it was very evident that Gia-Long's descendant, the present Emperor, would have little hope, if the need arose, in emulating his ancestor's feat. The real interest in this pagoda lay in a great cautionary fresco depicting the respective fates in the hereafter of the blessed and the damned. The old bonze, who by the way was much respected by the Commandant, was very proud of this, and there was a smile of gentle satisfaction on his face when the time came to show it off.

The rewards of evil-doing were portrayed with great fidelity to detail across the whole of one wall. Minor crimes that had escaped detection in life were punished here according to their gravity with the four prescribed degrees of chastisement: the facial mark, removal of the nose, amputation of the foot and castration. The duplication in hell of a felon's death began with the mere strangulation by devils of those who had erred, perhaps, rather than sinned, and included the varieties of slow death prepared for the perpetrators of such atrocious crimes as grossly unfilial conduct. Fiends worked on these offenders with knives marked with the bodily member to be sliced, drawn at random, according to the ancient penal practice, from the lottery sack. Tigers devoured others, and yet others, who had probably in their life-times questioned the heavenly mandate of the Divine Emperor, were being dismembered by the elephants specially trained to inflict capital punishment. Demon executioners stood apart, in corners, practising their aim on bamboo stalks, marked according to tradition with betel lines.

All the victims concerned were neatly dressed for the occasion, and did not appear to despair; a reflection perhaps of the Annamese custom of encouraging the condemned to meet their ends with as much dignity as the circumstances permitted, and insisting indeed on a show of composure which included the elegant performance of the five ritual prostrations in taking leave of the accompanying relations.

On the opposite wall the blessed were shown in their bliss. But as beatitude is less keenly felt than suffering, the rewards of virtue were insubstantial, even insipid. Heaven was one of those briefly sketched Chinese landscapes; a few misty, not altogether credible peaks, pine trees, a stream, a bridge. It was the heaven of the poet and the artist of one of the early Chinese dynasties, and the Annamese souls in glory wandered through it disconsolately and somewhat out of their element. The old bonze, too, was soon bored with this and lured us with gentle insistence back to the vigorous scenes of damnation, pointing out to us obscure refinements of torture that we had missed.

That a Buddhist pagoda could be decorated in this way, of course, was a measure of the distortion that the religion had suffered in the course of its slow propagation through India and China and finally into Cochin-China. Nirvana had become a picnic excursion to the hills, and the sorrows of the soul bound to the wheel of incarnation, a series of vulgar episodes in the torture-chamber. An illustration, indeed, of the barbarism that infects the great religious systems in their decline.

There was never, by the way, any cause for embarrassment in going boldly into any pagoda in Indo-China, prying curiously among its shrines, watching the rites, and even photographing them. The officiants, on the contrary, were delighted at any manifestation of interest. It is part of a genial Confucian tradition, which has spread to all the other cults. 'The Master having gone in to the Grand Temple, asked questions about everything. Someone remarked "who says that the Son of the citizen of Tsou (Confucius) has any knowledge of ceremonial observances. He comes to the temple and asks about everything he sees". Hearing the remark, the Master said: "This in itself is a ceremonial observance."'

Later, when alone, I would make a trifling donation to the pagoda funds, which would be enthusiastically acknowledged by the beating of a great gong, and the burning for my benefit of a few inches of one of the great spiralling coils of incense, suspended from the roof. And sometimes the old priest would throw in a minor piece of divination, shaking into my hand one of a jarful of what looked like spills, but which were assorted prophetic utterances from the classics, written on slips of screwed-up paper. Coming to my help with the elegant but inexplicable ideographs he would clearly indicate by his gleeful, congratulatory smile that at last Fortune was about to open wide its arms to me.

Than Phú, the exemplary village, was followed by the ideal French post. It had been the work of a *sergent-chef* who, like the Commandant, would shortly be returning, demobilized, to France, where it was obvious that they would both spend the rest of their days in a Kipling-esque nostalgia for Indo-China. And yet, much as the colonies had become his spiritual home, and depressed as he was at the thought of his repatriation, the *sergent-chef* was extremely proud of the fact that he had made his post a Corner of France. And at what a cost. He had imported bulbs by air-mail and there had been a painful sprouting of tulips, dragged inch by inch from that ochreous soil, their heads now hanging a little wearily in the nooses that attached them to their supporting canes. Over them reared up exuberant ranks of canna, grown only to afford shade for the European importation. A native hut, too, had been pathetically camouflaged as a *bistro*; a *rendezvous des sports* for the benefit of visiting N.C.O.s. Anything to shut out for a while the hateful sight of bamboos, the memory of which would become so dear in a few months time.

The *sergent-chef* also kept a boa-constrictor in a cage. It was fed monthly with a live duck, a ceremony which collected appreciative crowds. He said that the snake refused to interest itself in food that was not alive.

A new Vietnamese village had formed like a series of cells round the ideal post. In their tragic situation, the prey of every kind of gangster and bandit, the peasants' one craving is for protection and stability. Their village destroyed in military operations, they live uncomfortably dispersed in temporary shelters and eat the shrimps and undersized fish caught in the irrigation ditches. As soon as a military post goes up in their neighbourhood they are naturally attracted to it, and under the cover of its machine-guns they rebuild their huts, plant their vegetables, establish a market. They are encouraged to do this, and tragedy only happens when the Viet-Minh, first terrorizing the villagers, use its cover to attack the post. Massacres have occurred in the subsequent reprisals, which, since by this time the Viet-Minh have left, are directed against the villagers.

The new village without a name was, temporarily at least, prospering. The *sergent-chef* had appointed himself unofficial mayor and was insisting on European sanitary standards, which, to his surprise, were scrupulously carried out. He held a daily inspection of the streets and market place, made vendors mark the prices on their goods, awarded certificates of merit for the best-kept houses. He helped to fit up a town-hall and a theatre — the two essentials of Vietnamese communal life — and presented the information centre with a frivolous dragon which he found in a deserted ruin. The Vietnamese, who had probably seen their last village blown off the face of the earth, were as surprised, no doubt, as they were gratified. It was a pity, the *sergent-chef* said, that we had not been there the day before, because he had helped the villagers to celebrate the Têt by organizing a regatta, with sampan races for both sexes and all ages, and he had taken the liberty of offering a few tins of army rations as prizes. The Commandant nodded in benevolent approval.

This, I believe, was the average French soldier's attitude. If given half a chance he would make a kind of pet of anyone who was dependent upon him — even Vietnamese peasants. He soon began to feel as responsible for their welfare as the administrators I met did for that of the Moïs. The soldiers had none of the civilian prejudices towards the Vietnamese. I asked the *sergent-chef* if it was a fact that they had no sense of humour, and he was staggered by such an absurd suggestion. I wondered how the Commandant and his N.C.O. would have reacted if called upon to put into practice paragraph four of the military proclamation which says, 'every native quarter situated in the immediate neighbourhood of a point where an important act of sabotage has been committed, will be razed to the ground'.

The situation at Binh Long Dong was less favourable. I was in another Zone of command now, and the familiar warring factions in the neighbourhood had been overshadowed by a partisan-chief, an unsmiling mountain of a man, who had been decorated with the Croix de Guerre, and lived in a magnificent fortified villa, full of paddy and streamlined furnishings. The main piece of furniture, however, in the reception room was a rack, an intelligent adaption of the umbrella stand, on which guests hung their weapons. The room was gay with the most expensive artificial flowers of cloth and paper, and we were offered champagne and sweet biscuits. This man was a rare sport of nature, the archetype of a Vietnamese pirate turned Governor, or a Chinese War-Lord. One wondered if whatever factor it was that had produced all this bone and muscle from the slender Vietnamese stock had also created the fierce, resolute character. He was quite illiterate, but had recently begun to interest himself in the choicer rewards of success, and had built pillars of precious wood into his house, specially brought from Tonkin, at a cost of three thousand piastres each.

About half the land of this community was owned by big proprietors who had been finding it practically impossible to collect their rents. If they put the screw too hard on the peasant farmers, they were liable to be kidnapped by the Viet-Minh and receive a period of 're-education' and an enormous fine before being released. Nowadays they could hire bodyguards from the partisan-chief who specialized in protection for prominent citizens and industrial enterprises. But even this, they were beginning to realize, wasn't doing them much good, as the farmers had got into the habit of telling them when they called for the rent: 'Too late, I've already had to pay it to the Viet-Minh.'

A ferry nearby provided a racket for yet another petty regional boss. There he stood by the shore in his uniform of a lieutenant in the Bao-Dai army and bright yellow boots, prepared, for a *concussion* (most descriptive word), to grant priority to any vehicle not wishing to take its turn in the queue. If no *concussion* was forthcoming you waited in the line, perhaps an hour, perhaps half the day. The village at the ferry, overtopped with its crop of *miradors*, looked like a mean Siena, but rose-coloured pastors instead of starlings crowded sociably on the roofs. While we awaited the ferry-boat a partisan patrol passed, complete with their wives. Several of them carried bird-cages as well as rifles.

There was an undercurrent of artistic feeling in these harassed villages of Cochin-China that the quilting of poverty could not entirely suffocate. A tree grew in the garden of a fisherman's hut. The leaves had been stripped off and replaced by small, silvery fish, which from an aesthetic quirk he preferred to dry in this manner. Sometimes a lamp had been planted outside a hovel, graceful yet solid, like a reduced version of a London lamp-post, but with a golden-scaled dragon curled on the top. Or perhaps the usual platform set upon a post with offerings to the wandering and neglected spirits had been elaborated into a tiny pagoda, containing say, along with the tea-cup and the incense-sticks, a packet of Craven A. There were wayside food-stalls everywhere, and as much attention, one felt sure, was paid to the matching of the colours of the food displayed in the bowls, as to the flavour itself.

The sky above all these villages was full of grotesque and meaningful kites. Like miniature balloon-barrages they hung there, as if designed to frustrate the surprise attacks of fabulous aerial monsters.

The zone of French occupation in Cochin-China is shapeless and unpredictable. There is a small squid-like body which thrusts out groping tentacles into a vast no-man's land of canal-patterned paddy-fields and swamps. On a larger scale the country is hugely segmented by the mouths of the Mékong which leave great, ragged tongues of land projecting into the sea. The enemy is everywhere; in full strength and with complete organization in one of the great, estuarial peninsulas, and split into skirmishing groups in the next. Defence towers garrisoned by Bao-Dai troops control the main roads, but only in daylight hours. Traffic is withdrawn before sundown and only starts again at eight in the morning.

During the night hours, the defence towers, too, go out of business and their defenders lie low, while the Viet-Minh patrols pass by on their way to collect tolls or impose retribution, conducting their activities even in the suburbs of Saigon. There are supposed to be live-and-let-live arrangements, and sometimes, perhaps when these break down, the Viet-Minh arrive in force and lay siege to a few towers, which may or may not be prepared to hold out to the last bullet. In this pacified zone you can sleep in the towns at night, so long as you do not go out after dark, but you cannot stay in the villages some of which it is better to keep away from even in day-time. The enemy includes the regular army of the Viet-Minh, tough and brilliant in guerilla tactics, but lightly armed; innumerable partisans who follow respectable occupations in the day-time, but turn into guerillas at night; and, as well, all that farrago of dubious allies, including the religious armies, who accepted French arms in order to live by near-banditry, but who are ready and willing to administer a stab in the back and will go over to the other side as soon as the moment seems right. As for friends — they are probably few, since the logic of modern warfare involves the destruction of the guilty and the innocent, and friends along with enemies. On the anniversary of the signing — a year before — of the agreement with Bao-Dai for Vietnamese 'independence', the French declared a holiday and blundering on in a quite un-Gallic but wholly Teuton fashion, ordered spontaneous demonstrations of joy. The police would see to it, newspapers warned, that flags were hung out. Can it have been the influence of German occupation? Or is it the circumstances and not the race that make the Nazi. To be fair to them, the French themselves, reading this in their papers, were either amused or horrified. The day came, the celebrations were ignored, the streets were empty, no flags flew. And the police did nothing about it.

It was at the house of one of the remaining allies, a high official of the Bao-Dai government, that the banquet was given on the last night of my Cochin-China interlude. There had been no warning of this glittering occasion. I was caught in a state of total unpreparedness, my change of clothing when I made an inspection, being nearly as grimed with yellow dust as those I wore. And now to my alarm I found myself seated at the right hand of the Vietnamese provincial Governor, facing the *décolletée* lady of the Colonel and a row of senior officers and officials in gleaming sharkskin. But the French are a genial people, little troubled by starchiness and the rigours of social self-defence. Besides that, the nature of the banquet was in itself an all-out, frontal attack on the citadels of dignity.

Formal deportment is shattered and devastated by the manipulation of Vietnamese food, and although some people might have been merely embarrassed, the French headquarters' staff at Mytho and their womenfolk were prepared to treat the thing as a gastronomic romp. Undoubtedly in placing bowls and chopsticks before his guests, the *Chef de Province* knew his types.

Vietnamese cooking, like most aspects of Vietnamese culture, has been strongly influenced by the Chinese. By comparison it is provincial, lacking the range and the formidable ingenuity of the Pekinese and Cantonese cuisines. But there are a few specialities which have been evolved with a great deal of dietetic insight. The best known of these is *Chà Gió*, with which we were served as an entrée. *Chà Gió* consists fundamentally of very small, highly spiced meat-rolls, which are transferred easily enough with chopsticks from the dish to one's plate. But this is nothing more than a preliminary operation, and many dexterous manipulations follow. Two or three kinds of vegetable leaves are provided as salad, plus minute spring-onions. A leaf of each kind is picked up and — this is not so easy — placed in superimposition on one's plate and garnished with an onion, ready to receive the meat roll in the middle. And now comes the operation calling for natural skill, or years of practice, since the leaves must be wrapped neatly round the narrow cylinder of mincemeat. The *Chà-Gió*, now fully prepared, is lifted with the chopsticks and dowsed in the saucer of *nuóc-mâm* at the side of one's plate, from which, according to Mr. Houghton-Broderick, an odour resembling that of tiger's urine arises. The total operation takes the non-expert several minutes and involves as many contretemps as one would expect. On this occasion, the Europeans soon gave up the struggle, throwing dignity to the winds, and dabbled happily with their fingers. A spirit of comradeship was noticeable, a democratic kinship born in an atmosphere of common endeavour, frustration and ridicule.

When travelling I make a sincere effort to throw overboard all prejudices concerning food. Consequently after a brief period of struggle I had already come to terms with *nuóc-mâm*, about which almost every writer on Indo-China since the first Jesuit has grumbled so consistently. I felt indeed that I had taken the first steps towards connoisseurship, and it was in this spirit that I congratulated the Governor on his supply which was the colour of pale honey, thickish and of obvious excellence. *Nuóc-mâm* is produced by the fermentation of juices exuded by layers of fish subjected to pressure between layers of salt. The best result as in viniculture is produced by the first drawing-off, before artificial pressure is applied, and there are three or more subsequent pressings with consequent deteriorations in quality. First *crus* are allowed to mature like brandy, improving steadily with age. The Governor told me that he thought his stock, which he had inherited, was over a hundred years old. All the fierce ammoniacal exhalations were long since spent, and what remained was not more than a whiff of mellow corruption. Taking a grain of cooked rice, he deposited it on the golden surface, where it remained supported by the tension — an infallible test of quality, he said.

After the *Chà Gió* came a flux of delicacies, designed undoubtedly to provoke curiosity and admiration and to provide the excuse for enormously prolonged dalliance at the table, rather than to appease gross appetites. The Vietnamese picked judiciously at the breasts of lacquered pigeons, the sliced coxcombs and the tiny diaphanous fish, while the Europeans ate with barbarian forthrightness, finding their chopsticks useful to illustrate with fine flourishes — since shop-talk had crept in — the feints, the encirclements, the annihilation. The Governor had been presented with a remarkable lighter, an unwieldy engine, which commanded admiration by producing flame in some quite unexpected way. How this was done, I have forgotten, but I know that it was not by friction on a flint. Through-out the meal he could hardly bear to put this away and fiddled continually with it between the courses, while his guests stuffed themselves with the rare meats he hardly touched. For me there was an allegory in this scene.

The night of the return to Saigon I went with Vietnamese friends for the second time to the Vietnamese theatre. The first visit had been an appalling fiasco, although cruelly funny in its way; a pathetic attempt at a Wild Western musical, inspired perhaps by reports of *Oklahoma*. It was acted by fragile, slant-eyed beauties in chaps, wearing ten-gallon hats and toting six-shooters; their cheeks heavily incarnadined in representation of occidental plethora. The cowboys had coloured their top lips and chins bright blue to suggest a strong Western growth of beard. Provided with guitars which they were unable to play, they shrilled a strident Oriental version of hill-billy airs, which someone in the orchestra accompanied on some Vietnamese stringed instrument, punctuating the lines with a vigorous clashing of cymbals.

This second experience was a great improvement. It was a traditional play describing the tragic courtship by a Chinese Ambassador of an unattached medieval Empress of Viet-Nam. The costumery was the most gorgeous and obviously expensive I have ever seen. There was none of the dreamy symbolism of Cambodia and Laos in this performance. The acting was literal and never relapsed into ballet. When, for instance, the Ambassador and his rival the Chief Mandarin fought a duel, the fight was meant to be a real one; a dazzling display of traditional swordsmanship, and not a set *pas de deux* with each performer releasing symbolical thunderbolts. The culminating point was reached when, with a mighty cut, the Ambassador's arm was hacked off. Much blood flowed, some of which the Ambassador staunched with his handkerchief which he tenderly presented to the Empress. Afterwards, holding his severed right arm in his left hand, the Ambassador acted an energetic death-scene, lasting half an hour, finally expiring, still upright, in the arms of his followers. The dramatic high spots of the scene were accentuated by an orchestral supernumerary on a special perch who beat a cymbal.

Extreme despair at the Ambassador's fate was registered by all the company, including the Empress, hurling themselves to the ground and then performing a kind of frantic gyration. This was the moment when the curtain should have been rung down, but unfortunately it stuck half way. The orchestra had worked up to a deafening finale, with the cymbals man lashing out as if fighting for his life and the human catherine wheels whirling, with peacocks feathers and brocaded panels flying in all directions. And then the cast had had enough. Leaping as one man to their feet, the Ambassador still clutching his arm, they caught at the edge of the curtain and pulled it down. It was an exciting performance in the zestful tradition, I thought, of an essentially Northern people, whose culture had remained completely uncontaminated in their long sojourn in the South.

CHAPTER XIII

INTO CAMBODIA

THE Land-Rover bounded westwards over the road to Cambodia. It was the only road of any length in the country open to unescorted, day-time traffic, although it had been closed for a fortnight before the day we left, 'owing to damage caused by the weather'. We plunged through a bland and smiling landscape, animated by doll-like Vietnamese figures, and mud-caked buffaloes that ambled across the road, lowering their heads as if to charge, when it was too late. Children dangled lines from bridges, while their elders, gathered in sociable groups, groped for fish, waist-deep in liquid mud. The kites, floating over the villages, were pale ideographs against a deeper sky. There were miles of deserted rubber plantations.

It was better, said the driver, not to stop between the towers, and his method was to accelerate to about 65 m.p.h. until a tower was about two hundred yards away. He would then relax speed until we were past, and about the same distance on the other side. This confidence in the towers seemed not altogether well-founded. The papers had recently published an account of an attack by one of the garrisons on a car straggling behind a convoy in which the driver was shot dead and a lady passenger's finger was almost bitten off in an attempt to rob her of a ring. We frequently found that ditches had been dug across the road by Viet-Minh sympathizers, and subsequently filled in with loose earth. A series of such semi-obstacles taken at full-throttle was a fun-fair sensation, even in the Land-Rover. At one point we passed a newly burned-out car from which a tracery of smoke still arose.

Cambodia. It was a place-name always accompanied in my imagination by tinkling, percussive music. Although the Viet-

facing: VIETNAMESE THEATRE: THE CHINESE AMBASSADOR DECLARES HIS LOVE

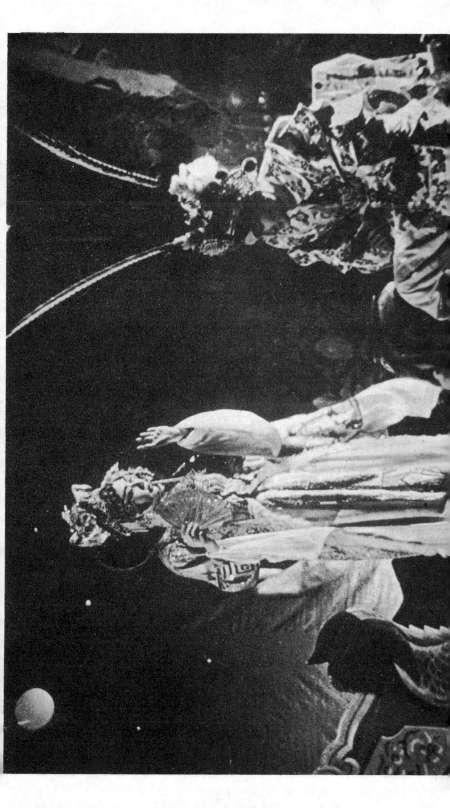

namese had been encroaching for centuries upon Cambodian land, there were signs of a true physical frontier at the present border. We came to a wide river; on one side was Cochin-China — which had once been Cambodia too — with the neat, busy Vietnamese, the mosaic of rice-fields and the plantations. Across the river was the Cambodia of present times, and what, too, must have been some early frontier of the ancient Khmer state, since everything changed immediately. It was not only the people, but the flora and the fauna. A cultural Great-Divide; a separation of continents. On one bank of the river were the ordinary forest trees, which, as amateurs of natural history, the Vietnamese would spare, if not compelled to clear them for rice-fields or plantations. The other bank bore sparse clumps of coconut palms — the first I had seen in my travels — and beyond them, a foretaste of the withered plains of India.

The bamboos and the underbrush had gone, and with them the dark-winged, purposeful butterflies of the Vietnamese forests. Here only trivial fritillaries fluttered over the white prairie grass. Great pied kingfishers as well as the large and small blue varieties encrusted the edges of yellow pools and ditches that served no economic purpose. There were no rice-fields. Cambodians lounged inertly about the rare villages that were no more than a few squalid African huts. In one village some women with dirty, handsome faces were pouring earth into some of the worst holes in this terrible road, while a group of bonzes stood by, watching them with saintly detachment. The trim pyjamas of the Vietnamese had given way to the dreary weeds of India; a drab, sarong-like skirt, pulled in the men's case into the shape of breeches by bringing the waist-sash through the legs. There might be, in addition to this, a jacket of some dingy material and a rag wound round the head as a turban. It was curious to reflect that under the barrack-room discipline of their spirits, the aboriginal Moïs — when left alone — were the best dressed and best housed people in Indo-China. After them came the Vietnamese, in their brisk, work-a-day turnout — you never

facing: PNOM-PENH: PROCESSION OF THE TWENTY-FIVE SPIRITS

saw a ragged one — and their flower-decked shacks. And last of all were these descendants of the great Khmer civilization, who quite clearly didn't care in the slightest how they lived or dressed.

But the Cambodians had one enormous advantage over the others. There were no plantations to be seen on this side of the river. So far, the Grendel of Colonial capitalism had been kept at bay. The Cambodians are practising Buddhists, and every man, including the King, must spend a year of his life as a mendicant novice in a Buddhist monastery. And the strength of this second of the world religions lies in the fact that it has produced a tradition, a permanent state of mind, which makes its followers neither adept as exploiters nor amenable to exploitation. The Cambodians, like the Burmese, the Laotians and others, no doubt, of the South-East Asiatic peoples, are, by their own design, poor, but supremely happy. In these rich and comparatively underpopulated countries there is no struggle for existence, and this provides the ideal atmosphere for the practice of the gentle faith in which their people have been reared.

The Vietnamese, whose Buddhism is diluted almost to the point of non-existence, has a competitive soul, is a respecter of work for its own sake, and strives to increase and multiply. As he will work hard for himself, he can be made to work hard for others, and is therefore the prey of the exploiter. There are a few uneasily conducted plantations in Cambodia, and while I was there, in fact, there was a serious revolt in one of them. But Cambodia has no surplus population and no proletariat. Every man can have as much land as he can cultivate. As far as I know no Cambodian has ever been shipped in the hulks to end his life toiling in some depopulated South-Seas island.

Spurred on by thoughts of what the French call isolated acts of piracy we reached Pnom-Penh, the capital, early the same afternoon. It is approached through unimposing suburbs: several miles of shacks among the trees, most of them reeling slightly on their supporting posts. There are a few pagodas, insubstantial looking and tawdry with gilt, which contrived to remind one of the Far-Eastern section of a colonial exhibition, and many graveyards of bonzes with tombs almost as showy as those of the cemeteries of Northern Italy. The dogs of India are here, one per house; an ugly yellow variety with a petulant expression, and sometimes in a state of utter decrepitude. Together with the pigs and occasional domestic monkeys they profit to the utmost, in their slow saunterings on the road, from the Buddhist aversion to taking life. Through the open doors one sees that the houses contain no furniture, in keeping with the Cambodian's indifference to material possessions. The occupants wash, dress and, of course, eat in public, and half-naked families are to be observed squatting round devouring the splendid fish that can be had almost for the taking away, down by the river. Refuse is thrown out of a window or pushed through the floor, collecting in massive mounds for the benefit of the kitchen-midden excavators of the future. There is none of the well-bred aloofness of the Vietnamese about these people. The Cambodians stare at whatever interests them and will giggle at slight provocation.

The centre of Pnom-Penh has, of course, been taken over by the Chinese, who have indulged in it to the limit their taste for neon-signs, opened many cinemas, too many radio shops with loud-speakers blaring in the doorways, and a casino, which, started in 1949, is said already to have bankrupted half the Cambodians of the capital. However, they are supposed to be a local breed of Chinese, cheerful vulgarians raised in the country, and very much to be preferred to the arrogant immigrants from Hong Kong that lord it in Saigon.

The matter calling for first attention in Pnom-Penh was that of the journey to Laos, which I still wanted to make overland, if this could be done from Cambodia. There was a road which followed the river Mékong, which in Saigon was thought to be impassable in places. In normal times one could ascend by the river itself, which, at the height of the rainy season, was navigable up to 1600 miles from its mouth by one sort of craft or other. This was the end of the dry season when the water was at its lowest. Nor did anyone in Saigon know if boats still went up the river.

First inquiries were unhopeful in result. There were many fine old river boats; picturesque relics of the first decades of steam navigation, moored along the bank by the King's palace. But there were no signs of activity, no polishing of brasses or clanging of bells, no evidence that the greenish hawsers would ever be loosened or the anchors dragged up by their rusting chains. The crews slept out of sight or had gone away. These ships would stay there for ever, one felt, a painted riverine background to the town's flattish silhouette.

But there was one boat actually about to leave, said a Frenchman I spoke to. He pointed to the one with an eye painted on the bows that lay alongside the King's state launch, and, sure enough, a curl of smoke rose from the tall, black funnel. Hastening up the gangplank I asked for the Captain and was led into the presence of an elderly gentleman in an old-fashioned Chinese gown, who half reclined on a bench in what I took to be the first-class passengers' saloon. At his side was a jam-jar containing a goldfish, which, while we talked, he prodded at absently with a fountain pen. I asked this venerable mariner when the boat was going and he answered, in good French, that it was making a journey of one night up the river. That seemed of little use, I explained, as it would take a week to get to Southern Laos. Did he connect with any other service? Not that he knew of, the old gentleman replied pleasantly. And the pirate situation? I asked. Were they ever attacked? The gown was lifted for access to an inner pocket, and a bullet produced gleefully for my inspection. It had been recovered, he said, from the body of one of the crew. But such attacks were infrequent now. Until a month or two ago he hadn't been able to leave his estate and this was only his second trip down to Pnom-Penh. I now at last realized that the boat was a private one, and later I learned that its owner was a well-known Chinese millionaire.

Nor were the prospects for road travel much brighter. The Royal Hotel had a special notice-board covered with what looked like Army standing orders. They were the constantly changing regulations dealing with travel on the various roads, and the minimum degree of precaution permitted vehicles to travel in pairs, at not more than one hundred metres from each other. Each car had to carry three passengers.

The situation looked even less promising when Valas arrived on the evening plane and we went down to the *cercle* together. The first piece of news that greeted him was that a business friend had been shot dead, two miles from the town's centre, and a few minutes later we were drinking with a man who had been captured by a band of Issarak nationalists. This man, a school-teacher, had been saved by his Sino-Cambodian chauffeur, who had convinced the Issarak in an argument lasting several hours, that his master, quite accidentally, observed the five virtues – proved by the fact that he accepted poor pupils without payment – and should be spared. He was, therefore, held prisoner, while the Issarak went for rides in the car until the petrol was used up, when they set him free, leaving him with the car.

On the next day's programme was a visit arranged by the enthusiastic members of the local information centre to the headquarters of General des Essars, who was in command of the French Army in Cambodia. I decided that if anyone knew what the prospects of getting to Laos were, it would be the General and that these preoccupations might, therefore, be postponed for that day

Pnom-Penh was one of those synthetic Chinese towns with all the warm glitter so cheering to the hearts of Sunday night Coventry Street crowds. The Chinese are not interested in South-East Asian towns until they have reached on their own initiative a certain level of population and prosperity. They then descend like a flock of gregarious birds, galvanizing its life with their crow-like vitality.

The feeble shoots of local culture wither away and what remains is a degenerate native slum round the hard, bright, self-contained, Chinese core. Valas and I went to look for the Cambodian ballet. In addition to the King's private troupe there had been another in a fairly flourishing state as late as 1946 when Valas had lived there. We found the house, but it was empty, and neighbours said that the corps de ballet had disbanded. It evidently couldn't compete against such attractions as 'Arsenic et Vieille Dentelle', currently showing at one of the Chinese cinemas.

But Madame Shum's was still going strong. Madame Shum's is Pnom-Penh's leading opium den, or *salon de désintoxication* as they are now, with a kind of prim irony, renamed. The salon was a great bamboo shack among the trees, its empty window-apertures glowing feebly with death-bed light. In these romantic surroundings the raffish élite of Pnom-Penh meet together at night over the sociable sucking of opium pipes.

We were received by Madame herself, who possessed all the calm dignity of her social position. There was evidently a certain snob-value in being on calling terms with the head of the house, comparable to the privilege of being allowed to address a well-known head-waiter by his Christian name. The rank and file of patrons were dealt with by underlings, but the socially prominent always made a point of calling at the administrative headquarters to present their compliments to Madame. We were served with highballs on the veranda while Madame showed us the latest portrait of her son, who was studying medicine in France, and of her daughter, an extremely beautiful girl of seventeen who was at college in Saigon. They were by different French fathers, she mentioned. Valas produced the formal banter the occasion demanded, including mild, chivalrous overtures to Madame herself and a request for the daughter's hand.

One went to Madame Shum's, Valas said, first because it was the thing to do, and secondly because you met all kinds of business and other contacts there. We did in fact run into one man who hoped we might be induced to buy a certain American car from him. He had imported this car with a particular client in mind, a wealthy Chinese, who, since it was the only one of its kind in Indo-China and loaded with chromiumed accessories, was expected to jump at the chance. Before seeing it the Chinese had asked all the questions covering the essentials. Was it fitted with radio? — Yes. Press button hood-operation? — Yes. Parking and pass-lights? — Yes. Two-tone horn? — Yes. Air-conditioning? — No, but it could be fitted. Only at the last moment when the man was sure the sale was in the bag had he turned up with a tape-measure. He was sorry, it was too small; several centimetres shorter than a Buick he had been offered. Thus have the provincial Chinese of Pnom-Penh, separated from the mainsprings of their culture, turned away from the curious and the exquisite, and embraced the standards of taste which are impressed by fashion, by glitter and by sheer size.

As a concession to the atmosphere at Madame Shum's patrons were supposed to remove their clothing and put on a sarong. At first one felt childish and self-conscious, like a timid experimenter, per-haps, in a nudist colony. But among all these corpulent officials, these chiefs-of-staff and under-secretaries padding to their pleasures down the creaking corridors, the feeling soon passed. It was nothing more than a casual encounter of elks in semi-regalia. There seemed to be no desire for privacy. The sarong was the badge of a temporary inward and spiritual state. One showed one's determination to go native for a couple of hours after dinner and one was expected to flop down quite unconcernedly wherever there happened to be a vacant mat.

The actual smoking, a tedious process, brought no reward it seemed, unless persevered with. I was promised that with six pipes I could expect to be reasonably sick, which was as far as a beginner got on the first few occasions. However the smell of the stale smoke-impregnated compartment of a 'workman's special' was enough for me. It was another convention that one stretched oneself out on a mat while the blob of opium was toasted over a spirit lamp before being transferred to the bowl of the yard-long pipe. These preparatory rites were performed by a corps of uniformly ill-favoured young Cambodian ladies, whose looks Madame excused by saying that all the pretty ones had recently been abducted by some ex-bandits newly formed into a patriotic army. Valas smoked three pipes and was ready to move. No one seemed in the slightest affected by their indulgences, despite the fact that two civil servants and a very high ranking officer in the same room had smoked fifteen pipes and said that they would smoke thirty before leaving. Apart from the sheepish good-fellowship of shared weakness, there was nothing in their manner — I met the officer later on duty — that seemed in any way other than normal.

Valas was highly suspicious of the quality of the opium, and asked whether it was contraband rubbish from Siam. The original wrapper, marked with the government stamp, had to be found to convince him.

Valas could find no one among the opium smokers who wanted to buy the car, but there was at least news of the disbanded ballet. The girls had gone to work in the *Lap ton* dancing places. Breaking away from Madame Shum's sombre haven, we therefore got into the car and plunged back again into the vast, brazen clamour of Pnom-Penh's centre. It must have been a great day for the Chinese, who have always enjoyed noise, when the principles of electrical amplification were discovered. Here, as at Cholon, the crowds had an air of exultation, of crisis. Heralds with banners stood at the cross-roads. Trumpeting loudspeakers yelled an actor's lines, their rhythm fiercely marked by the crashing of cymbals. Stone-faced men in flapping silk bowed their heads beneath the thunder of celestial drums, and sing-song girls sobbed an immense cosmic anguish from the open casements of good, first-floor restaurants.

But the places where the Cambodians go to dance are quite properly a little withdrawn from all this Tartar fury. We found a quiet back street with waste paper kicked about all over its dusty surface, and a few sad, yellow dogs. The noise of someone banging a drum came to us through a broken fence, on the other side of which was a kind of beer garden. There were a dozen marble-topped tables and a stage with a row of Cambodian girls sitting with their hands in their laps at the back of it. Out in front was a microphone and a band in the form of one man who was beating a drum. The centre of the stage was marked by a small table with a bunch of fleshy red blooms in a large whole-milk tin. The place was lit by the early-type, ghastly fluorescent tubes, and there were notices about minimum *consummations* in French, Chinese and Vietnamese. All the customers were Cambodians but the Chinese who ran the place didn't even bother to put up a notice in their language. The Chinese management sat at a table right up by the stage, with their backs to the patrons, doing the accounts, while the Cambodians sipped their blood-coloured lemonade and smiled as if delighted by inner visions. The Cambodians kept arriving on bicycles that were decorated with pennants and all kinds of gadgets. They came from those shacks we had seen on the outskirts of the town and were very dapper-looking with their sports-shirts, American ties and slicked-down hair.

Someone on the management table struck a small gong and the drummer started up again. A moon-faced young Cambodian, who had been egged on by his friends, went up on to the stage and began to croon into the microphone a Tino Rossi song called 'Gardien de Camargue'. After the first verse he was handed a pair of maracas and, still singing, began to slash out some kind of un-recognizable rhythm which the drummer did his best to follow. It was now the turn of the ex-members of the Cambodian ballet to go into action. As soon as one of them caught the eye of a patron, she got up, left the stage, went over to his table and putting her hands together in the attitude of prayer made a solemn-faced bow. The young man then followed her back to the stage and joined her in a kind of processional dance round the centre table with the flowers in the milk-tin. The couples kept three or four feet apart, their hands and arms weaving about in the formal gestures of the

Ramayana and their feet doing their best to conform to a rhythm which was not quite a fox-trot, a rumba or a béguine. No charge was made for the dancing. It was all included in the price of the beer.

The girls' faces wore the frozen expressions demanded by tradition, since in the classic dances the emotions must be interpreted by a repertoire of postures. Their partners seemed to have emancipated themselves from this courtly discipline and did not mind looking as if they were having a vulgar good-time. When a girl felt she had given her partner his money's worth she just turned back while the dance was in progress and bowed to him. The pair then turned away and left each other without so much as exchanging a glance. This dance had been imported in recent years from Siam and in it were enshrined thus, on the verge of oblivion, the gestures from the mimes of the Cambodian kings.

Valas pointed out the star performer, whom he remembered from the old days. She was not the best-looking of the girls and the extraordinary mask-like effect of her features was heightened, rather grotesquely, by a red stain, the size of a five-shilling piece, caused by cupping, in the dead centre of her forehead. For all that she had the truly impressive sinuosity of a girl who had spent more than half her short life contorting her body into the strange rhythmic moulds demanded by the representation of the fabulous serpents, birds and apes of the Ramayana. In the interval, the half-hour relief from the doleful conspiracy of crooner and drummer, the girls wandered off the stage. Valas caught the prima ballerina's eye and she came down to us swaying slightly as she moved through the tables, with the undulation of a charmed cobra. As she lowered herself into a chair there was the faintest tinkle of concealed ornaments. With the gesture of a drowning arm raised from the surface of an enchanted lake, a silk head-shawl was discarded. It was most unfortunate that we spoke no Cambodian and the lady knew only two words of French: soupe Chinoise. The soup was served and we had reached a conversational impasse. However, the universal language of art came to our aid. The controlled face relaxed in the beginnings of an anxious, half-smile. A bond was to be created that would defeat the barriers of speech. Sita, the beloved of Rama, opened her plastic handbag and groped in it for a picture which she passed across the table to us. It was an indecent photograph, of the Port Said kind, vintage about 1925.

We finished the evening with a visit to a night-club called, I believe, the Florida, or something equally absurd. Valas had endured mild heart-burnings for several years over a Vietnamese dance-hostess who worked there, known as 'La Panthère'. He paid her an immense sum to come and sit at our table for about half an hour. She was immaculate, regal and rather surly. They soon fell out over the provenance of some jewellery she was wearing, and the atmosphere became heavy with suppressed recrimination.

But the Florida was well worth a visit for a study of its patrons. A French woman in a sarong was pointed out who had married a Cambodian prince and had gone so completely native that she refused to speak anything but Cambodian. There was a Chinese millionaire of seventy, a grave little fellow, who came there every night to rumba with the same statuesque professional partner. Two representatives of distinguished Cambodian families with Portuguese names were present — descendants of Fernao Mendes Pinto's two shipmates, left behind when he escaped from slavery in the country. The owner of a small fleet of *cyclos* had come here to relax. He made the equivalent of £1000 per month from the hundred coolies who worked for him and was therefore able to spend ten months of the year in Paris. From this it was clear that a rickshaw coolie who owned his own *cyclo* could live comfortably. But on further inquiry I learned this was ruled out because only Europeans with a great deal of pull could get the licences, which were strictly limited. In any case, whatever the coolies earned, said Valas, they would only gamble it away; and the only difference as things were was that one man squandered the money instead of a hundred.

CHAPTER XIV

KING NORODOM'S CAPITAL

NEXT morning, I saw General des Essars, who was in command of French troops in Cambodia. Like all the official personalities I visited in the country, he seemed to be enjoying life, and he gave the impression of being no more than faintly amused by the preposterous difficulties of the military task.

A London newspaper had been interested to know what were the possibilities, in the event of the French being obliged to leave Indo-China, of Viet-Nam, Cambodia and Laos lining up together to form an effective barrier to what was called the southwards march of communism. Put into plain language, this meant, could these three countries combine to keep out an invasion by Chinese communists? The General said that he would not wish to have his opinion quoted on such a point, and would content himself with supplying figures to give some idea of the Cambodian war-potential.

The regular army, he said, consisted of three battalions, comprising 2500 men. There was also a national guard which wasn't particularly well-trained or well-equipped. These short-time warriors also numbered about 2500, and the General quoted Wellington's remark about not knowing whether or not they would frighten the enemy, but, by God, they frightened him. He felt nervous about giving them up-to-date arms, because if they had anything worth taking they would clear off — *ils foutraient le camp*. Besides this there was an officers' school with twelve students and a police force whose armoury contained one medium machine-gun and two tommy-guns. On the whole the General said it wasn't famous. But there you were, what could you expect in a country where every man-jack of them had done a year in a monastery, where they taught you that thou shalt not kill had to be taken literally?

'They defend themselves — sometimes,' the General said. 'But that is about the best you can say for them.'

As for the other side of the medal, there were the Viet-Minh, who held the coastline, solidly, all the way from the frontier of Siam to Cochin-China. And then there were five bands of Issarak nationalists, all well armed with fetus amulets and automatic weapons, and they were only getting a little peace round the capital itself since the sixth band, that of Dap Chhuon, had surrendered, and Dap Chhuon himself had been given the governorship of the province of Siem-Reap. I remembered seeing propaganda pictures at Saigon of the ceremony that had accompanied Dap Chhuon's submission. It had been a well staged act of fealty. Dap Chhuon, thin and tough, with the ravaged face of an anchorite, knelt before the King, who, dressed I believe in the uniform of a French admiral and smiling like a Bodhisattva, was leaning over to hand him back his carbine. This was the thing in a nutshell. You committed a single murder and you were probably shackled hand and foot, thrown into a dark hole in the ground and left to rot. You went in for large-scale slaughter, called yourself an Issarak and managed to keep a whole skin for a year or two, and it was cheaper to buy you off. The King himself made the nation's peace with you and you got a provincial governorship. And now, with Dap Chhuon and his three hundred and fifty men keeping order, tourists could come again — for the first time for several years — to visit the ruins at Angkor Vat.

But the General pursed his lips and shook his head over future prospects. It seemed that a certain, quite unforeseen element had suddenly cropped up. It was to be feared, in fact, that Dap Chhuon was no decent, reliable, straightforward bandit after all. Either he had never been one of the old school of dependable tiger's-liver-eating thugs, or in some mysterious way he had been corrupted, being now, indeed, suspected of having turned communist. The latest news of him was that he had put one of his men in each of the villages, who had presented the notables with a list of reforms to be carried out. That was the state of affairs. Apart from all the bother the Viet-Minh gave, they now had their own people, who used to be satisfied with looting pigs and rice, going in for all this silly nonsense. The General wondered how long it would be before he had to send the planes to Siem-Reap.

It was clear that this account of the military situation in Cambodia contained the death of my hopes about the overland journey to Laos. Of the five Issarak bands still active, one, controlled it was thought by the Viet-Minh, operated on the Cambodia-Laos border. This would have been the same band that was reported in the neighbourhood of Stung Treng, when I had tried to reach Laos from Central Annam. They were mounted, the General said, well-armed, and very mobile. By the time he could get planes to any district where they were reported to have been seen, it was always too late. Land operations were almost useless, because you had to fight with soldiers who expected to be fed regularly and generally mollycoddled. But the bandits didn't worry about creature comforts. While you were dragging your baggage trains about after them, they just slipped off into the mountains, or some god-awful swamp, and that was that.

General des Essars's absence of confidence in the ability of Cambodia to stand on its own feet was certainly not shared by its Prime Minister, S. E. Yem Sambaur, whom I visited next. Since the accumulation of wealth is considered rather ill-bred in post-Khmer Cambodia, there are few large fortunes and little ostentation among the Cambodians. The head of the State, beneath the King, lived in what looked like a six-roomed villa, furnished in European style with a sober good taste rarely seen in Western imitations in the Far East. I was surprised to find that although said to be about forty, His Excellency looked rather like a not too serious-minded undergraduate of about twenty-three. This extraordinary youthfulness was a thing I continually noticed about the people of Cambodia and Laos, my impression entirely contradicting that of the thirteen-century Chinese traveller Chou Ta-Kouan, who wrote a unique account of the Khmers at the height of their power. Ta-Kouan found that the Cambodians of his day — and the race has suffered not the slightest change — aged very quickly. A Cambodian lady of twenty or thirty looked as old as a Chinese of forty or fifty. This is so far from being the case today that one wonders whether that heavy burden of glory the Khmers carried, the constant warrings and the exactions of task-masters and divine kings, may not have been wearisome to the flesh as well as a vexation of spirit. Their descendants are without a care in the world and wear wonderfully well.

Yem Sambaur had the face of a dusky fawn. He laughed continually, especially when describing the atrocities committed by the French Foreign Legion in Cambodian villages. I found it surprising that the Prime Minister should express himself with such complete lack of restraint in political matters to a foreigner and an utter stranger. It was even odder that a French official of the Information Bureau should have arranged the visit. It was all very Cambodian; the unquenchable good humour of Sambaur, and that of the Frenchman too. He had been several years in Cambodia, he said, and would never leave it, if he could help it. He was literally turning into a Cambodian before one's eyes and could have mingled quite easily with that serene group of functionaries I saw later at the Palace, and have avoided detection.

His Excellency, addressing me continually as Monsieur le directeur, spoke very seriously about relations with the French, although the sharpness of remarks never ruffled his seraphic expression. The Cambodians had refused to sign the agreement by which Cambodia became 'independent within the framework of the French Union' because of several quite unacceptable provisions. The fact that Bao-Dai, the Emperor of Viet-Nam, had signed, did not influence them in the least. The first serious obstacle was that the minorities in Cambodia, including the French, and of course the Chinese, could not be brought before Cambodian courts — an insult to a legal code recognized as one of the most humane in the world. The second objection was that French troops were to be allowed to operate on Cambodian soil. 'We can take care of the Issarak, without French help,' the Prime Minister said. 'If the country were really independent there would be no Issarak. There would be no reason for them.' As it was the French air force on the mere report that Issarak had been seen in them, bombed Cambodian villages off the face of the earth, or the Foreign Legion went into them and massacred the villagers; men, women and children. I asked if His Excellency were referring to isolated incidents, and still smiling broadly he told me that cases were reported to him every day.

And as a result, he said, the country people were turning to communism. Communism, Yem Sambaur thought, was singularly unsuited to the people of Cambodia; a country without industries and an urban proletariat, and with few rich landowners. But now it was being presented to the people as a way of salvation. That was why you had the phenomenon of Cambodian Issarak chiefs coming to terms with the hitherto detested Vietnamese — a totally unprecedented state of affairs. The best way to convert a villager to communism was to burn his house down and kill one or more members of his family. In this way you abolished a man's inducements to lead a quiet, respectable existence. When you cut the bonds that tied a man to the existing order, he naturally became a bandit, and if you could persuade him that the communists would fight his enemies more ruthlessly than the others, well, he would be a communist too. And that was how the Issarak bands grew, and that was also why they were quite ready to provide themselves, if the Viet-Minh suggested it, with political commissars. 'But then, of course,' said His Excellency, still smiling, 'the transition to communism is less difficult for an Asiatic, even for members of the upper classes. Perhaps we have less to lose. In any case, the prospect does not alarm us. There are times when one feels that perhaps it would be even better to be a little poorer, if at the same time one could be a little freer.'

Western architecture has always been impressed with the *kolossal*. Cities are dominated by dome, tower or turret; the acts of faith or monuments to fear. The spires of gothic cathedrals rising cliff-like above the roofs of a medieval town, are visible in some cases from such a distance that the surrounding buildings are concealed by the curvature of the earth's surface.

In South-East Asia the motives that found their expression in this kind of building are absent, and it is only to be found in the ruined temples and mausolea of Angkor. Apart from the houses in European quarters, all buildings must be of a single storey, since there is an ancient and universal prohibition against standing directly above another's head. This is so scrupulously observed that in Cambodia it is even illegal for a manacled prisoner to be lodged temporarily under the raised floor of the typical Cambodian house.

The Royal Palace at Pnom-Penh, then, is a single-storey affair, and quite obscured, except from the river's bank, by other buildings. It is pagoda architecture and one feels that if the pinchbeck glitter of the gilding could be subdued it would provide, perhaps, a charming and discreet lakeside ornament. We have seen buildings of this kind so often in Colonial exhibitions that we have come to associate them with impermanence, and even suspect that they may be supplied in sections with simple instructions for erection. It comes as no surprise to learn that the Palace was built by the French soon after Cambodia became a protectorate. But even the ancient and notable pagodas of Luang Prabang turn out later to be not very much better as buildings, however far superior their decoration may be.

Behind the high, screening wall, the palace proved to consist of several separate buildings, all of which, except those containing the private apartments, could be visited on a set tour, for which a guide was provided. Among this cluster of lacquered, box-like edifices, their roofs curled up as if by the scorching sun, there was one of solidly incongruous stone. This was a house presented by Napoleon III to Queen Eugenie and then taken down and sent here as a gift to the Cambodian monarch of the day. It looked like the permanent administrative offices, stolid and matter-of-fact, on an exposition site, squatting among the lath and plaster which after a few months would be taken down and cleared away. The presence of the European interloper gave a clue to the contents of the pavilions themselves.

These were frankly museum exhibits of the past two centuries of royal history. Some of them were strangely revelatory. The only building which could be described as internally impressive was the Silver Pagoda, and then it was impressive rather as a curiosity. Here for the first time one glimpsed the East of the traveller's tale; prodigious, garish and wasteful. If the kings of Cambodia had never felt the urge to build an Escorial or a Caserta they had at least floored a pagoda with 5000 blocks of solid silver, and although the aesthetic effect was no choicer than that to be had from walking on the polished deck of a battleship, there had at least been fine, profligate squandering of precious metal.

The purpose of the Silver Pagoda appeared to be to house the royal treasure, consisting principally of a great collection of Buddhas, in gold and jade and other precious materials; some with diamonds in their foreheads. Whenever a Buddha happened to be of solid gold, the guide, padding relentlessly in the rear, inevitably announced the exact weight of the metal that had gone into its construction. Below the ranks of Buddhas, with their smiles, placid, ironic or even supercilious, were lined up rows of pawnbrokers' counters. In these, behind the scratched and dirty glass, had been assembled for inspection the gifts of foreign potentates of the past, together with what looked like nothing more than a great miscellaneous collection of family bric-à-brac.

One brooded over enormous jewelled watches, full of whimsy and misplaced ingenuity in their methods of working; Victorian compositions of wax flowers, fruit and sea-shells under bell-jars; a miniature Buddha studded with perhaps ten thousand pounds-worth of diamonds seated uneasily on the back of a tortoiseshell hairbrush; reliquaries of cloisonné and beaten gold; an ivory back-scratcher; more jewelled Buddhas; china eggs of the kind that are supposed to induce hens to lay; a string of Christmas-tree decorations — tinsel and silver balls. One imagined the queen, or perhaps a succession of queens, making a periodical clear-out of their cupboards and then tripping down to the Silver Pagoda with all the attractive, useless things that had to be found a home somewhere. The family photographs were perhaps the most interesting thing about this magpie's hoard. There were the monarchs and their queens in faded sepia, staring of eye and stiff of pose in the European clothing into which they had just been buckled and laced for the occasion. Among them was one informal and dashing scene, probably taken by one of the courtiers, of the old King Sisowath waltzing round with a very aged lady. And sometimes, under the influence perhaps of Edward VII, the ruler of Cambodia was displayed in knickerbockers, the oddest of all garments for an oriental potentate, possessing, one supposed, a plurality of wives.

Of the other pagodas' contents I remember less, but of the wax-works jumble of exhibits two things caught the imagination. One was the genial cynicism with which the French had sent the reigning king when they had taken over the country, a statue of himself ... only all they had done was to find a spare statue of Napoleon III, knock the head off and replace it with one of the Cambodian monarch roughly chiselled-up from a portrait. The other thing that impressed me was the extraordinary variety of the king's regalia of state, which changed in style according to the manner in which he showed himself. Thus there was an assortment of crowns, with varying numbers of tiers, for use according to whether his majesty was riding on an elephant, or on horse-back, or being carried in a palanquin. To these there had been recently added a new form of ceremonial headgear, to meet the case of the motor car. For such public occasions he wears a bowler hat, decorated with a diamond cockade.

It was soon clear to me that the enthusiastic Monsieur Salis of the Bureau of Information, who had arranged this visit, would never rest content until he had obtained for me an audience with the king. And as he seemed to be on the best possible terms with everyone at the palace, a man who liked Cambodians and was equally liked by them, I felt quite certain that he would succeed. However, as nothing definite had been arranged by the time we left the palace, I went off for a walk, hoping to be able to find a booth where they sold theatrical masks, which I had seen from the car on the previous night.

Thereafter there was some similarity between my experiences and those of the French explorer Mouhot — or at least the first part of his experiences — when he interviewed the king of Cambodia in 1859. Mouhot had just arrived in the capital and his luggage had not caught up with him. However, weary and travel-stained as he was, the king sent for him. To quote his account, 'I objected that I could not visit him in my travelling dress. "Oh, that is nothing, the king has no dress at all, and he will be delighted to see you," was the reply.' When after an hour or so's chase round Pnom-Penh, Monsieur Salis finally found me, with the news that the interview had been arranged, these were practically the words he used. The temperature was at least a hundred in the shade, and I was wearing shorts and covered in grime and perspiration, but it was nothing, Salis said. The people at the palace were all 'des braves gens', and they expected a traveller to look like one. We would go up there right away.

In Mouhot's account, the ancestor of the present king is shown rather in the light of one of these comical stock-figures of an African paramount chief. ' "Good brandy," said the king in English (the only words he knew of that language)' and, 'His majesty then displayed to me his European furniture, mahogany tables covered with china vases and other ornaments of a commonplace description; above all, he pointed out, as worthy of notice, two old looking-glasses in gilt frames, a sofa and various similar articles. "I am but beginning," said he; "in a few years my palace will be beautiful." '

The present king appeared to me to be of a quite different calibre.

Salis led the way up the steps to the ante-room of the audience chamber and introduced me to the members of the royal staff. We had hardly shaken hands before the king skipped into view through an open doorway on the right. He was wearing the smile that one saw in the photographs, and it was considerably less complaisant than that of any of the Buddhas in the Silver Pagoda. The king shook hands vigorously and we went into the audience chamber together and sat down on a settee.

King Norodom of Cambodia is spiritual and temporal head of his people, the ultimate possessor of all Cambodian land — which, however, he bestows freely upon the petition of those who wish to cultivate it — and the inheritor of all who die intestate. He is the only person in the kingdom entitled to a six-tiered parasol and being semi-divine, and above the law, his privileges include the right to contract incestuous marriage with an aunt or a half-sister. In return for his prerogatives he performs the many ancient ceremonials in use since the days of Angkor, such as the ablutions of the Brahmanical idols, which assure the well-being and prosperity of the people. Being without debts, free of crime or bodily blemish, he was permitted to serve the customary year as a mendicant novice in a Buddhist monastery. My only previous interviews with royal personages had been with Arab princes, and the King of Cambodia in his informality was like somebody whose acquaintance one had just made in a bar, by comparison. The personal splendour of the past had been reduced to mere sartorial impeccability, in the form of a well-cut grey flannel suit.

Norodom, who is a man of thirty and looks twenty-one, is said by some of the French to be the most intelligent Cambodian. It was, in fact, quite astonishing how easily he brushed aside all the polite generalities accepted on such occasions, to embark without further ado on a competent half-hour's lecture on Cambodian politics. It was much the same story as Yem Sambaur's, but couched in less forthright terms. Sambaur's bloody massacres became 'incidents of violence'. It was difficult to associate the king's gentle manner with harsh, uncompromising words like murder. The king's thesis, to which he returned continually, was that the French continually lagged behind the times. 'Ils ne marchent pas à la tête des évènements; ils se laissent dépasser par les temps.' As King of Cambodia and a Buddhist gentleman he would engage his word that French commercial interests would remain untouched if only they would get out — just as the English had done in India. France had failed in its engagements as the protecting power when the Japanese had been allowed, without resistance, to overrun the country. The old treaties were therefore invalid, and in future Cambodia would prefer to protect herself. France, said the king, could not boast of having brought civilization to Cambodia. The phrase 'l'œuvre civilisatrice de la France' was an insult to their ancient culture, especially when the Cambodian countryfolk who made up nine-tenths of the population could only judge this civilizing task by what they saw of the Foreign Legion.

When it was clear that the interview had run its normal and reasonable course, there was an awkward moment. The conversation lagged and the king's smile became a little fixed. The time had come to withdraw and I waited for the king to indicate, by rising, that the interview was at an end. But it was becoming evident that innate politeness was too strong for the conventions of royal deportment. Forming the conclusion that if I did not make the first move we should both be condemned to sit there indefinitely, exchanging painful smiles and trying to think of something to say, I got up. I am sure that His Majesty was grateful.

That evening, which was my last at Pnom-Penh, I had an extraordinary piece of good luck. In the course of my travels I was coming to accept that wherever I was I was fated to experience a sub-normal amount of the customary activities. The theatre would be closed, the custom abolished, the service discontinued, the road cut by bandits, the tiger invisible, the season just over — or not yet started. But at Pnom-Penh, I was in luck. I went out of the hotel at about five in the evening and walked right into the most rampageous of Chinese celebrations — the procession of the twenty-five spirits, which the police had done their best to prevent and which had now broken loose, providing as fair an example of the medieval Chinese idea of a good time for all as it would have been possible to see in these days.

There is an alien northern vigour about such Chinese divertissements which is quite outlandish in the languorous and debilitating tropics. Moreover a century or two's sojourn in the deep South has done nothing to calm the Chinese temperament, nor caused them to develop any relish for the sedate posturings of Indonesia. When the Chinese dance, they leap and twirl, a spectacle I had observed before at the Mardi Gras *comparsas* in Havana, when the Chinese community decided to participate, suddenly appearing on the streets with their dragon, and startling even the bloodshot-eyed negroes of Cuba with their exertions. Wherever there are Chinese communities such celebrations as the twenty-five spirits tend to be discountenanced, as they disrupt all activities while they are in progress, and produce a state of exaltation which sometimes ends in riot. There had been an official attempt at interference with the Pnom-Penh procession which should have accompanied the Chinese New Year, and was some two weeks delayed.

By five o'clock the non-Chinese citizens had long since given up trying to go about their business and had resigned themselves to calling it a day. All the cars were taken off the roads and the shops were shut, while the twenty-five spirits, incarnated in their human representatives — both male and female — were carried round and round the town, in palanquins, on thrones and on stages accompanied by their altars and cult objects from the various pagodas. Each spirit was preceded by a dragon, a rabble of standard bearers, and a horde of attendants running amok with gongs and drums.

The spirits themselves looked like the old-fashioned idea of Chinese pirates, even to the sashes tied round their foreheads. They kept up a lusty howling, twirled their swords and frothed at the lips. Occasionally a particularly energetic spirit would make a flying leap from his throne or platform, seize a bystander and join with him in a frenzied Tartar dance, while the surrounding cult devotees clashed their cymbals and howled like damned souls. Other spirits confined to their palanquins swayed from side to side in the throes of cataleptic seizure, pausing only to inflict slight self-mutilations with their knives or to thrust skewers through their cheeks. I was told that the celebrants had all drugged themselves with hypodermic injections before setting out, five hours previously; but now it was evident that some of the effect was wearing off, as under the strain of carrying the altars and palanquins, some of the bearers were beginning to collapse. When this happened a spirit would be thrown into the crowd with even more violence than he bargained for.

At this stage the rickshaw coolies were beginning to reap the harvest. They lay in wait in the side-streets ready to pick up the victims of syncope, self-inflicted wounds and various types of seizure. By the time the procession had disintegrated they had done a roaring trade. That night half the coolies in Pnom-Penh were gambling in the Casino and owing to a temporary hold-up in the workings of the laws of average a lot of them actually won. For the first time in its short history the syndicate found themselves down on the evening. This shocking circumstance was followed next day by the dismissal of all those girl croupiers who intone so melodiously the winning numbers; not because they were suspected of cheating, but because they were unlucky.

CHAPTER XV

ANGKOR

I GOT a lift on a French military lorry that was going to Siem-Reap, the nearest town to the ruins of Angkor Vat; arriving there without incident — by courtesy of Dap Chhuon — on the evening of the same day.

Siem-Reap was another slumbering Shangri-La, perfumed slightly with putrid fish-sauce. In a palm-shaded river meandering through it both the sexes bathed all day long, lifting up their garments with extreme modesty as they allowed their bodies to sink below the level of the milk-chocolate-coloured water. When they had had enough of bathing they sat on the bank and caught occasional fish with lengths of cotton and bent pins.

With the ingeniousness of clever, lazy people, the Cambodians had worked out an irrigation system that looked as if a comic artist had had a hand in its construction. There were hundreds of great, rickety water-wheels turning slowly all day and splashing tumblers-full of water into conduits, that in their turn ran into a crazy network of bamboo tubes and finally reached the pocket-handkerchief-sized gardens that people bothered to cultivate. It was all very inefficient and wasteful and probably only a quarter of the water taken out of the river eventually got to the gardens. Some of the scoops only scooped up a thimbleful of water and others were set in the wheels at such an angle that they missed the collecting chute and the water went back into the river again. But all the open bamboo channels leading to the gardens had a trickle running through them and, until that dried up no one would be disposed to worry.

There were many baleful looking dogs, like miniature hyenas, with wrinkled snouts and foreheads; almost hairless and sometimes tail-less. Each house possessed one of these small, ugly creatures, which seemed to lay claim to a certain area round the house and therefore advanced with a hideous snarling and yapping when one entered it. One was then escorted with furious menaces to the boundary of the next cur's territory and so passed on down the road. The dogs never barked at Cambodians.

Everywhere the air was filled with the sweet creaking sound of the irrigation wheels mingled with the song of some bulbul that sang like a blackbird. The houses were the normal Cambodian shacks, standing on piles above their refuse. Beside each was the usual receptacle raised on a post with the offerings for wandering and neglected spirits — those who had no descendants on earth left to provide for them. But in this custom the Cambodians had bettered the Vietnamese, furnishing as a temporary sanctuary for these ghostly paupers most elegant little multi-tiered pagodas.

I found that the girls of a Cambodian country town were liable to smile at and even address strangers, especially if their courage was fortified by numbers. Dressed in sarong-like skirts of plain colours, with a blouse hardly reaching the midriff or perhaps just a scarf concealing the breasts, they would come sauntering out of the most squalid hovels, clean, bright and pretty, and with a ready smile of welcome. It was strange to see one of these gliding shapes suddenly galvanized into efficient action at the sight of a cow in her vegetable garden, which she chased out, throwing sticks at it with an accuracy and force that no Western woman could ever hope to emulate.

Valas had told me that when in Siem-Reap it was more important to see the Cambodian theatre than Angkor itself, because the ruins would wait. But once again it was too late. The Chinese had been granted a month's licence to run a gambling casino and they had taken over the theatre for this purpose. Anyway, I was told, it was doubtful if the theatre would open again. They were arranging for weekly cinema shows and who would be bothered with going to watch people they had known all their lives dressed up as gods and devils, when they could see a *pa-wé* for the same money.

But I was at least lucky in one small thing. I had noticed in the king's audience room a curious decoration consisting of a delicately fretted-out scene from some well-known episode of the Ramayana. The intricate lacing of motives looked, until the rear-illumination was switched on, as if it had been punched out of brass; but when lit-up it proved to be semi-transparent and was actually made from treated hide. The king mentioned — and it surprised me that an oriental sovereign should have any appreciation for the arts of his country — that this was a typical pattern used in the old shadow plays, and that they could still be found in Siem-Reap. And in Siem-Reap despite the fact that I was assured that the workshop had long since gone out of business, I tracked it down. There were the artists, squatting on the ground dressing the leather, marking the surface out with chalk, and punching out the traditional patterns. No more orders would be forthcoming for the shadow-theatre of course, but a few private persons still bought their work for decorative purposes. They sold me their show-piece, a delightful Lokesvara, for about fifteen shillings. I learned later from a visit to the Musée de L'homme at Paris that this art is still practised, though in a less finished way, in Siam and in Java.

Although the basis of Cambodian art is Indonesian and there are many recognizable affinities between the decorational motives of Cambodia and of all those countries where the Indian artistic influence has at some time been paramount, the Cambodians have undoubtedly added a flourish of their own, a recognizable style, generated in their aboriginal past, that asserts itself above the general pattern. Unfortunately, as M. Henri Marchal, Conservator of Angkor has said, the Cambodian aristocracy, who were the only patrons of Cambodian art, have abandoned it in the last half-century in favour of European importations. After the loss of their independence rich Cambodians developed an inferiority complex about everything their country produced. European cannons were more effective than the sacred and invincible sword of Cambodia;

therefore nothing Cambodian was worth having. The mandarins dismissed the goldsmiths and the sculptors who formed part of their normal households, and bought themselves gilt mirrors and Victorian tasselled furniture.

Perhaps the two most valuable and altruistic works the French have done in the Far East have been the creation in 1930 of the Institut Bouddhique at Pnom-Penh (after Catholic missionaries had succeeded in several years in making only one convert), and the establishment in the same city of the École des Arts Cambodgiens. The latter institution has made a desperate and successful attempt to save the situation, by encouraging the production of goods of high artistic value that can be sold in the ordinary way of commerce. The utmost difficulty was experienced in reassembling the artists with whom the old traditions would have died. They had returned to their villages and taken up the cultivation of rice, or fishing. When they were tracked down, it was found that some of them, who were already ageing, had not touched a tool for a quarter of a century. However, the happy fact is that the effort was made just in time, and that the Khmer arts which were on the point of vanishing for ever were given a vigorous artificial respiration and are now in fairly good shape. Naturally enough, they are now directed to commercial ends, and are largely applied to the rather banal objects demanded by the tourist and export trades. It is a stimulating reflection that the imaginative verve and faultless technique of modern Cambodian art at its best is considered by experts to rival that employed in the ornamentation of Angkor, and that this creative ability is now placed within the reach of a wide public in the form of such articles as cigarette cases and powder boxes. According to M. Marchal the present danger lies in the fact that the Cambodian is determined at all costs to be absolutely up to date, and is therefore inclined to turn his back on his own impressive artistic heritage, and allow himself to be too deeply influenced by movements in Europe, purely because they are fashionable and would-be audacious.

As there was nowhere to stay in Siem-Reap, I had to go to the Grand Hotel outside the town, which draws its sporadic nourishment from visitors to Angkor. I returned to the town — a blistering, shadeless walk of a mile — for occasional meals. In the whole of Cambodia there is not a single Cambodian restaurant. True Cambodian dishes, just as Aztec dainties in Mexico and Moorish delicacies in Spain, are only to be eaten in the market booths and wayside stalls of remote towns, which are the last refuges of vanishing, culinary cultures. While from fear of infection, one dared not at Siem-Reap risk those brilliant rissoles, those strange membraneous sacks containing who knows what empirically discovered tit-bit, there was always a restaurant serving what came vaguely under the heading of Chinese food. This is, at least, light, adapted to the climate, and consequently less burdensome than the surfeit of stewed meats inevitably provided by the Grand Babylon hotels of the Far East.

The Grand Hotel des Ruines had had several lean years. It was said that one or two of the guests had been kidnapped. The necessity, until a few months before, of an armed escort, must have provided an element of drama not altogether unsuitable in a visit to Angkor. Now the visitors were beginning to come again, arriving in chartered planes from Siam, signing their names in the register which was coated as soon as opened with a layer of small, exhausted flies falling continually from the ceiling. Perking up, the management arranged conducted tours to the ruins. In the morning the hotel car went to Angkor Thom, in the afternoon it covered what was called the Little Circuit. The next morning it would be Angkor Thom again and in the afternoon Angkor Vat. You had to stay three days to be taken finally on a tour of the Grand Circuit. Naturally in the circumstances the hotel wanted to keep its guests as long as possible. And even Baedeker would not have found three days unreasonable for the visit to Angkor.

There were many remoter temples, such as the exquisite Banteay Srei, thirty kilometres away, which the bus did not reach, as it was doubtful whether the writ of Dap Chhuon ran in these distant parts. The forces of the tutelary bandit seemed to be concentrated in the immediate vicinity. There was a sports field under my window and every morning, soon after dawn, a party of Dap Chhuon's men used to arrive for an hour's P.T. Against a background of goal posts, they failed to terrify. They were thin from the years spent under the greenwood tree and as they 'knees-bent' and 'stretched', each piratical rib could be counted. Beyond the playing-field and the gymnasts, was the forest, tawny and autumnal, from which in the far distance emerged the helmeted shapes of the three central towers of Angkor Vat.

The existence of Angkor was reported by sixteenth-century missionaries, although the ruins were not fully described until Mouhot's visit in 1859. They are probably the most spectacular man-made remains in the world, and as no European could ever be expected to rest content with the comfortable attitude taken by the Cambodians who assured Mouhot that 'they made themselves', the details of their origins have provoked endless speculation and many learned volumes.

At its maximum extension at the end of the twelfth century, the Khmer Empire included, in addition to the present kingdom of Cambodia, parts of the Malay Peninsula, Burma, Siam and Cochin China, but for practical and metaphysical reasons the capital has always been in the vicinity of Angkor. There are important Khmer ruins scattered through the forests over a hundred miles radius. The principal monuments are the colossal mausoleum of Angkor Vat, the shell of the city of Angkor Thom, with its fantastic centre piece, the Bayon, and a few scattered temples and foundations; some pyramidical, but all built on a strictly rectangular plan and carefully oriented with doors facing the cardinal points. Between these are clear open spaces, since permanence was only desired for religious edifices and only those could be built of brick and stone. All these buildings were erected between the ninth and twelfth centuries.

Savants of the late nineteenth century have argued with compelling logic that Angkor Vat took three hundred years to build, although the figure generally accepted at the present time is nearer thirty. Divergences of opinion regarding the completion dates of other monuments ranged over several centuries, and there was a similarly fierce conflict of theory over the purposes of the buildings and the identity of the statuary. The arguments have been slowly resolved and many a dogma demolished by the periodical discovery of steles, on which the monarchs of those days have left a record not only of their achievements but of their motives. Thus Udayadityavarman II informs posterity that he built the Baphûon, which was then the centre of a city which pre-dated Angkor Thom, 'because he had remembered that the centre of the universe is marked by the mountain of Meru and it was appropriate that his capital should have a Meru in its centre'.

This statement presents one with a key to the whole situation. All Khmer building was governed by an extravagant symbolism. The first Khmer king, who, returning from Java, had thrown off the suzerainty of that kingdom and unified Cambodia under his rule, had promptly declared himself a god. Under the aspect of Siva he took the title of 'Lord of the Universe'. He was obliged, therefore, to order his kingdom, or at least his capital, along the lines of an established precedent — provided in this case by Buddhist mythology. The Buddhist universe included a central mountain of Meru, which supported the heavens and was surrounded by an ocean, and finally a high wall of rocks which formed the barrier and enclosure of space. There was a lot more in it than this, but these were the reasonable limits to which the king's symbolism could be pushed. He built his artificial hill, the wide moat round his city, and the wall. This probably helped to convince him that he really was a god. It was wishful thinking on a cosmic scale.

Yet there was a curious sense of dependence shown by these self-created divinities upon the observance of their cult by their successors and their subjects. It was a grotesque magnification of the belief underlying so many Eastern religions that the fate of the dead is in some way linked to the living, who must provide them with regular offerings if they are to remain prosperous and contented in the land of souls. This idea, lodged in the ruthlessly energetic mind of a Khmer king, was translated into action on a huge scale. The king erected temples and consecrated statues to his divinized parents while leaving behind him inscriptions which positively implore his successors to follow his example. His immortality, King Yaçovarman admits on one of his steles, depends upon the maintenance of the cult. Seen in this light these deities were not comparable to the unassailable gods of the ancient Mediterranean world. For a neglected and forgotten god-king passed into oblivion. He became no more than one of the great multitude of nameless and forgotten spirits for which the pious erect those tiny shrines outside their homes.

So the king came in time to devote the whole of his efforts to the preservation of this shaky immortality. The royal megalomania reached its height with Jayavarman VII. Ta Prohm, built to house the image and the divine essence of the Queen mother and 260 attendant and lesser deities, required for its service 79,365 persons of whom about 5000 were priests. The gold plate used in this temple weighed five tons and the temple establishment lived upon the revenues of 3140 villages. The king's obligations to his father gave rise five years later to the erection of Prah Khan. This time, according to the stele discovered in 1939, there were 430 minor divinities included with the old king — nobles who as a kind of promotion for meritorious services had been either granted apotheosis or raised posthumously to the divine status. The responsibility for the upkeep of this establishment fell upon 5324 villages, the total number of persons involved being 97,840. Among the dependencies of Prah Khan was the little sanctuary of Néak Pân, built upon one of those sharply rectangular artificial lakes the Khmers were so fond of digging out. This symbolized a lake situated, according to a Hindu legend, somewhere in the Himalayas,

facing: THE SINISTER SMILE OF THE BAYON

which was supposed to possess extraordinary purificatory powers. Its construction was no mere poetic conceit, but followed a formula by which it became, in essence, the original lake. In this way the Khmer king saved himself the kind of gigantic wild-goose chase sometimes undertaken by the Chinese Emperors in their searches for similar legendary sites.

These are the games of children, who by a slight imaginative effort can even transform inanimate objects into living ones; a broom into a horse. But the children's games played by the Kings of Cambodia were backed by monstrous and freakish power. Néak Pân, of course, was a trifle for those days, probably not occupying more than 10,000 men for a mere three or four years.

But the king was not, and never could be satisfied. Hounded on by furious compulsions he reconstructed his capital in such a way that the Baphûon — microcosm of Meru — was no longer in the town's geometrical centre. This called for another sacred mountain, a great extension of the moat and entirely new walls. After only ten years of his reign there were already 13,500 villages comprising 306,372 men at work on these projects. The new sacred mountain was the Bayon, the most singular of all the Angkor monuments. It was Jayavarman's last work begun in about 1190, and it marked the height of the Khmer power and foreshadowed its end. From its towers sixty-four colossal faces of the king, now represented as one with the Buddha, smiled, with rather savage satisfaction, it seems, towards the four quarters of the kingdom. Even Pierre Loti, who knew nothing of the Bayon's history, found it very sinister.

With inexorable will-power at the service of mania the Khmer kings called into being whole populations whose only ultimate function, whether directly or indirectly, was the furtherance of their insatiable cult. In the early period, the economic basis of this efflorescence was the inland sea of Tonlé Sap, close to which all the successive capitals had been situated and which contained, and still contains, so many fish that when in the dry season the waters sink to their low level, the oars of boatmen are impeded by them. The

225

Tonlé Sap provided food for the whole populace through the exertions of a few fishermen, and the king saw to it that all the spare hours were occupied with profitable labour. An agricultural people, efficiently tilling fertile soil – and one is reminded of the pre-Columbian Mayans – can live fairly comfortably on an aggregate of forty or fifty days labour a year. Inevitably, however, some organizing genius comes along to make sure that the spare three hundred days are occupied in impressive but largely wasteful undertakings.

With the flying start provided by the Tonlé Sap the kingdom was expanded in all directions, covered with rice-fields, nourished by a brilliant irrigational system and linked up by a network of roads, with elaborately equipped staging points providing shelter for the buffaloes and elephants used as beasts of transport, as well as their masters. The great building king, Jayavarman VII, in addition to his religious foundations and influenced perhaps by the fact that he was a leper, established 102 hospitals. He did not omit to furnish on the great stele of Prah Khan the most detailed catalogue of the medicaments with which they were stocked. It was a huge piece of organization, controlled finally by a vast machine of state, with its Domesday Books and its army of accountants, to keep track of the activities of every single man in the interests of the maximum production. One can be quite sure that there was a police force and that the minds of the young were carefully moulded by the priesthood to fit them for the efficient fulfilment of their duties. The Khmer Empire was nothing if not totalitarian.

A great deal of unnecessary mystery has been made about the downfall of the Khmers, followed by the abandonment of Angkor. It has often been attributed to spectacular Acts of God. The facts, simple enough, are related by the Chinese traveller Chou Ta-Kouan, who visited Angkor when its decadence was already well advanced, and when, partly because the sand-stone quarries were exhausted, even the building mania had petered out. It seems that the Khmers, attacked in retaliation by the Siamese, had been obliged to apply the principles of total war. 'They say,' said Chou Ta-Kouan, 'that in the war with the Siamese, all the people were forced to fight.' One notes that Ta-Kouan speaks of compulsion, and suspects that if any were spared conscription it would have been those tens of thousands of temple servants who ministered to the royal cult. If the report is true that the Khmer army was several millions strong, it must have been by far the largest in the world of its day. But these peasants torn from their rice-fields and forced into uniform fought with little enthusiasm and the wars dragged on until final defeat.

In the meanwhile the irrigation systems were allowed to fall into ruin and the rice-fields on which the enormous, swollen population depended, quickly reverted to forests. The highly productive paddy-field system was progressively abandoned in favour of that present scourge of Indo-China, rice-cultivation in 'rays', which involves the annual burning of the forest. It was a method, since it occupies the minimum of labour, which must have been tempting to a nation at war, but results are poor and decrease rapidly, and ultimately it results in the sterilization and exhaustion of the soil. The process of decline, once under way, could not be halted, and defeat was made absolute by the victor's introduction of the primitive apostolic Buddhism of the 'Little Vehicle', the religion of withdrawal, of renunciation, of tranquillity; which was so utterly destructive to the perverted power-cults of the divine kings. It was the subtlest of Carthaginian Peaces.

It is possible that the ruins of Angkor are in many ways more impressive than the city itself was in its heyday. Time has wrought wonders with the sandstone, which must have been garish enough when freshly cut. And vandalism and the flailings of sun and rain have done much to mute that excessive symmetry, that all-pervading symbolism, that repetitiousness which I find so irritating in far-Eastern art. There is evidence of an obsession with the magic of numbers and of the dignifying, under artistic forms, of primeval superstitions. One feels that the Khmer must have reasoned that if it was a good thing to erect one statue to Vishnu or of a Devata, then it was fifty times better to have fifty of them. Adepts of magic never seem to be convinced that their magical practices are completely and finally effective. The causeway which leads into Angkor Vat is, or was, flanked at exactly spaced intervals by pairs of nagas — seven-headed serpents. I do not find seven-headed serpents particularly decorative, and much prefer the lions *couchants* of which there are many hundreds. However, they represent the serpent beneath which Buddha sheltered. They are, therefore, in essence, protective; and it is necessary to have as many as can be fitted in. I think that it is an aesthetic advantage that the majority of them have been broken and are missing.

The causeway conducts one smack into the centre of the whole architectural composition. It could not be otherwise, since all considerations had to be subordinated to that of symbolism; and to have built the formal approach from any angle but this would have been to risk throwing the universe, or at least the kingdom, out of balance, by sympathetic magic. Angkor Vat, however, is best viewed from across the water from one of the corners of the moat. Immediately the tyranny of the matched-pair is broken. The towers, many-tiered like the head-dress of an Indian dancer, are re-grouped in majestic nonchalance. The Vat gathers itself from the lake, raised on a long, low-lying portico. Above that the unbroken lines of the roofs rise one above the other, to be capped by the towers, which are somehow jaunty in spite of the sad harmony of the old, disintegrated colours. A lotus-broken reflection is carried on the mildewed waters of the lake.

And all the monuments of ancient Greece could be enclosed in this one building.

Within the Vat miles of goddesses and heavenly dancing girls, de-humanized and amiable, posture in bas-relief round the gallery walls. They are all exactly of the same height and physique, hands and arms frozen in one of the dozen or so correct gestures. Since Khmer art is never erotic — and one remembers de la Rochefoucauld's 'where ambition has entered love rarely returns' — they do not exhibit the development of breast and hip which is so characteristic of similar figures in Indian art.

The triumphant existence is portrayed in a series of set poses. The king or god out hunting adopts the wooden pose of a dancer to shoot a deer — in itself depicted with admirable realism. Victorious princes and warriors parade for the ascent to heaven (success being identified with virtue), heads overlapping in three-quarters profile, left hands on breasts and right on hips. Nothing, however, could be more realistic than the treatment of the defeated and the damned, who are naturally consigned to hell. The postures of these bodies being trodden underfoot by horsemen and torn by wild beasts have been observed and carefully copied from the life. Only the devils are permitted a hieratic stance.

But it is when the artist is left to his own devices in his treatment of the ordinary citizen, and his everyday life, that he shows us what he can do. Gone is the processional dignity and the frigid smile of power. The peasants and fisher-folk are shown as thick-limbed and grotesque, with coarse, clownish faces. With gleeful licence the artist depicts their buffoonery as they haggle over tripes in the market, slaughter their pigs, smirkingly watch a cock-fight or visit a palmist. These are the trollish faces that medieval church-sculptors carved on almost invisible bosses as a relief from the insipidity of righteousness. The vulgar of Angkor are shown taking their pleasure on the Tonlé Sap — capering on the deck of a becalmed junk like day-trippers on the river boat to Southend; or hunched over a game of chess. With lower-class respectability most of them have put on short jackets for the occasion. Meanwhile a boat-load of the better people passes, all seated with decorum, fashionable in their semi-nudity, facing one way, and smiling with the refined beatitude induced by the knowledge that sooner or later they will appear in the honours list as minor gods.

Cormorants and herons are shown competing with the fishermen for their catches while crocodiles menace them from the water. The Khmers made much decorative use of flora and fauna. The anarchic quality of trees is subdued and subjected to a Byzantine stylization, but the animals that lurk among them are seen in a lively naturalism comparable to palaeolithic cave-art. And the intention that animated cave-art is roughly identical with that which produced these miles of bas-reliefs. Their object was magical and their decorative effect quite incidental. Angkor Vat was the funerary temple of Suryavaraman II divinized under the aspect of Vishnu, and this world in sculpture replaced the great funeral holocausts of earlier days. That aesthetic pleasure had no bearing upon the question is proved by the fact that many scenes have been sculpted with scrupulous care in places where they are quite invisible, or even — as in the case of the Bayon — on the building's subterranean foundations.

Ta Prohm, which Jayavarman VII built to house his mother's cult, and which occupied the working lives of 79,000 of his subjects, was scheduled to detain the thirty tourists from Siam for one hour.

The temple was built on flat land and offers none of the spectacular vistas of Angkor Vat, nor the architectural surprises of Bayon. It has therefore been maintained as a kind of reserve where the prodigious conflict between the ruins and the jungle is permitted to continue under control. The spectacle of this monstrous vegetable aggression is a favourite with most visitors to the ruins.

Released from the hotel bus, the thirty tourists plunged forward at a semi trot into the caverns of this rectangular labyrinth. For a few moments their pattering footsteps echoed down the flagstoned passages and then they were absorbed in the silence of those dim, shattered vastnesses, and I saw none of them again until it was time to return.

Ta Prohm is an arrested cataclysm. In its invasion, the forest has not broken through it, but poured over the top, and the many courtyards have become cavities and holes in the forest's false bottom. In places the cloisters are quite dark, where the windows have been covered with subsidences of earth, humus and trees. Otherwise they are illuminated with an aquarium light, filtered through screens of roots and green lianas.

Entering the courtyards one comes into a new kind of vegetable world; not the one of branches and leaves with which one is familiar, but that of roots. Ta Prohm is an exhibition of the mysterious subterranean life of plants, of which it offers an infinite variety of cross-sections. Huge trees have seeded themselves on the roofs of the squat towers and their soaring trunks are obscured from sight; but here one can study in comfort the drama of those secret and conspiratorial activities that labour to support their titanic growth.

Down, then, come the roots, pale, swelling and muscular. There is a grossness in the sight; a recollection of sagging ropes of lava, a parody of the bulging limbs of circus-freaks, shamefully revealed. The approach is exploratory. The roots follow the outlines of the masonry; duplicating pilasters and pillars; never seeking to bridge a gap and always preserving a smooth living contact with the stone surfaces; burlesqueing in their ropy bulk the architectural motives which they cover. It is only long after the hold has been secured that the deadly wrestling bout begins. As the roots swell their grip contracts. Whole blocks of masonry are torn out, and brandished in mid-air. A section of wall is cracked, disjointed and held in suspension like a gibbeted corpse; prevented by the roots' embrace from disintegration. There are roots which appear suddenly, bursting through the flagstones to wander twenty yards like huge boa-constrictors, before plunging through the up-ended stones to earth again. An isolated tower bears on its summit a complete sample of the virgin jungle, with ferns and underbrush and a giant fig tree which screens the faces of the statuary with its liana-curtains, and discards a halo of parakeets at the approach of footsteps.

The temple is incompletely cleared. One wanders on down identical passages or through identical courtyards — it is as repetitive in plan as a sectional bookcase — and then suddenly there is a thirty-foot wall, a tidal wave of vegetation, in which the heavenly dancers drown with decorous gestures.

But there are still some signs of life in the temples and mausolea of Angkor, besides the sinister and stinking presence of myriads of bats. The people now come to these once exclusive places and burn incense-sticks before the Buddhas, which probably started their existence as idealized representations of various members of the Khmer aristocracy. Parties of bonzes stroll through the ruins. They carry the inevitable yellow parasols and sometimes box cameras with which they photograph each other, for the benefit of their friends back at the monastery, against some particularly sacrosanct background, such as the corpulent shape of a man who had once made a corner in fish.

My last daylight hours at Angkor were spent by the lake of Sram Srang. The Khmers were always digging out huge artificial lakes, which, if the preliminary surveying had been correctly carried out, and temples and statues were erected according to accepted precedents round their margins or on a centre island, could always be declared to possess purificatory qualities. For this reason Sram Srang was supposed to have been a favourite royal bathing place, with its grand approach, its majestic flight of steps, flanked with mythical animals, and its golden barges.

Now the lions were faceless, and the nagas had lost most of their heads. The severe rectangularity of old had been softened by subsidences of the banks, which had solidified into little peninsulas on which trees were growing. Buffaloes stood motionless in the virtuous water with only their heads showing. Sometimes even their heads were withdrawn for a few moments below the surface. Giant kingfishers flashed past, linked to their reflections; twin shooting stars in a grey-green firmament. Until forty years ago the Cambodians exported these birds' skins to China where they were made into mandarins' jackets, taking in exchange pottery and silk.

And then the vogue for European goods grew up, and the industry languished.

As if from nowhere a group of boys materialized. They were selling cross-bows. They were better looking and their physique was better than either the nobles or the commons on the Angkor Vat bas-reliefs, but six hundred years ago they would have worked twelve hours a day, and now they probably worked an hour a week, if at all. Three or four of them always lurked forlornly in the vicinity of the various ruins in the outrageous hope of one day selling a crossbow to a tourist.

One of them surprised me by speaking understandable French, and this was such a rarity that I asked him if he would act as a guide to one or two of the outlying monuments I wanted to see. At the same time I thought that I would be able to question him as to the existence of legends, and particularly about the legend of the leper-king which was supposed to be the only memory of the Khmer rulers that had survived. The boy said he would be delighted, but when? I said that night, as it was practically full-moon, and I believed that I could get a rickshaw in Siem-Reap·to bring me out to Angkor. His face fell. He was sorry, it couldn't be managed. I asked why not? Were the ex-bandits unreliable at night? Oh, no it was not that. On the contrary they were very disciplined, and with Dap Chhuon in command you were in fact safer at Angkor than at Phom Penh. Well, then, what was it? . . . the tigers, perhaps? No, it wasn't the tigers, either . . . but the fact was that after dark Angkor was a very bad place for the *néak ta eysaur* and the *néak ta en* — in other words, the spirits Siva and Indra.

Thus had the powerful Brahmanical gods of the Khmer Empire shrunk and shrivelled along with the Empire itself. And now they were no more than *néak ta* — mere tree spirits to frighten babies with; of no more importance than the *khmoo pray* — the wicked dead, such as women who have died in childbed; the *beisac* — the famished souls of those who have died violently, who return from hell to implore food; the *smer*, who, losing their reason, have become werewolves, and the *srei ap*, beautiful girls, who through dabbling in black magic have inadvertently turned themselves into heads, accompanied only by alimentary canals, and live on excrement. The Khmer gods have accompanied their worshippers in their decline.

A rumour existed in Siem-Reap of the survival of a troupe of heavenly dancers. At the hotel there was a knowledgeable hanger-on who had learned enough English from American visitors to describe himself as an officer's pimp. From him I made inquiries.

His first reaction was to produce the slow compassionate smile of the sensitive man who dislikes to disappoint. There were dancers, but they were very old — at least fifty — and quite ugly. On clarifying the nature of my inquiry, he said that they were not only old, but charged a lot for their services, that he did not know where they could be contacted, and that they had no proper clothes to dance in. These had to be hired from a Chinese, who 'would not be there'. It was clear that my informant's services as an intermediary would only cover the simplest arrangements and that he had now retired behind this squid-like effusion of negatives. But at this point, some of my fellow-guests became interested. Among them was an Anglo-American business executive from Bangkok, who had lived a number of years in Siam and said that he was used to tackling situations like this. The Chinese, he said, was the key to the problem. The thing was to find the Chinese . . . if possible the one who hired out the costumes. There was no doubt about it that this man could make arrangements for us to see a Cambodian dance.

Down to the town, therefore, went my friend, and in due course a suitable Chinese was discovered. He was one of those octopuses of commerce that plant themselves squarely in the centre of the business life of such towns; the kind of man — Tes Heak, I believe his name was — whom anyone could lead you to, and who was to be discovered sitting unassumingly, pencil behind ear, on a sack of dry fish, surrounded by his stocks of dried milk, his cobra skins, his coffins and his Algerian wine. Tes Heak also ran the bus services, conducted an undertaking establishment, with a hearse most lavishly equipped with miniature puppet theatres, and supplied an American car for weddings, to the wings and roof of which gilt dragons were attached. Taking in the situation with a saurian flicker of the eyelids, he produced a number of reasons overlooked by the officer's pimp why it would be infeasible to persuade the heavenly dancers to perform. He even complained that they had artistic temperaments, hastily adding, however, when it looked as though he was being taken seriously, that a performance would cost 1500 piastres — about £27.

This seemed an enormous fee for a short demonstration by the five ladies, who, Tes Heak said, might be induced to go through a short repertoire. My hopes had been to arrange something that would be as spontaneous and unselfconscious as possible — perhaps in a back yard. But Tes Heak was revolted at so shoddy a proposal. Such a spectacle, he thought, should be staged in the forecourt of Angkor Vat itself, and by moonlight. It was clear that he knew his tourist, and that this negligently sown seed would probably fall on fertile soil. Just as there is a collective crowd-mentality which is a little more (or less) than the sum total of the mentalities of its individual members, so the single traveller multiplied by thirty becomes a tourist with a certain garishness of taste that he did not possess before; a kind of temporary distemper provoked by gregarious indulgence, that commits him to extravagances. The idea of a spectacle in the grand manner was, therefore, enthusiastically acclaimed.

Having easily won the first round, Tes Heak now suggested drummers, a local orchestra, and an escort of torch-bearers — at a slight extra charge, of course. This too was agreed, and finally, at a cost of 3000 piastres, the thing was arranged.

At ten o'clock that night, therefore, the hotel bus stopped at the end of the causeway leading to Angkor Vat. News of the performance had spread, and to my surprise what must have been most of the population of Siem-Reap, and probably of the neighbouring villages as well, had put in an appearance. A fiesta atmosphere prevailed with stalls selling hot sausages clamped between two slabs of bread, sugar-cane juice — crushed out while you waited — mounds of pale green jelly, and mineral waters. In addition to the hundred small shaven-headed torch-bearers, in the old style, who awaited our coming along the causeway, waving bundles of resin-soaked rags, at least five hundred of the hurrying crowd flashed electric torches as they walked, to the natural detriment of the archaic effect.

The passengers, mostly women, who had dressed with painstaking informality for the occasion, stepped down gingerly into this carnival scene. With their charming, defeated smiles, the sellers of cross-bows pounced upon them and in the background a group of Dap Chhuon's men, lean from their peace-time rations and physical jerks, eyed the occidental display with the wistful sincerity of tethered peregrines.

Along the causeway the torch-bearers, descrying a European among the padding Cambodians, would gesticulate and wave their flaming rags. A small group had deserted their post and clambered down into the water where, torches aloft, they were looking for something — a living fountain-group in bronze. Shutting out half the horizon was the long, low mass of Angkor Vat, moonlight glinting feebly in its towers. There was a certain poetry in the scene, and the ridiculous march of the tourists, flinching from its wan escort of bow-sellers, was part of it.

By the time we arrived at the forecourt the Cambodians were already installed on the best vantage points, riding the mute lions and perched on the necks of beheaded serpents. The torch-bearers now broke away and stormed raggedly forward; the rearguard of a triumph. Four acetylene lamps lit up a white amphitheatre of expectant faces and a player seated himself at a semi-circular xylophone and began a discursive tinkling.

Although I had no standards by which to judge, the dancing seemed lifeless — a mime of embalmed postures. Only four dancers had appeared, and two — as we had been fairly warned — were indeed past their prime. Although no doubt perfectly correct in their rendering of such episodes as the fight between Hanuman and the Demon King, the two fifty-year-old ladies could hardly be expected to galvanize us with the impetuosity of a combat which, according to the Epic, was conducted chiefly with thunderbolts, aerial javelins and arrows of wind. But if the old ladies were lacking in vigour, their youthful pupils showed no signs of having been schooled in such elementary feats as going through fairly long interpretative passages while balancing on one leg, the other being bent backwards from the knee, and held at right angles. There were some perilous wobbles, causing on one occasion an elderly lady to animate the powdered mask in which her features were set by the most unclassical of grimaces.

But the girls came into their own soon after, deposing the heavy, multi-tiered crowns, and exchanging the stiff, hired finery for sarongs and blouses. Joined by several more girls and partners from the audience they gave a sparkling demonstration of the *lap ton*. It was a dance with a sense of humour — an extraordinary thing in these countries — particularly the version which mimicked a husband and wife quarrelling, and there was as much of Eastern grace as could be combined with the vigour of the West. There was no dead symbolism here, nor were there traces of ritual intended to assist the growth of the crops. But the performers were thoroughly enjoying themselves, skipping about and twirling their hands, evidently relieved at the release from the puppet-antics of a pre-historic tradition. These were the low-class caperings on the junk in bas-relief . . . and it was soon clear that this was what the audience had come to see.

CHAPTER XVI

BANDIT COUNTRY

THERE was an intrepid American girl at the hotel. She was not a member of the tourist party from Siam, but had straggled in unobtrusively from Tokio, via Macao and Saigon and many other intermediary China-Sea ports with remote and evocatory names. She was writing, and living on a small, carefully managed allowance and appeared never to stop travelling. One of the motives for these uneasy wanderings was her connection with the *Des Moines Register*, the leading newspaper of her home town. Her assignment was to look up all the Des Moines citizens she could find living in the Far East and write a chatty, human account of their doings for the benefit of the people at home. So far she had only found one exile from Des Moines in Indo-China.

She was brave and indefatigable with an appetite for regular achievement. The spirit she enshrined, with its voracity for random facts and experiences, was rather that of the late twenties than the early fifties. I came across her continually in the ruins. Guide-book in hand, waving guides aside, she tracked down all the most obscure pieces of sculpture ('Say, have you seen Indra on a three-headed elephant?') and the isolated temples, half-submerged in the jungle, that others overlooked. She was as preoccupied with numerology as the Khmers themselves, checking up on the exact numbers of gods and demons and marvelling, as the great kings would have had her marvel, at the sixty-four faces of the temples containing the sixteen images and all constructed in best selected sandstone, with the regrettable laterite patching kept well out of sight.

Now this dauntless girl, having digested all that Angkor had to offer, had decided to go on to Siam, but had no intention of going all the way back to Saigon and flying from there by the regular route. Instead she was determined to cross country somehow or other to the Siamese border, a matter of a hundred miles or so, where she could get a train to Bangkok. There was, in fact, a road through Sisophon which joined up there with the railroad, and doubled it to the Siamese frontier town, but there were no trains on this side of the frontier owing to the presence of one or more of the five bands of Issaraks who had not yet shown signs of surrendering. Nor, according to reports, was the road safe for most of its length; but she had persuaded the French army, who were always delighted to oblige in such matters, to take her on the first military transport to go through.

I mention all this because I had to get back to Saigon fairly soon now; either to go on the trip to the Viet-Minh occupied territory or to take up the seat I had booked on the plane to Laos, and I had learned that if I wanted to return to Pnom Penh by the safe road — the one policed by Dap Chhuon — which runs along the eastern shore of the great lake, it would mean a wait of several days for transport. But there was another way of returning more quickly, although apparently with some risk, down the west-shore road. Under some kind of sub-rosa arrangement Tes Heak ran a bus which slipped out of Siem-Reap in the early morning hours and took this route. It occurred to me that if the American girl-journalist was prepared to take the chance in a French military car, there was no reason why I should not do so under Tes Heak's auspices, as a man with his business flair would undoubtedly have an arrangement with the bandits through whose territory we passed.

The bus to Pnom Penh stole out of the town at four in the morning. Like all Asiatic buses it was packed solidly with passengers, and only by paying nearly twice the right fare had I been able to obtain one of Tes Heak's attractive tickets, covered in red ideographs. In the bus I was given the place of honour on the right of the driver, who was obliged to jostle me continually as he changed gear. Three distinguished citizens of Siem-Reap were squeezed in on his left and a complete row of yellow-robed bonzes sat, with cultivated impassivity of expression, immediately behind. Although vowed to lives of self-abnegation there were certain minor bourgeois affectations which they were not forbidden. One was the wearing of sun glasses, which they and all the other passengers of distinction put on as soon as the dawn came.

The passengers carried with them strings of dried fish, just as they might have carried sandwiches. These, hung up within easy reach, filled the bus with a rich, sea-shore tang. As soon as we were under way, one of the bonzes, bothered by his parasol, leaned over and hooked it over the windscreen. The others followed suit, leaving the driver with half his normal field of vision. He paid no attention to this handicap; in any case, it would have been unthinkable to criticize the holy men.

It was a bad thing if you were in the least mechanically minded to sit next to the driver because you couldn't help noticing some of the things that were wrong with the car. In these countries cars are driven on relentlessly until under the strain something goes. Patched up with ingenious makeshifts they are put back on the road again where they carry on, come what may, until finally, with elliptical cylinders, worn-out bearings, burnt valves, crippled transmissions, flattened springs and shattered bodies, not another mile can be forced out of them. In the meanwhile, and until this final disintegration, their drivers handle them with confidence and verve.

In this case the engine seemed to be loose in the chassis as the control pedals jiggered about quite independent of the floorboards. The driver was obliged to hold the foot-brake off by hooking his toe under it, and to drive with one hand on the gear lever, to prevent its jumping out of gear. The steering wheel turned freely through about ninety degrees before the steering was affected, and the lights went off and on as we hurtled over the bumps. None of these inconveniences seemed to worry the driver in the least. He was a small, elderly Chinese, who conducted the bus with quiet determination. Whatever happened and however terrible the road, he drove straight on at the bus's maximum speed — a bellowing forty-five miles an hour.

facing: FREE DRINKS FOR THE BONZES

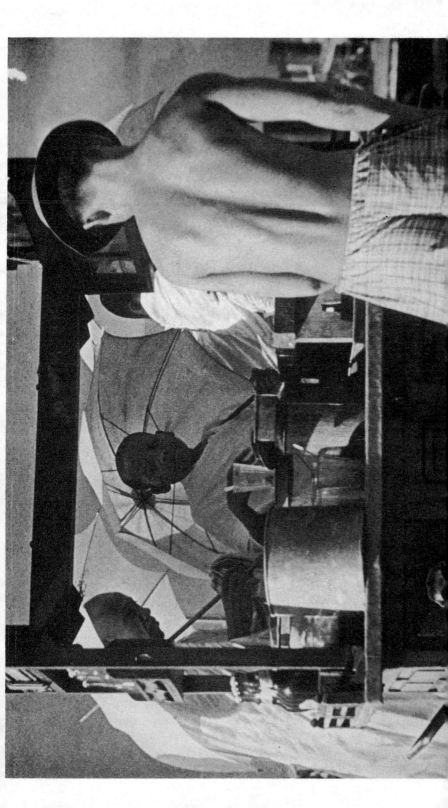

It seemed that we had taken a cross-country cut, avoiding the towns I had expected to pass through, because somehow or other we missed Sisophon. A few miles away over on our left would have been the shores of the great lake which, although in the present dry season was only about ninety miles in length by about twenty in width, has the habit of tripling its area and flooding many square miles of forest at the height of the rains. It is this flooding of the forest which produces the enormous annual increase in the number of fish, which are so concentrated when the shrinkage takes place that they are practically scooped out of the water, rather than fished. At this season when the waters were at their lowest (and when this great exterminatory fishing was actually going on), the water had receded from ten to fifteen miles, leaving behind sticky prairies, with temporary villages where they grew a few vegetables, and temporary roads. On the lake itself, always out of sight, was a fringe of floating villages, which moved backwards and forwards across the map with the expansion and contraction of the waters.

Soon after sunrise we found ourselves on a main road. You could tell it was a main road because, although the surface was even more awful than that of the temporary track, there were permanent villages and bridges. One modern bridge we passed over was a reconstruction of an ancient Khmer one with the remnants of a balustrade formed from the body of a seven-headed serpent. In a few places the jagged stumps of ruins rose above the ground.

We stopped at a village for breakfast, a half-circle of slate-coloured shacks with all the uprights newly plastered, as if for the visit of a circus, with vermilion Chinese New Year posters. A few day-dreaming Cambodians had found posts to lean against and there was a great collection of the hyena-faced dogs in the street — which our driver carefully avoided.

Since eating in strange surroundings is half the pleasure of Asiatic travel, the passengers all tied their dried fish to the backs of the seats, got down and made for the dark cavern that was the local café. Two of the senior bonzes seated themselves together at a

facing: Top: LAOTIAN DANCERS AMUSED BY THE CAMERA
Bottom: AUDIENCE IN ANGKOR

table. One got out a fountain pen and began to write a letter, while the other took a snack out of an American mess-can.

The four other junior bonzes who were travelling with us now lined up in the gutter, graded in order of height, each one holding his basin. Walking a few paces until they were opposite the first house, they stopped and left-turned. A woman came out of the house, ready as if warned by premonition, with a bowl and ladle. Facing the line for the moment, rather like a sergeant inspecting a parade, she then squatted down and raised the bowl for a moment to her forehead. Getting up again, and starting at the leading bonze, she passed briskly down the line, depositing a ladleful of rice in each bowl. This completed, the bonzes right-turned and marched in single file to the next house.

Having a fad for the interior decoration of such places, I preferred to go right into the café's forbidding interior instead of sitting outside. I was rewarded with a picture of Sun-Yat-Sen (Chiang-Kai-Shek had quite disappeared and Mao-Tse-Tung had not yet arrived), a badly cured tiger's skin, a collection of imitation rhinoceros's horns and an advertisement for the Khmer National Lottery, consisting of four pictures of Cambodian family life. The first scene, shortly entitled 'Misery', showed an ordinary household, its members squatting about on the floor of their house, doing, as you would expect, nothing in particular. In the second picture the husband, struck by an idea contained in a balloon floating above his head, suggests buying a lottery ticket. In spite of their misery, the money is found for this. In picture three — they win, and, on being told the grand news, express their joy with the hand-flourishes of temple dancers. Fourth picture, 'Happiness', is refined and sedate. The wife wears a red jumper, a short skirt and carpet slippers. Her man has put on a coat with lapels, a collar and tie. In the ordinary way both of them would now die of heat-stroke; but the lottery has taken care of that too. They sit in front of an electric fan.

I was now more and more embarrassed by my speechlessness in such places as this. In the remote interior of Indo-China it is a good thing, for both one's comfort and one's safety, to speak a few words of one of the principal languages; Vietnamese, Cambodian, Laotian or even Chinese. But the first and last present great difficulties, owing to their tonal system. One must be willing to sing as well as speak. And Cambodian, although poverty-stricken in words expressing abstractions, is bewilderingly rich in other respects. There are, for instance, seventeen different verbs replacing the English verb *to carry*; according to whether one carries on the head, the back, the shoulders, the hip, in the arms, suspended from a cord, etc. There are also seven forms of address, reflecting, one supposes, the old Khmer social order, which take into account both the social and moral standing of the person one is addressing — and give grave offence if improperly used. This is not a simple matter like using the polite form in a Latin language. The differences are so great as almost to divide the language into seven separate dialects.

In the case of one's food requirements, the remedy is to try to draw what one wants (my stylized sketch of a bird produced not a chicken's wing, but two fried sparrows on a skewer), or point to what others are eating — invariably Chinese soup, from which the tentacles of small river octopi tend to trail. All this gives the greatest amusement to the customers, although, with the chiding finger of several thousand years civilization behind them, the Indo-Chinese have far too much maiden-auntish control over themselves to laugh uproariously, as Africans might. In this case one of the heads of the family was fetched, who with dignified bows invited me into the kitchen, where in the antechamber to Dante's hell I selected some brightly dyed mincemeat, which was delivered to me wrapped — in Hungarian style — in a cabbage leaf. Salt was always rare and precious in these places, and one was expected, in its place, to dowse one's food in rancid sauces or to nibble between mouthfuls at salted fish. This café, however, supplied what was described in English, on the tin's label, as Ve-Tsin Gourmet Powder, a yellow and pungent spice, which, if you used enough, produced a faint salinity.

Something like a state of emergency seemed to have been proclaimed in the neighbourhood, and several members of the National Guard were mooching round looking for somewhere to sleep. One of them slumped into a vacant chair at my table, and his rifle clattered to the ground. He groped for it, picked it up, leaned it against the table and stuck a flower down the barrel. It was an oldish weapon with a rusty bolt, but the butt had been most tastefully carved with a close, intricate design of leaves, through which a helmeted horseman charged with raised sword.

When it was time to set off again, the driver himself went round the village to look out each passenger, tracking down with difficulty some who, wanting to make the most of the excursion, had wandered off to see the local sights. We were leaving some of our fellow-passengers behind and collecting some new ones – Cambodian women who arrived carrying their belongings in beautifully woven baskets. Their good looks were subdued by the determined composure they adopted to cover all traces of excitement. The girls' hair was done up in thick, glossy chignons, but the older women wore their hair in the close, ragged crop which happened, quite by chance, to correspond to the European fashion of that time.

Leaving the village, we thundered on through dead-flat country. On each side stretched a milky slough with deep pools, the colour of pale yolk, in which buffaloes squirmed like fat, grey maggots. The sky was iron-grey over this waste of tempera. For the first time I saw glossy ibises, in extraordinary partnership with eagles, paddling awkwardly in the shallows. The villages here were quite different, and for a short distance each house had a kind of totem pole with a carved, wooden cock raised in front of it. The country manners, too, were informal. At a hamlet stop an exquisite lady in black knickers descended the steps of her house, and, stationing herself with her back to us, before a large earthenware jar, began her morning toilet. Properly, the bonzes averted their eyes. Across the road the building of a new house had been started – a combined village enterprise which would take three or four days — and the solemn moment of the insertion of the central pillar, flying its red banner, was being fêted with flutes and drums.

And so we went on, the driver, it seemed, feeling his way with quiet perspicacity across the gentle, sunlit, dangerous landscape, stopping sometimes to make inquiries from a peasant, and then making perhaps a detour into the white waste to avoid some doubtful village. The bus took terrible punishment. We developed electrical troubles and without slackening speed the driver sent his mate out to repair them. With the bus leaping and lurching beneath him he crawled bare-footed all over the front end, opening first one and then the other side of the bonnet, wielding his pliers to strip and join wires and insulating the joints with oblongs of tape he carried stuck to the skin of his legs. People who wanted rides were always trying to stop us. The driver took no notice of ordinary civilians, shouted polite excuses to bonzes, and stopped for soldiers.

In the early afternoon there was another pause. Once again there was a Chinese restaurant, and the family, until the invasion from the bus took place, could be seen taking their siesta on the tables in the background. It was a very enterprising concern; probably under new management. The food was served in splendid gold-edged bowls, splashed over with Chinese lettering, and stylized cocks and dragonflies had been painted on the spoons. But in spite of its amenities the restaurant did not object to patrons bringing their own food. While I was busy with my salted prawns one of the passengers, a frugal Cambodian, sat down at my side, ordered a glass of tea, and unwrapping a banana leaf produced a small bird, looking as if it might have been fried in bread-crumbs, which, holding by the beak, he devoured in two bites. When we had both finished our meal he got up, smiled and beckoned to me to go with him. We walked a short way down the street and he pointed to a house which consisted of a framework only supporting several intricately carved doors. There were no walls, and just as we arrived, the occupant, who had been reclining on a mat under a parasol, got up, opened one of the doors and came down the step-ladder into the street. From his dress, which included a thick, black pullover and a topee, I judged him to be a man of importance. My companion grinned and said, *pirate*.

This village was on a river bank and had a market selling a great deal of fish. There was a particular species which I saw here for the first time, but continually thereafter. What was remarkable about it was that it was always displayed for sale alive; in this case neatly lined up on banana leaves with others of its sort, price tickets balanced unsteadily on the flattish tops of each head between the eyes. Sometimes the fish, which I was told lived for about three hours after being taken out of the water, would start to move unsteadily away on ventral fins that were evolving into flippers. This happened particularly when they were chivvied by dogs. They would make a yard or so's progress before being recovered and gently replaced by the Cambodian maiden in charge. When a sale was made the fish were tied up, using a length of thin bamboo, with a neat bow, and taken away suspended from the buyer's finger. The only dead fish on offer were very large, and these, by way of placation, had their jaws forced wide apart and a propitiatory prawn thrust between them. It was a village of animal-lovers, and two great pink buffaloes — the lucky kind — had the run of it and had stopped at the market for a feed of choice vegetables, while the vendors looked on admiringly.

It was here that a rather ill-boding incident took place. Three soldiers had been travelling with us and now suddenly they came rushing up, breaking through the group of passengers who waited in the shade of the bus for the driver's signal to take their seats. Scrambling into the bus they threw their possessions out of the window into the street, jumping after them — upsetting as they did so a pyramid of hens in bottle-shaped wicker baskets — and then dashed off up the road, trailing belts and bandoliers.

A clucking excitement now spread among the passengers, and

some of them, following the soldiers' example, tried to unload their packages. They were frustrated by the arrival of the driver, who, abandoning his normal phlegm, and waving his arms like a goose-herd, drove them back into the bus. When I tried to follow, the way was barred and the driver explained possibly in mandarin that some difficulty had arisen. His arguments were supported by help-ful translations into Cambodian by the passengers, speaking with the exaggerated slowness and clarity which they felt sure would more than compensate for an actual ignorance of the language. The senior bonze joined in, respectfully removing his sunglasses before beginning a low-voiced exposition of the circumstance in some scholarly lingua-franca — probably Pali. The man of the restaurant clambered down, and pushing his way to the front, said *pirate* again, but this time with a sadly apologetic smile. One of the market people called to interpret, asked 'toi parler Français?' But when I said yes, shook his head in confusion and, having exhausted his vocabulary, was allowed to escape.

Once again the man of the restaurant was back, determined to break this impasse, while the driver cranked the starting-handle furiously. Hearing the word pirate again I pointed up the street to where the master of the skeleton house, who I supposed had retired on the proceeds of Dacoity, having made a dignified re-ascent of his step-ladder and passed through his front door, was stretched out on his mat. But the man shook his head. Raising both arms he laid his eye along the sights of an invisible gun, pointed in my direc-tion, pressed a phantom trigger and produced with his tongue a sharp, conclusive click. Then placing a finger on each eyelid he drew them down over his eyes, sighed deeply and gave a final puff, as if in dismissal of something, perhaps a soul. The passengers, who had all crowded over to our side of the bus, were much impressed with this piece of theatre, and shook their heads sympathetically.

The driver had now started the engine and was making gestures of impatience, but my friend persevered. From further sign lan-guage, some of which was international — such as the laying of both hands, palms together, under the cheek, to represent sleep — it was conveyed that as there were bandits ahead it would be better for me to stay in this village and to spend the night there, because if they found me on the bus, they would shoot me. This did not seem a very good idea, because I felt that if the bandits heard that I was in the village, as they probably would, they would most likely come for me, and I should be alone. Whereas if I went on with the bus and the worst came to the worst, I might be to some extent protected by the natural human sympathy, the bond of neighbourliness, however slight, that begins after a while to exist between fellow-passengers who are thrown together on such journeys. I therefore succeeded in making it clear that I wanted to go with the bus.

As soon as my determination to continue with them had sunk in, the driver, aided by several of the passengers, began a re-organization of the baggage at the back of the bus. This was piled up round a kind of priest's hole, in the opening of which I crouched in the manner of a hermit-crab, refusing to withdraw myself entirely from sight unless an emergency arose.

There followed two stifling but uneventful hours, by the end of which I was half-anaesthetized by the fierce gases from the bales of dried fish. The bus then stopped again. We had come to a ferry and the driver beckoned to me to come out. It seemed that the danger point was past. But we were just on the point of embarking on the ferry barge when a young man came up. He was dressed in a new American G.I. uniform, and in spite of his air of easy authority, appeared to be weaponless. Going up to each of the passengers he made a collection. When my turn came, I smiled and shook my head. The young man repeated whatever it was that he had said, and I shook my head again. With an expression of slight embarrassment he then gave up and went off. 'Pirate,' said my friend of the restaurant again, nodding his head after him.

Three days later I reached Saigon, just in time to claim my seat on the plane for Laos.

CHAPTER XVII

LAOS

LAOS from 10,000 feet was a grey-green frothing seen through a heat-mist that was like a pane of dirty glass. As we came into Vientiane in the late afternoon the mist thickened and the pilot came down as if to look for landmarks. For the last half-hour bundles of rags kept whirling past the cabin. They were vultures — bad things to hit at two hundred miles an hour. We landed bumpily in a haze, as though bonfires had been lit round the field; and in this the sun wallowed — a diffused yellow disc. As the door of the cabin was opened, the heat rolled in.

In most journeyings there stands out the memory of days of discouragement; when the enthusiasm flags under the strain of petty physical discomforts. The introduction to Laos was spent in such a period. This was the earthly paradise that all the French had promised; the country that was one vast Tahiti, causing all the French who had been stationed there to affect ever after a vaguely dissolute manner. To be fair to Laos I was seeing it at the worst of all possible seasons — it was late March — when the air is burdened with the presage of storms and the landscape blighted with autumnal sadness. Heat lay like an interdict on the town of Vientiane, although the sun was wrapped until late morning in a sweltering mist. At certain hours, out of the stillness, a hot wind rose suddenly and skirmished in the streets, producing a brief, false animation, flapping huge leaves in the faces of passers-by, who were half disembodied by the swirling dust, above which they floated like genii. Sometimes the grey, swollen sky squeezed out a few drops of rain.

I was lodged in the government guest-house, a European villa — since it had two storeys — which at some time had gone native, with earthenware dragons crawling on its roof. Hornets had started cellular constructions in the window shutters and armies of cockroaches marched across the floors. Precious, expensive water was brought in large pots and left in the subdivision of the room where, using a gourd with a hole in its bottom, you could take a shower. The main advantage of having this open pot of water in the room was that it collected a gauzy layer of mosquitoes which were content to stay there in harmless concentration, unless disturbed. The Mekong could be seen from the window, a sallow strip of water across half a mile of whitened river-bed. Perhaps this drought had something to do with the town's electrical generating system, because only occasionally — and never at night — would the filament of the electric light bulb consent to glow feebly. Whenever the hot wind sprang up, stirring the trees round the house, great dry leaves as big as dishes came tumbling down and fell with a crash in the layer already deposited on the earth. It was the death-rattle of the year, which in Laos expires in croaking senility, to be re-born with the raging storms which were about to break.

Vientiane is a religious centre, one of the two ancient capitals of Laos. It abounds with pagodas, many of them deserted and in ruins; and colossal Buddhas, with dusty half-obliterated smiles, sit in the tumbled brickwork.

Since at this time, when the earth had dried up, there was no work to be done anywhere, it was the season of *bouns*; the Laotian festivals. Each pagoda holds one, as a means of collecting funds. They last for three days, and although an attempt is made not to hold two *bouns* at the same time, there are so many pagodas that duplication cannot always be helped; so that every night for several weeks the sky over one or more districts of Vientiane glows with the reflection of thousands of lights, while from a distance one catches the gusty, carnival sounds of Laotian rejoicings. *Bouns* start at about eleven, and go on all night.

The first night after my arrival I went to a *boun*, which I found by following a crowd. It was about two miles from the town's centre and I passed several pagodas on the way, where carpenters were working by lamplight in preparation for a future festival.

An enclosure had been built round the pagoda in which every kind of light, from hurricane lamps to fluorescent tubes, had been concentrated in an anarchic glare. The pagoda had hired a generator for the occasion. There was no entrance fee, but young ladies with demurely lowered eyes waited just inside to accept donations, in return for which you received a candle, a posy of Japanese lilac and two joss-sticks in a bamboo container. Among the many attractions was a free theatre show, lasting for many hours, indistinguishable, except to an expert, from the theatre of Siam. Actors remained on the stage for what seemed interminable periods, occasionally advancing or retreating a few steps. Meanwhile their babies played happily round their feet, and quite frequently a stage-hand would walk across and interrupt a scene for a few seconds to pump up the pressure in the hurricane lamps.

On a nearby platform the *lap ton* was being danced. Once again it was the major attraction, but as it was still incorrect for Laotian girls to dance in public, religious enterprise had arranged for hostesses to be brought over from Siam, just across the river. The pagoda hired the girls for the three nights and lodged them in a nearby building. It cost a piastre to cavort round the stage for about fifteen minutes with one of them. They were dressed in hideous knee-length frocks, and some seemed to have permanent waves. The backward Laotian girls in their dowdy finery, their silk scarves, their skirts woven at the hem and waist-band with silver and gold thread, and their abundant jewel-decked chignons, could only look on wistfully. As I arrived the organizers were having trouble with the microphone — indispensable adjunct to any social occasion in the new Far East. A young man chanted a soft, nasal melody which could only be heard within the *boun* enclosure itself. But suddenly the electricians were successful with their tinkerings and all Vientiane was flooded with a great, ogrish baying. The electricians hugged each other, and, enchanted by the din, the audience began to drift away from the theatre and make for the dancing floor.

The second attraction in order of popularity was a love-court. A quadrangular arrangement of tables had been formed, covered by a thatched roof raised on posts decorated with woven bamboo representations of animals, weapons and phallic emblems. Seated round the tables in the interior of the square were the girls, and their suitors sat facing them. Between the couples had been placed offerings of food, brought by the girls. Originally a tribute to some ancient, forgotten fertility god, a primeval Thai Venus, the offerings would be given, next day, to the bonzes. All through the night the bantering of witticisms, the singing and the exchange of improvised verse would go on, accompanied by the accordion-like wheezings of the Kène, the Stone Age gourd pipes of Laos. Sometimes through a happy fault in the circuit the splutter and bellow of the loud-speakers would suddenly lapse, and you heard the beehive dronings of the communal love-making, the kènes, and the voice of the presiding bonze, preaching continually in an archaic, incomprehensible language from the wicker cage into which he had been fastened. The cage symbolized the protection of his religion from these earthly distractions. As soon as inspiration failed he would be relieved by the next on the rota of preachers, waiting now to take his place.

Love-courts are the accepted preliminary to the consummation of affairs of the heart, which — despite European conviction that romantic love is a Western invention — are accompanied in Laos by much versifying and mild, self-imposed frustrations. When, for instance, a well-known beauty is wooed by a number of suitors, a serenading match may be arranged on the veranda of her house to permit her to test under competitive conditions the poetic and musical capabilities of each of them. Complete pre-marital freedom is recognized, but much outward reserve is maintained. There is a time and place for everything. It is incorrect, for example, to acknowledge in the street a lady with whom one happens to be on particularly good terms. These things in Laos are fraught with an etiquette which is the legacy of a highly organized society not too far gone in decay.

The charm of Vientiane lies in the life and the customs of the people. Unless one is an amateur of pagoda architecture there is little else to be seen. The Laotians have preferred to work in wood, rather than stone, and their art, confined chiefly to the decoration by religious artists of the doors, pillars and interiors of pagodas, quickly perishes in such a climate.

Outside the town there is a great, grey, half-decayed *stupa*, built as a tomb for a hair of the Buddha. It is surrounded by a cloister, containing perhaps a thousand Buddha images; a collection of which the people of Vientiane are very proud. But even here, where the religion is practised in its purest form, there is a little degeneration, a little backsliding from the lofty philosophic conception; and the taint of magic practices shows itself. Selecting one of the numerous images as a personal tutelary divinity, the devotee subjects it to a kind of bribery similar to that sometimes practised in Southern Europe with images of the saints. In this case the image's chief function is healing, and when the sufferer recovers from any complaint he hastens to the pagoda to apply gold-leaf to the part of the Buddha corresponding to that where he has felt the pain in his own body. I was interested to deduce from this practice that the people of Vientiane are much plagued by headaches – perhaps those which accompany malaria.

Standing in a corner of the sanctuary was an ancient ithyphallic statue, an old Hindu divinity, no doubt, which had been worn smooth in the appropriate parts by the feminine adoration of a thousand years. I was told that the women of the French colony who wish for a child frequently emulate their husbands' pose of Laos-ization by coming here secretly to pay their respects. I wondered whether this clandestine tribute might not be extended eventually to the Buddhas to solicit their curative powers; and if so what we should learn from it about the prevalence of disease among Europeans.

The museum of Vientiane, which I visited in the hope of learning something of the living art of the country, has also little more to show than a collection of Buddhas. There is a tranquillity, a lack of compulsion in the Hinayanist Buddhism of Cambodia and Laos — so different from the neurotic deformation practised by the later Khmer kings — which is not propitious to the development of religious art. There was no violence or drama in the life of Buddha comparable to that of Christ, and the Indian Epics have been eschewed in Laos as improperly secular. It has been enough to carve Buddhas, and more Buddhas *ad infinitum*, seeking perhaps to multiply in this way the magic virtues which each image contains. The curator takes you round, explaining the characteristic postures — there are seven or eight — all of which can be appreciated in five minutes. After that there are minute differences of physique and physiognomy to be noted that reflect the influences of India, of Java, of Thibet or of Ceylon. That is all.

By the time the museums turn to the art of the people, the grotesque animals in bamboo, the carved movable figures which are obscene to European eyes — all of which become a pagan burnt-offering at the end of each *boun* — it will be too late. The microphone is an infallible sign of what is to come. Nothing of this kind will survive the era of materialism, under whatever form it arrives.

These are the sights of Vientiane, but in addition there is a spectacle which is popular with Europeans, who, remote, isolated, and living under difficulties, tend to shut themselves up within the protective social rituals of people in exile.

This spectacle is the slaughterhouse at work. I do not know whether or not it is illegal in Laotian law to kill animals, but certainly it is thought shameful, and the killing for Europeans is done at the dead of night on the outskirts of the town. The slaughterers are obliged to work by flares, which is responsible, the French think, for an unusually picturesque effect. It is 'not done' to go along while the actual killing is in progress, but shortly after, when the carcasses are suspended from hooks to be cut up, and the workers, stripped to their loincloths, and garishly splashed, paddle about in a vermilion sea. Cars are stationed just beyond the reach of the steaming odours, and one is recommended to see the thing as one views a nude in a picture gallery — that is, divorced from all but a disinterested abstraction, in this case the colour.

The possibilities of Vientiane, it was clear, would be quickly exhausted. Thao Nhouy, the Laotian Minister of Education, lent me his jeep to see some of the surrounding villages, but the roads were so appalling that it broke down after being driven for about five miles. He then suggested that I might like to see the local schoolgirls dancing, and when I said that I would be delighted, and asked for permission to take photographs, the girls were sent off home, on their bicycles, to get their best clothes. An hour or two later they began to trickle back, wearing their mothers' jewellery as well as their own and with their silk finery done up in paper parcels. When they had dressed and were ready they made a glittering sight. One girl wore a scarf ornamented with real gold thread said to be worth about £50 in English money. They danced under the supervision of a teacher whom I recognized as a professional actor, from the *boun*, and who occasionally intervened when a girl failed in some minor feat, such as bending her fingers back at an expressive ninety degrees from the palm.

All these girls, dressed as they were like princesses, came from shacks in the forest. Each one had a bicycle — infallibly fitted with dynamo lighting, and sometimes 3-speed gears. It seems that a bicycle for his daughter is one of the essentials for which a Laotian will work. It is considered ill-bred and irreligious in Laos to work more than is necessary. The father of a family cultivates an amount of land, estimated, by a bonze who is expert in such matters, to be sufficient for his requirements. If there are six members of the family, six standard, equal sized portions of land will be cultivated. If a child is born into the family another piece of land is cleared and worked. When a member of the family dies, whether it be a baby or the grandfather, cultivation of his portion will be stopped. Just enough is produced for the family to eat and to provide a small surplus sold in the market — *with the bonze's approval* — to buy occasional strict necessities, like a silk shawl and a bicycle for the daughter. There is no social insurance and there are no poor. The old and the sick are supported by the young, or, where they are left without able-bodied providers, by the community, and the bonzes give instructions for the necessary land to be placed under cultivation for them. The accumulation of wealth which is not to be used for definite, approved purposes, causes a man to lose prestige among his neighbours, just, as in the West, the process is reversed. The main difference, it seems, between Buddhism in Indo-China, and Christianity — apart from any question as to their relative merits — is that, whether we admire it or not, the former is largely put into practice.

It is a stimulating reflection that the Western millionaire, obsessed for the sake of social distinction with the amassing of enormous possessions — little of which he can personally consume — would attain the same ends of personal celebrity under a Laotian Buddhistic order of things by his priestly austerities — by embracing the most abject and prestige-conferring form of poverty.

For this reason perhaps the local Evangelist missionary and his wife have made no converts. Like all who have lived among the Laotians they are charmed with them — although, of course, disappointed at their blindness. They also deplore their immorality.

In the matter of converts the Evangelists have been no more unsuccessful than their Portuguese, Spanish and French forerunners. The Laotians having little capacity for abstractions, either in their language or religion, cannot follow the subtlety of Western religious concepts. They have a passion for taking things *au pied de la lettre*. Being told that the basic commandment of Christianity as well as Buddhism is 'thou shalt not kill', they cannot swallow such reservations as capital punishment and 'the just war'; while casuistry repels them. Moreover, a bonze, the spiritual leader of the country people among whom he lives and works, occupies by virtue of his rigorous fulfilment of the principles of his religion, a position in their esteem accorded in the West, say, to a boxing champion. The Laotians have come to associate the prestige of sanctity with certain abstinences and uncomfortable practices. The bonze gives an example of utter renunciation which is awe-inspiring by comparison with the minor self-abnegations of the villagers. The Laotians, therefore, although tolerant in the extreme, are not impressed by the worth of a would-be spiritual leader who presents himself to them loaded with material possessions. And this negative attitude deepens into a certain aversion if, as usually happens, the holy men of the West spend most of their time hunting in a country where animals must be allowed to die of old age. I fear that where the austere Dominicans, and the Jesuits failed, there is little hope for the Evangelists.

However, the missionary was far from despondent. There were Meos in the mountains not far from Vientiane, and just as in the plateaux of Viet-Nam the Moïs had not rejected the Gospel, so here the primitive peoples of the mountains seemed promising material for evangelization. There would be no risk of jeopardizing conversion by hunting, among such hearty amateurs of open-air sports as the Meos, and if the missionary had more of this world's goods than they — well, that was a sure sign that his *ai* (or spirit), was stronger, and it would be a good thing to imitate him. Before the Meos could trouble themselves with renunciatory religions they would have to create a comfortable and abundant civilization for themselves. There was no chance of becoming sated with prosperity at the top of their mountains.

The missionary had made one trip to the Meos and was well pleased with his reception. The Meos, he said, were delightful children. Since tribes at this cultural level are hospitable to the last degree and much given to humouring strangers' whims, the whole village seemed to have foregathered and listened most attentively while he preached. It seemed to me that if the missionary had preached in Meo it was rather an achievement and I asked him whether, in fact, he had done this, or had contented himself with Laotian, which most Meos understand. 'I did neither,' he said. 'I preached in English, and from the way my words were received I feel that we may have started something up there.'

It may be doubted that in thus boldly treating the language barrier as non-existent the evangelist had succeeded in communicating anything of the Christian point of view to his Meo audience. But this performance was, in fact, no more than the *reductio ad absurdum* of a situation which had arisen even with the first Jesuit missionaries. The separating gulf of language, of thought and of tradition, was too wide and deep. Father Buzome, for example, the first missionary to be sent to Indo-China by the Society of Jesus at Macao, was, if possible, even less effective. The Father preached with the aid of phrases prepared in advance for him by ships' interpreters, and as a result carried out a number of baptisms. It was only by the accident of watching a farcical theatrical performance in which he saw himself represented, that he found out to his sorrow that his converts had no idea, even, of what the term Christian meant. One of the players was dressed to represent the Father, but was provided with a great artificial stomach. He had a boy as his assistant. The turn consisted in asking the boy 'whether he would go into the Belly of the Portuguese?' The boy then replied that he would, and the player stuffed him into the artificial stomach; repeating this ridiculous procedure many times, to the great diversion of the onlookers.

To his horror Father Buzome realized that the invitation to enter the belly of the Portuguese was precisely the phrase he had been accustomed to use when asking potential converts if they were willing to accept Christianity. Thus, by his linguistic industry, the Father had done no more than bring his religion into secret ridicule; while the Meos, at least, are not likely to have felt anything other than slight bewilderment at the evangelist's quite unintelligible discourse.

Laos, they said at Saigon, was happily free from those disorders that made travel so chancy in the rest of Indo-China. The only difficulty was getting to Laos. Once you got there all was well, and there was nothing to stop you going about the country as much as you liked.

This account proved to be cruelly fictitious. You left Vientiane in the same way as you came — by plane. Either that, or you waited an indefinite time for the military convoy which provisioned Xien-Khouang in the north and the posts between — islands in perilous seas. The only way to get to Luang Prabang, the second of the ancient capitals of the country, which was about 300 miles away up the Mekong — or about 250 miles across country — was by one of the occasional motor pirogues. It now remained to find out what were the possibilities of making the trip in this way.

Providing myself with a Chinese interpreter — the pirogues being, of course, Chinese owned — I went down to the river. By walking a mile or two along the thirty-feet-deep bank you came to a place where the main stream floundered over from the Siamese side, so that a few barely connected stagnant puddles lay directly beneath. In one of these the pirogue lay, cracking in the sun and seemingly abandoned. It was an ugly, shapeless craft; a small junk, with its deck-space entirely covered over with a kind of hutment, so that travellers were confined to a stinking semi-darkness for the duration of their journey. It was arranged so that air and light could be kept out by the lowering of rush-matting screens over the few apertures in the sides.

A few corpse-like figures lay strewn about the fore-shore and the interpreter, raising the rags that covered one face, awoke its owner. An absurd conversation now took place, complicated by the interpreter's refusal to use any medium but pidgin-French.

N. L. Is that the owner of the boat?
INTERPRETER. Yes.
N. L. Tell him I want to go to Luang Prabang.
INTERPRETER (*to* BOATMAN). Him content go Luang Prabang.
BOATMAN (*in French*). Yes.
INTERPRETER. Him say yes.
N. L. Ask him when he expects to start.
INTERPRETER. Yes, possible you go. Him say.
N. L. I know, but when?
INTERPRETER. When? Ha! Today, tomorrow. Maybe you content to go. All right.
N. L. Do you mind asking him?
INTERPRETER (*determined not to lose face by speaking a word of Chinese, puts this into a long incomprehensible rigmarole of pidgin.* BOATMAN *replies similarly.*)
INTERPRETER. Him say engine no good. Sick. Soon he cure.
N. L. When?
INTERPRETER. Today, tomorrow, maybe. You content go — you go.
N. L. (*converted to pidgin*). How long trip take?
BOATMAN (*in French*). Ten nights.
INTERPRETER. Fifteen nights.
N. L. Why you say fifteen? Him no know?
INTERPRETER. Ten nights runnings maybe. Stoppings too.
    (*Another Chinese arrives and does his best to spread confusion.*
    He describes himself as a Hong Kong Englishman.)
H. E. (*in English*). This boat good. First top-rate class. You come back tomorrow, after yesterday gone. How?
N. L. Why come back tomorrow?

LAOS

INTERPRETER (*suddenly falling into line with* H. E., *and pointing to* BOATMAN). Him no say go. Him brother say.

N. L. Him brother where?

INTERPRETER *and* H. E. Him brother gone.

N. L. When him come?

BOATMAN. Today, tomorrow, approximately.

INTERPRETER. Approximately.

CHAPTER XVIII

THE ROAD TO XIEN KHOUANG

THE struggle with the pirogue men, which I expected would become a daily routine, was suddenly broken off by news of a convoy going to Xien Khouang. And better still there was a spare seat in a car which would leave the convoy after the danger point was passed and carry on to Luang Prabang. This was a jeep belonging to a French official called Dupont, a flamboyant, red-bearded figure I had often seen hurtling through the streets of Vientiane. Dupont had been on a mission in Vientiane and was now returning to his home in Luang Prabang.

He arrived at the villa at about 3 a.m. next morning — a tornado approach, through the foot-deep carpet of dead leaves. Shrouded in protective clothing as the driver of an early Panhard-Levasseur he could be seen through the bare frangipani branches, tooting his horn continually, and waving his arms with excited exasperation at the thought of things he had forgotten. There was a platform built between the driver's and passenger's seats on which a dog which looked like a samoyed perched uneasily. Dupont said it was a race bred only by the Meos. In the back of the jeep a Laotian driver sat buried in luggage. He was asleep, and as we took the corners his head rolled from side to side like a freshly cut-down suicide.

So far I had met French intellectuals, soldiers, politicians, but Dupont was the man of action, although action that seemed often without motivation or relevance. He was a corsair out of his day; an adventurer who was swaggeringly going native and whose ardours Laos would tame and temper. Dupont had married a Laotian wife in Luang Prabang and said that he would never return to France. His children would probably be brought up as Buddhists, and by that time, no doubt, Dupont himself would be paying some sort of lax observance to the rites. In the meanwhile he had reached the point of respecting in a light-hearted way all the superstitions of East and West combined; sometimes perplexed when they were in conflict, as happens, for example, with Friday the 13th; since in Indo-China all odd days are fairly lucky, and Friday is the luckiest day of the week. He carried a Laotian sorcerer's stick, engraved with signs and symbols enabling him to cast a rapid horoscope, but was only affected by verdicts in support of decisions he had already taken. Dupont was in a great hurry to get back to Luang Prabang, because his wife was pregnant and he was afraid that she would hurt herself on her bicycle, although he had dismantled it and had hidden some essential parts. We were supposed to stay in the convoy until the Xien Khouang embranchment was reached, about a hundred miles from Luang Prabang, but Dupont said that if I had no objection we would clear off on our own at the first possible opportunity. He then made some fatalistic remarks about death and predestination.

At the convoy assembly-point, we found a great show of discipline. Tight-lipped officers were walking up and down examining tyres and checking guns and ammunition. Drivers were assembled and lectured on convoy discipline. A soldier's Laotian wife, being observed to be pregnant, was refused permission to travel. The infantry escort was carried in five or six lorries and as many others were loaded with supplies. A dozen jeeps were placed in the middle of the convoy, which was guarded at each end by an armoured car. Dupont was turned back when he tried to bluff his way to the head of the column behind the leading armoured car, from which position he had hoped to be able to sneak away at an early opportunity.

Although by the time we got under way it was shortly before dawn, all Vientiane was still awake. Grinding our way through the streets we passed a *boun* in full swing with its temple-dancers still trapesing round their stage, and the magnified sobbings of a crooner not quite drowned in the roar of thirty exhausts. The streets were full of torch-carrying crowds.

No sooner had we left the town than the dust, released from its covering of fallen leaves, rose up in an all-obliterating fog. It was useless to rebel, to attempt evasion, to muffle up the face and cover the mouth with a handkerchief. In the end you gave in. Dust erupted in seemingly solid cones from the wheels of the preceding cars. In an hour we were turned into reluctant millers. Dawn revealed Dupont falsely tranquil beneath a yellow mask. Our Laotian driver slept peacefully and drifts had filled in the hollows of his upturned face. The Meo dog cleared its fur occasionally with a violent muscular spasm, and, sneezing continually, spattered us with its saliva. Dupont comforted it in Laotian, which he said the dog understood, as well as some Chinese.

Beyond the veil which the convoy spread about itself, the forest took shape dimly, or rather, disclosed its leafy anarchy. Stems, trunks and flowers — if there were any — were all contained in a grey carapace of leaves. Once or twice, a silver pheasant, its plumage dulled in the haze, passed over our heads and splashed into the foliage again. Only when we stopped and the ochreous fog slowly settled, could the colour seep back again into the landscape. Somewhere beyond the barricade of trees, the sun had risen and was greeted by the mournful howling of monkeys. Small, dull birds had awakened in every bush and produced a single melancholy note. The soldiers, forming dejected groups, scooped the dust from their ears, rinsed out their mouths with vacuum-flask coffee, and were professionally pessimistic about the outcome of the journey. Dupont came to an understanding with the drivers immediately ahead, and in this way improved his position in the convoy by two places. He had just found a stream in which he was about to throw his dog — the animal was terrified of water — when the officer in charge blew his whistle for the convoy to get under way.

Until mid-day we slithered and bumped along the track, walled-in by the monotonous forest. Then at last the forest diminished and shrivelled into bush, then scrub, and finally a savannah of coarse grass. Here crouching among cyclopean boulders were the few huts of plaited bamboo which made up the first village. Into this we thumped, bursting out of our envelope of dust and swerving to avoid naked babies and senile dogs. A canopy of vultures driven into the air by thundering wheels hung in suspension above us.

This was the lunch halt. We had been eating dust for eight hours and had averaged seven miles an hour. It was from this point onwards that trouble might be expected. But I told Dupont that there would be no trouble. However many times the convoy might have been attacked previously it would not be attacked when I was travelling with it. For once I found someone in hearty agreement with me. Dupont said that the convoy system was a ridiculous waste of time. You could travel up and down this road with not much more hope of running into bandits than on Route Nationale number seven. Anyway, if you were craven about such things, what was wrong with travelling at night only, when bandits — especially Laotian ones — were in bed. He said that we would really have to think seriously about how we were going to get away from the convoy, because the risks we were incurring in swallowing germ-infested dust were several thousand times greater than stopping the odd bullet if we went off by ourselves.

Dupont, who refused to eat army rations while there were cooked meals to be had in the neighbourhood, led the way to the sombre Chinese hovel masquerading as a restaurant. He ordered three portions of Soupe Chinoise; one for his dog, which to his dismay was missing when the food arrived. The Chinese apologized for the poor quality of his soup, being deprived by his isolation, he said, of every accepted ingredient. He promised to send out for some tree-frogs to enrich the flavour if we could give him half an hour. Owing to the time limit set by the convoy-commander, we had to reject this offer, declining also to select for grilling one of a group of live lung-fish hastily lined up for approval.

The proprietor had not been over-modest. The soup was utterly negative in flavour. We were sipping our coffee, which tasted of earth and bitter herbs when a commotion aroused us. Hurrying from the restaurant we saw Dupont's dog busy with carrion in a nearby field, surrounded by an excited huddle of vultures for whose benefit it had been exposed there. Dupont's cries of horror were interrupted by the whistle of the convoy-commander, who this time signalled for all officers to gather round him. He told them that seventy Issaraks were reported to be in ambush, awaiting us at Kilometre 115 — about twenty miles further on. They were turned out in new American uniforms, he said, and were well armed. At Kilometre 115 a cross-country track leading from Siam into Viet-Nam crossed our route. It occurred to both Dupont and myself that if this report was several hours old, it was not likely that the Issarak would be in the place where they were first seen. However, the official view taken was that they would not have moved more than five kilometres down the road in our direction, because orders were given for the infantry escort to dismount from their lorries at Kilometre 110 and to precede the convoy on foot for the next five kilometres. We noticed, too, that the officer assumed that the Issarak, if they had moved at all, would have inevitably marched towards us, and not in the other direction, because, once Kilometre 115 had been reached, the danger would be officially declared at an end, and the infantry ordered back into their lorries.

We now entered a country of low, bare hills; a whitish land-scape, rarely animated by wandering pink-skinned buffaloes. In the hollows there were islands of splendid vegetation — flamboyant trees, arranged as if by design, with giant ferns and feathery bamboos. Peacocks gleamed in abandoned paddy fields, and storks, flapping away at our approach, trailed their legs in pools of yellow marsh-water. The vegetation was sensitive to quite small variations in altitude. The valley-bottoms were choked with bamboo thickets, and slender, segmented canes, wreathed in blue convolvulus, curved over our path like coachmen's whips, flicking us as we passed beneath. At this level the ditches were full of dead butterflies which seemed to have completed their lives' span while in the act of drinking. But a climb of only a few hundred feet was enough to break right out of this hot-house profusion; to pass through the curtains of liana and to reach the first pines.

Approaching the portentous kilometre, the road became steadily worse. It was only just wide enough for the six-wheelers to pass and there were frequent tyre-bursts. Whenever a vehicle was put out of action, it was manhandled off the road and left to its own devices. There was continual trouble with the bridges, which were temporary affairs, put up at the end of the rainy season and only intended to last until the weather broke again. The most rickety-looking of the bridges had to be tested first with a jeep, followed by an unladen lorry. When this precaution was neglected, a lorry loaded with supplies crashed through and fell into the river below. This meant a painful detour through the water for the rest of the convoy. Several vehicles also got stuck and had to be hauled out. Any of these moments would have provided an ideal opportunity for an attack.

The Meo dog suffered from the heat just as badly as, according to report, its original owner would have done. Its tongue lolled from its mouth and, laying its head either on Dupont's lap or on mine, it dribbled on our bare knees. It could not stand the dust, and wetted us further with its continual sneezings.

Some of the drivers were showing signs of tiredness, and probably nervous strain. The standard of driving was going down. We were once again in the bamboo thickets, and the road was no better than a ledge round the flank of a low hill. On our right was a precipice, but the vegetation was so thick that you could get no idea of the drop. Dupont, having profited by casualties in front, had now worked his way up to a position immediately behind the last of the lorries, and we were nosing our way round the hill, keeping a look-out for occasional gaps in the road left by subsidences, when the lorry ahead suddenly turned off the road and went over the side. Gently, almost, it was lowered from sight amongst the bamboos.

Up till the last fraction of a second before a thousand graceful stems screened it from our view it was still upright and quite level. The soldiers in it had hardly risen from their seats and raised their arms not so much in alarm, it seemed, as to wave farewell.

Soon after, the infantry climbed down from the lorries and began their march in single file along the sides of the road in front. This manœuvre seemed to me not only useless but dangerous, since nothing could have been easier for ambushers than to let the soldiers go by and then destroy the defenceless vehicles. In the spirit of one who whistles in the dark to keep his courage up, the armoured car ahead occasionally opened up with its machine-guns and 2-cm. cannon, provoking, to the great discomfort of the following cars, one small forest fire. We never heard that the enemy was other than imaginary. At five in the afternoon we crawled into the village of Vang Vieng, having done about twenty miles since mid-day.

Vang Vieng was just such another village as the one where we had had our mid-day Chinese soup, but it was set in the most staggering surroundings. Overhanging it was a range of mountains which were not very high, since the peaks only reached 8000 feet, but which did not look like any mountains I had ever seen before. There was no visual preparation by a gently rising foreground of foothills. These were stupendous walls of rock rising 4000, 5000 and 6000 feet sheer out of an absolutely flat plain. We were overhung, as it were, by a huge scrabbling in the sky, which at its base had been erased by mists. Dupont said that we would pass over these mountains that night.

It was at Vang Vieng that Dupont had planned to slip away. His resolution was only slightly shaken when it was announced that the whole convoy would stay in the village overnight, owing to the presence of a small force of Viet-Minh, which the infantry would have to clear out, in a village fifteen kilometres further along the road; but as all the men were thoroughly tired this operation would be postponed till early next morning. Dupont was determined not to stay in Vang Vieng, but even he seemed to think twice about deliberately disobeying the convoy-commander's orders, and when he finally did so it was done in gentle stages, rather than in one flagrant act of insubordination. The excuse given for this phobia about Vang Vieng was that all the sleeping space would be taken up and we should find nowhere to stretch out comfortably.

We were still filthy from our travels; sweat-soaked and covered in bright yellow dust, through which the perspiration trickled down regular courses. As part of his campaign Dupont suggested that we should have a meal first and after that get permission from the convoy-commander to go for a bathe in a river, twelve kilometres down the road, where we should still be three kilometres short of the village with the Viet-Minh. Dupont described this river as if it had magical curative properties. It came out of a cave not far away, he said, and the water was icy cold. This course being agreed upon, we went to the usual Chinese eating-house run by one Sour Hak. Taken by surprise by our invasion, Sour Hak found himself short of food. However, as these villages are completely cut off during the six months' rainy season, there are always standbys for emergency. Reaching to the top of the cupboard he found a hunk of venison *boucané*, dusted it off and set it before us. This meat, prepared in a manner similar to that employed by the Argentine gauchos, was black, fine grained in texture as cheese, odourless and tasted slightly of liquorice. According to the usages of life in the bush, strips were cut off it with one's clasp knife. Fortunately, Sour Hak was found, quite mysteriously, to have a stock of first-rate Burgundy; doubtlessly bought in the belief that it was Algerian. Dupont's sudden optimism was only lowered by Sour Hak's refusal at any price to sell a green parakeet, which had flown in one day and attached itself to the house. Since tasting civilization nothing could persuade this bird to use its wings again, although like a true Laotian it enjoyed being taken for a ride on a bicycle. Dupont's process of going native involved a craze for collecting animals. By the time the parakeet had bitten him several times, he was ready to offer anything for it – including a worn out Citroen car he kept at Luang Prabang – but it was all of no avail.

When we left Sour Hak's place there was no one in sight in the street. Dupont said that the officers would be eating, so why worry them? We would motor off quietly down the road, have our bathe, and then see how we felt. So, driving quite slowly and pretending to take an interest in the sights, we edged our way out of the village; past the sentries, the last house, the last Laotian girl squatting on her veranda looking into space; out into the splendid and menacing amphitheatre of the landscape; very much alone, but invulnerable with the good red burgundy awash in our stomachs.

The river was there, as Dupont promised, and we swam about in it for half an hour, while the Laotian driver sat on the log bridge holding his Sten between his knees. People always alarm you with stories of the perils, the leeches and the parasites to be picked up from bathing in these countries, but as far as could be seen, the River Song – tributary of the Mékong – looked like any river in the south of England. The water poured with a swift, black, curling surface round the boulders and under the bridge. It was cold and there were long, flat, trailing weeds just below the surface. As we went into the water great mustard stains spread from us, were thinned and borne away. The Meo dog, yelping in protest, was thrown in over and over again.

Dupont now made mention of the next part of his programme. Since things had gone so well, why not stroll over to the village of Pha-Tang, half a mile off the road, down the river, and ask permission to sleep there? In this way we should at least get a comfortable night's sleep, and then, in the morning – if, of course, we felt like it – we could re-join the convoy without more ado, and no one would be the worse.

Pha-Tang was a cluster of palms and thatched roofs under the high scrawled translucent mountain shapes. A flourish of cranes deserted the village paddy fields at our approach. Dupont told the driver to wait behind as we went into the village. As a convert to the Laotian way of life he paid much attention to local etiquette; he said that we must on no account appear with arms. There were no signs of life in the village and Dupont found this disconcerting. We must keep a careful look-out, he said, for a white thread across the path, or a cross decorated with red flowers. Either would mean that the village was taboo to strangers; in the first case because of a violent death or the presence of epidemic disease and in the second because the feast of the tutelary spirit was being celebrated. It was for reasons of these periodical taboos that Laotian villages, although built as near as possible to roads, were not actually on them. The places where we had stopped that day were not true Laotian villages at all, but military posts, around which a few store-keepers, mostly Chinese, had grouped themselves.

Although Dupont could find no signs of a definite taboo, he was still very uneasy that no one had come out to greet us. The correct thing on entering a Laotian village with the intention of staying the night was to ask for the headman and obtain his permission to do so. Unless this were done it would be a grave discourtesy to enter any house. Dupont emphasized that while the Laotians were tolerant, civilized and hospitable, there were certain indispensable forms, and as we mooched about the deserted village, he poured out information on the subject; even describing the position for correct sleeping; body stretched out at right angles to wall containing door, feet pointing to the door. When I suggested that we might find an empty hut and sleep in it, he was startled. Although the villagers might overlook minor breaches of custom, he said, this would be a grave one, involving them in an expensive purification ceremony before the hut could be occupied again.

I offered no more suggestions and in the end we found a rather scared looking woman who said, when Dupont spoke to her in Laotian, that the headman was away, and was not expected back. It was quite clear now that we were not welcome, and Dupont said that perhaps it would be better, after all, not to sleep in the village. Thinking about this experience afterwards, I concluded that the villagers dared not welcome us in the usual way, being unable to guarantee our safety, with the Issarak bands and the Viet-Minh in the neighbourhood. I expected that Dupont would now resign himself and return to Vang Vieng, but he began to produce arguments for carrying on. The worst thing about the convoy, he said, was that it prevented our seeing so many things and doing so many things that we could otherwise do. Up in the mountains there were Meo villages, he said, and he badly wanted to get another Meo dog. They were rare and hard to come by, but he knew one of the Meo chiefs who would oblige him. Having found out that I was very ready to be interested in such things, Dupont produced this Meo village as a kind of gaudy enticement. The only thing that separated us from the leisurely enjoyment of such pleasures, was a single village, not more than three kilometres away, which, once passed, was the last until we reached the military post of Muong Kassy, fifty kilometres away, over the mountains. Dupont's final suggestion was that we should stay where we were until about an hour after dark, then creep up to the outskirts of the village – Pha Home was its name – with lights off, switch on the lights to make sure there was no barrier, and rush through it.

At about 8.30, then, by which time Dupont was convinced that the village of Pha Home, with its Viet-Minh visitors, would be peacefully sleeping, we started off. It was difficult to approach the village quietly, as the road was uphill all the way. Dupont stopped and tried to quieten the exhaust, by squeezing the ends of the pipe together. This certainly reduced the exhaust note to a strangled snuffling, but through it sounded too plainly the miscellaneous rattlings that nothing could stop, and as soon as the headlights were switched off there was no way of avoiding the pot-holes and the small, loose boulders, over which we crashed continually. It was lucky for us that the village lay back about a hundred yards from the road. In spite of the hour, it was full of light and animation. As

facing: THE FANTASTIC LANDSCAPE OF NORTHERN LAOS

we sneaked past we could see a bonfire with a group silhouetted round it. Our passing appeared to go quite unnoticed.

We reached Muong Kassy about two hours later and slept in a large, barn-like Laotian building of thatch and bamboo, which served as the officers' mess. Insects had been at the bamboo and the slightest movement filled the air with a powder which had the effect of snuff. The building swayed slightly with each step, but no more when there were twenty occupants, as there were next day, than when there were only two.

Muong Kassy was the headquarters of a company of Engineers whose job was the upkeep of the bridges. They were uncomfortably isolated here on top of a small hill rising only partially free of the forests, with magnificent views in all directions, which nobody noticed any longer. There was no doctor, so that casualties of any kind might have to wait several weeks for a convoy going in any direction. In the rainy season, when roads and bridges disappeared, the garrison was confined to barracks for five or six months. Outside the stockades the usual straggling collection of Laotian and Chinese huts had formed, with saloons selling 'shoum', a fire-water made from maize. Everything was brought by convoy and was in short supply, except the shoum which was a local speciality. The store-keepers also had a stock of what was described in English on the label as 'fruit tonic'. The fruit tonic was made in Siam and was probably an industrial by-product; but the garrison had found out that shoum plus fruit tonic was more effective than either separately, and that stunned by a good stiff early morning dose of this, the day's boredoms could be better supported. A shoum-and-fruit-tonic relaxed the nerves too. It was after we had been introduced to this Muong Kassy custom that Dupont changed his plans, and quite forgetting about his pregnant wife, and the bicycle she might succeed in putting together, he said we would stay the day, and leave next morning.

Taking a guide from the camp, we went for a dip in the river.

273

facing: MEO WOMAN

There was a recognized place about a mile up the river, which was free from weed and rock, and once again, because the water was deep and swiftly running, it was very cold and refreshing. We had been swimming round for an hour or so when we noticed a number of Laotian girls hanging about. They were not watching us, but sauntering backwards and forwards in twos and threes, chatting to each other. By the time there were twelve of them, Dupont, keeping well in the water called to them and asked if we were disturbing them in any way. One of the girls came to the edge of the bank, bowed, and looking down at her feet said that it was their usual bathing time, but that there was no hurry, of course. Dupont asked the girls if they would retire for a moment, and they walked a short distance away and stood in a preoccupied circle while we got out of the water. We then dressed quickly and walked on down the path leading to their village. After about a hundred yards we looked back. All the girls, quite naked, were in the water. At that moment two bonzes were strolling slowly along the bank past them; but the girls paid no attention. The bonzes were wrapped in the mantle of holy invisibility.

When we reached the village, Dupont asked punctiliously for the headman, making the excuse that he wanted to visit the pagoda. It was quite evident that this headman was in the good graces of the garrison, and probably supplied them with labour. He was very dignified and had a fine house, with European furniture. Although barefooted, he wore a French suit. On the suggestions of the soldier from the camp he took down his trousers and showed us his legs, which from ankles to thighs were tattooed, in the local manner, so closely that he seemed to be wearing stockings. The annual *boun* had just been celebrated at the local pagoda and a bonze was in the act of sweeping into a heap the votive offerings with which the floor of the courtyard was littered. There was a great collection of elephants, buffaloes, peacocks and tigers, all woven in basket-work. The kind of thing that Picasso produces when he is not painting, but perhaps rather better. They seemed to me to be of the greatest artistic interest. I asked the headman if it would be possible to take any, as the bonze was crumpling and smashing them vigorously with his broom. But the chief shook his head regretfully. Buddhism had degenerated in these remote provinces and was swamped with re-emergent spirit cults. These objects had been dedicated to the *phi* and would have to be burnt in a ritual fire. The *phi* would also receive the burnt essence, I noticed, of a large, very obscene, and no doubt magically valuable picture.

At about this time when the bonze was treading underfoot the village's artistic output of several months, a party of Issarak or Viet-Minh, timing their action to coincide with the convoy's arrival at Moung Kassy, had set fire to the forest just south of the post. A steady breeze was blowing from that quarter, and the fire, started over a width of about a mile and fanning out as it advanced, moved slowly towards the fort.

Coming up over the river bank it took us some time to realize what was happening. There was a haze; but then there was always a haze in Laos, although by this time of day it should have been clearing and not thickening. And then we heard the crackling, punctuated with the sharp pops, which might have been distant rifle fire, but which were the explosions of thick stems of bamboo. Looking up then we saw the curtain of smoke hanging over Muong Kassy, white at the top, and black at its base and streaked occasionally by lance-points of flame, which were still two miles away.

We ran to where the car was parked, started it and tried to drive down the road towards the fire. Dupont was as pleased with it as July 14th. In about fifty yards we got tangled up with the convoy and had to leave the car on the side of the road and run on. The fire was advancing on a ragged front and was as irresistible as a volcano. Black smoke was being blown before it so that at first the flames were out of sight; but when they came through they were two hundred feet high — twice the height of the tallest tree. It went forward in zigzagging rushes; eating its way quickly through the bamboo thickets, which went up like oil wells. A lane of fire had broken right out of the general advance and its spear-point was wandering up over the hill-side, already level with the fort. Large clumps of green forest were being left behind or encircled and then consumed at leisure as the fire went through the bamboo. It caught at the lianas, too, and went up a tree from top to bottom in shrivelling streamers — just like Christmas decorations catching fire. The noise of the exploding bamboos was becoming deafening and the sky was covered in a cloud through which black ash streamed up like flotsam carried on flood-waters. I noticed, though, that only the tops of some of the trees had caught on the other side of the road.

Orders were given to prepare to evacuate the fort. There was a great deal of ammunition and thousands of gallons of petrol, stored in cans, and the soldiers were swarming like ants stacking it in the road and loading the lorries. Confusion developed and matured into chaos, largely caused by the arrival of half the convoy, which blocked the road and prevented the lorries being driven out of the fort. Before an evacuation could be made the convoy had to be moved on through the village, but half the drivers couldn't be found. They had wandered off to look at the fire and taken their starting keys with them.

In the meanwhile the Laotians and Chinese rushing out of their houses with their beds and bedding, and piling their stocks of groceries between the wheels of the cars had made rapid movement impossible, even when the drivers could be rounded up. One family was actually at work taking their house down.

And then as an hour passed in struggling tumult with the convoy at last bludgeoned on through the village and safely parked on the other side, and hundreds of crates and cans loaded on to the lorries, the wind veered and the main front of the fire went by, about half a mile away. A few offshoots coming in our direction burned feebly for a while among the bamboos, and it was all over.

Next morning we left before dawn. But when daylight came there was no sunrise for us. For hours we went on climbing and dropping through the haze-dimmed mountain shapes. We were travelling at between 3000 and 4000 feet and there was no under-brush. Instead, a few trees straggled up the mountain sides, bearing sparse blossom like the flowering of an orchard in early spring. As the haze cleared a little we could see that the mountain tops bore caps of yellow grass. Dupont said that this was the work of the Meos and that it meant that we were getting into their country. Shortly we would go up to a village and try to buy a dog.

CHAPTER XIX

INTO THE MEO COUNTRY

IN the sense that least is known about them, the Meos are the most mysterious of the twelve principal races of Indo-China. This Mongolian people is to be found at altitudes higher than 3000 feet over the whole of Indo-China north of the 21st parallel of latitude. They are utterly incapable of bearing, even for the shortest time, other than cool and temperate climates. Being self-supporting, they rarely come down to visit the markets of the plains and valleys, and when obliged to cultivate fields below the 3000 feet line, they always return to their villages to sleep.

The Meos' territorial aspirations are purely vertical. By their disastrous method of cultivation, which completely exhausts the soil in a few years, they have been forced steadily southwards from China. In migration, as in the year 1860, when they crossed the frontier of Indo-China, they will fight their way savagely and effectively across low-lying country, only to split up and disperse immediately the mountains are reached. An ethnographical map of northern Indo-China is pock-marked with groups of Meos. Since 1860 they have travelled about 400 miles and are now filtering slowly southwards down the Annamite Chain, where from time to time a new group is reported on a mountain top. They are said to have been attacked in recent years by government forces in northern Siam, but it is unlikely that anything short of extermination can stop their slow. silent movement through the mountains. Europeans who have studied them superficially believe them to be of Esquimaux origin; a theory which is offered to explain their horror of warm climates. These authorities report that they possess legends of eternal snows and of arctic days and nights. But the short description published in 1906 by Commandant Lunet de Lajonquière says nothing of this, and no other scientific account of the Meos has appeared.

Besides the Meos' predilection for mountain tops they have other claims to distinction. They are utterly independent and quite fearless. Their passion for freedom compels them to live in the smallest of villages and, apart from such rare events as the invasion of 1860, they will not tolerate chiefs or leaders. If forcibly brought to lower altitudes they are soon taken ill and die. They are normally pacific, but if compelled to fight are apt to eat the livers of slain enemies.

The Meos are the only people in Indo-China who are not in the slightest concerned with evil spirits, although they admit their existence. Their complete indifference to all the ghouls and devils that plague the races surrounding them has invested them with enormous prestige, which they are careful to cultivate. They like to encourage the belief, prevalent among the Thais, that they are were-wolves and can turn into tigers at wish. They have no funerary cults but celebrate a funeral — or any other event providing the slightest excuse — with orgies of drinking. Husbands and wives keep their own property. Children are given the greatest degree of freedom; and sexual promiscuity before marriage — even with strangers — is general. 'Sacred groves' exist — there is a celebrated one at Dong-Van in Tonkin — to which Meo girls resort, and offer themselves freely to all comers. It is said that large-scale maps, upon which the locations of such groves have been scrupulously plotted, are the prized possessions of most French garrisons in Tonkin. Besides breeding fine, white dogs, they are experts at taming monkeys and birds, particularly a kind of minah which they teach a wide repertoire of imitative sounds. The Meos will only part with their animals for an enormous price — payable in solid silver which they immediately convert into massive jewellery.

But the first village beyond Muong Kassy, perched on a bare hill-top and reached laboriously up a long winding path, proved not to belong to Meos but the 'black' Thais — so called from the distinctive dress of their women. It was like climbing up to an eagle's eyrie and finding crows in possession. A rare species of crow though. Checking up on the ethnographical map, you saw that these were the only black Thais in Laos, although you could follow their tracks in isolated, coloured blobs right down from the frontier of Yunnan where they had crossed over from China. The Thais are the aboriginal stock from which both the Laotian and Siamese nations developed, but the black Thais are the only tribe with a taste for the high mountains, with the hard life and the freedom.

Their village was a philosopher's retreat. Ten or fifteen huts clung to the flattened summit of the hill, silhouetted, whichever way you looked, against white mist. Ten paces away the slopes went plunging down and were dissolved in vapour. Across the sky was a wavy, unsupported line of peaks. A few ravens flapped about the thatches, and babies, peering at us through the stockades, howled with horror at what they saw.

The headman received us in his hut, which marked the village's centre. He was dressed in Chinese-looking clothes of some coarse, black stuff, wore a black turban and was smoking a foot-long pipe with a bowl the size of a thimble. We had seen a number of fine white Meo dogs bouncing about in the village and Dupont, speaking Laotian, asked if he could buy one. The chief sent out to see if anyone would sell a dog, and while we were waiting produced a large dish of roasted chicken, already dissected in the Chinese style. This provoked such a lengthy exchange of protestations that the chicken was cold before Dupont decided that we could politely eat it. He presented the chief with some army rations in exchange, and this, too, set in motion a chain-sequence of reiterated offers and mock refusals. Dupont asked if there were any ceremonies taking place in the vicinity. The chief replied that a marriage fair had been organized in the next Thai village, but that you had to cross a range of mountains to reach it.

This custom, widespread in mountain tribes which are split up into scattered, isolated hamlets, is practised by the Meos as well as the Thais. Once a year eligible bachelors and maidens gather at some convenient central point, and each one in turn, the boys alternating with the girls, describes in verse, to the accompaniment of *Kènes*, their possessions, their accomplishments, or their virtues. Formal offers of marriage then follow, and according to eye-witnesses of the custom, the metrical form in no way inhibits the most banal cataloguing of articles to be included in the marriage contract.

We were still eating when the chief's messenger came back with the only dog on offer. It was a poor forlorn animal, suffering probably from some wasting disease, and an enormous price was demanded.

As there was no dog to be had from these intermediaries, there was nothing for it but to go to the source itself, even if it meant another stiff climb on foot. Instead of turning left, therefore, at the junction of the main road to Luang Prabang, we took the right-hand fork towards Xien Khouang, which, although it led us out of our way, went right through the heart of Meo country in Laos. Shortly after, we came up with a Meo family, who were struggling up a hill loaded down like beasts of burden with their possessions. The Meos threw down their bundles and looked us over with puzzled amusement. One of them, who wore pigtails to show that he was the head of the family, came over, cut the choice centre out of a sugar cane he was carrying and presented it to us, roaring with laughter. This was typical Meo conduct. The Meo is grateful to strangers for amusing him with their clownish faces and ridiculous clothes, and his first impulse is to look round for something to give them. Shouting with joy, the children leaped into the car and were cuffed out again by their father. The woman who, if a Thai or a Laotian, would have stood apart with downcast eyes, bent down to examine Dupont's sandals. She wore several pounds in weight of solid silver jewellery round her neck and had had her head recently shaved.

Meo finery at its best is the most extravagantly colourful in Indo-China. The women are stiff with embroidery and heavy silver necklaces and chains, and are half-extinguished by enormous turbans that look like Chinese lanterns. But this family was in its workaday clothes, as its head was very anxious to explain to Dupont. They had been away a week, working in their opium-poppy fields, and now they were on their way home for a flying visit. Dupont asked about a dog, and the head of the family invited us to come up and see for ourselves, as he had no idea who was home and who wasn't.

It was a long, slow climb up to the village, although the Meos, as they skipped along by our side, seemed in no way to notice the slope, nor their huge burdens. The coarse grass — usual legacy of Meo occupation — was replaced here by a noxious thorny scrub. For miles, in all directions from the village, nothing would grow but this ultimate of austere vegetations. This village was at the last stage before it would have to be moved. The fields under cultivation were now so far away that the villagers lived dispersed in temporary shelters where they worked. Very soon they would be too far from the village to return at all and it would be moved, ten or fifteen miles, always south; leaving behind the prairie grass and scrub. It only wanted the Mans to arrive here from Tonkin — the Mans cultivate on Meo lines between 1000 and 3000 feet — to reproduce eventually in Laos the denuded wilderness of southern China.

The Meo village consisted of nothing but a few most decrepit hovels. They were the lowest and the most barbarous examples of human dwellings that it would be possible to find. Why should the Meos be the most elegantly dressed and the worst housed people in the country? They are superb at the few handicrafts they undertake, but they just can't be bothered about how they are sheltered or how they sleep. There is no compulsion; no household genie — like those of the Mois — demanding high standards of order and cleanliness in the house; no canons of taste and refinement spreading slowly downwards from an idly exquisite aristocracy, since all Meos are kept hard at work; no spirit of bourgeois emulation, since this is total democracy, with no betters to imitate. The Meos have only themselves to please, and the result is anarchy.

In the hovel we were taken to, the contents of a thousand schoolboy's pockets lay strewn about; the lengths of string, the broken penknives, the buttons, the mirror glass, the tins, the bottles and the burned out lamp bulbs. Here was accumulated the jackdaw harvesting, the valuable glittering rubbish which was all a Meo wanted of civilization, and which he was free to take, while leaving the civilization itself severely alone. What foolish, generous people, these town-dwellers were!

Our host's wife, a child of fifteen, was lying with her baby on a heap of rags in the corner. The baby was sick, he said, but the only thing necessary was to keep it away from the light — and air — as much as possible. Most Meo babies die in their first two years, and one wonders what would have happened by now to the fertile land of Indo-China, if they didn't.

There was a gun in the corner — a muzzle-loader of the kind it takes a Meo two years to make. They are copied from the guns first supplied by the Jesuits to the Chinese, but are turned out by an endlessly laborious process involving boring out a solid bar by twirling a white hot iron in it. It was enormously long, like an old-fashioned Arab stove-pipe gun, and when Dupont took notice of it the Meo offered to show it to him in use. We went outside and he loaded it with powder and shot he made himself. This process took about five minutes. Before pressing the trigger he warned us to stand well away because of the muzzle blast. The target was a small banana-leaf, skewered against a bank at twenty paces. There was a tremendous bang when he fired, but the leaf remained intact. He blamed this on the maize-spirit which we had just drunk, and was quite delighted when Dupont, giving a demonstration with his American light carbine, also missed.

There were no dogs at all at this village. They were all down at the poppy fields with their owners, the Meo said.

Luang Prabang lies at the end of a long, curling descent from the mountains and through smoking bamboo groves, on the banks of the Mékong. It is built into a tongue of land formed by the con-

fluence with the river of a tributary; a small, somnolent and sancti-
fied Manhattan Island. A main street has turnings down to the river
on each side and a pagoda at every few yards, with a glittering roof
and doors and pillars carved with a close pattern of gilded and
painted designs. There is an infallible sense of colour, a blending
of old gold and turquoise and of many greys; but the bonzes are
continually at work, painting and carving and refurbishing, so that
everything is just a little too new (an extraordinary complaint in
Laos), too spruce, too odorous of freshly applied varnish. The roof
finials glisten with new applied glass and china mosaic. The ancient,
blunted features of lions and dragons get regular scrubbings, have
their teeth painted dead white and are re-fitted, as required, with
new eyes of green glass. A year or two's neglect might greatly
improve Luang Prabang.

For all the briskness with which its holy places are maintained,
the silence in Luang Prabang is only disturbed by the distant, class-
room sounds of bonzes chanting in Pali, and the slow, mild booming
of gongs. It is the home-town of the siesta and the Ultima Thule
of all French escapists in the Far East. Europeans who come here
to live soon acquire a certain, recognizable manner. They develop
quiet voices, and gentle, rapt expressions. This is accompanied by
the determined insouciance of the New Year's reveller. It is an
attitude which is looked for and is put on like a false nose or a carnival hat. Laos-ized Frenchmen are like the results of successful
lobotomy operations — untroubled and mildly libidinous. They
salt their conversation with Laotian phrases, all of which express a
harmoniously negative outlook. *Bo pen nhang*, which is continually
to be heard, means no more than, 'It doesn't matter'. But said in
Laotian it takes on the emphasis of a declaration of faith. Single men
instantly take to themselves Laotian wives, completing their bride's
happiness with the present of a superb bicycle, covered with mas-
cots and pennants, and with chaplets of artificial flowers round the
hub-caps, instead of the leather, dust-removing strap one sees in
Europe. Several painters have retired here to escape the world,

and to produce an occasional tranquil canvas, but Luang Prabang has not yet found a Gauguin.

On the day after our arrival I was invited home by Dupont to meet his wife, whose bicycle was still in pieces when he got back. They lived in a charming Mediterranean sort of house that had nestled down well among the pagodas. It was full of animals, including a large, handsome, domesticated goat that delighted to lurk behind furniture and charge unsuspecting guests.

Madame Dupont was pretty and gay, tall for a Laotian and evidently as nearly European in type as Dupont had been able to find. They seemed very attached to each other. Dupont assured me that jealousy was quite unknown in Laos, and that his wife not only expected him to have adulterous adventures while away from home, but actually advised him in the precautions to take. He did not know whether she allowed herself similar liberties, but thought it likely that she did. At all events he didn't see how he could very well show himself less civilized about it than was she. I was sorry not to be able to understand anything his wife said, except the inevitable *bo pen nhang* which was repeated several times. In a polite effort to make me feel at home, Madame Dupont brought out the family snapshot album and we turned the pages together. There were one or two photographs, evidently taken by her husband, of not fully dressed ladies who were also not Madame. She drew my attention to these, giggling slightly.

After supper, an army officer came in with another Laotian lady. Speaking in an extraordinary whisper, he told me that she was a Princess — a member of the royal family — and entitled to a parasol of five tiers. He admitted, quite frankly, that there was no shortage of princesses in Luang Prabang, and all genuine. They had been friends for fifteen years now, he whispered, although they had never troubled to marry . . . why, he couldn't think. It was easy enough. Dupont agreed with him here, mentioning the case of a subordinate of his who had recently arrived. 'At six o'clock,' Dupont said, 'he expressed the wish to get married. My wife went out to look for a suitable girl, and was back with one by six-thirty. At seven the bonzes came and performed a marriage ceremony which took half an hour. At seven-thirty we opened a bottle of champagne and drank to the health of the bride and bridegroom, and by eight they were already in bed.'

The evening was rounded off by a routine visit to the local opium den, which, probably by design, was as decrepit and sinister as a waxworks exhibit. We stayed only a few minutes in this green-lit, melodramatic establishment, but it was clear that the unprofitable puff at the pipe was not to be avoided. One had to make some show of going to the devil.

I was lodged in the minor palace of the *Conseiller de la République*, the senior French official in Northern Laos, a Monsieur Leveau. The *Conseiller* was a man whose shyness and slight reserve of manner failed to mask a quite extraordinary hospitality. He never, for instance, issued a formal invitation to a meal, preferring with an air of casual assumption to say something like: 'Of course, you'll be dining at home tonight.' Monsieur Leveau was married to a Laotian wife, to whom I was not presented, and the huge official building always seemed strangely empty. We dined facing each other across a darkly gleaming wasteland of ambassadorial table. Sometimes a Laotian servant stole into the room carrying dishes; trailing behind him the distant sounds of a domestic interior. These were immediately sealed off by the closing of the door, leaving us to the vault-like silences of the huge room. As we sat there the light bulbs gave out in various parts of the room and were swiftly replaced. In Luang Prabang the electric current was switched on at the same time as the water was turned off — at seven-thirty. But the result was no more than a feeble striving of the filament, and the lamp in my bedroom produced a light considerably less than that of one candle. Monsieur Leveau partly got over this difficulty by enormously over-running lamps intended for a much lower voltage, but they did not last long.

After dinner, when the Conseiller relaxed for an hour, he could sometimes be persuaded to talk about some of his problems. These were the chronic worries of the Issarak and the Viet-Minh. To the west of Luang Prabang the frontier with Burma started, and Burmese irregulars crossed it from time to time. Chinese opium smugglers conducted a regular trade with the Meos, and turned pirate when business was bad. But now that the communists had taken over in Yunnan there was some signs of this traffic slackening. And then the Meos themselves. They were passing like a blight through the mountains. Leveau's ambition was to change their agricultural habits. If they could be persuaded to come down to 1000 feet he could give them irrigated rice-fields to cultivate, and had offered to provide the buffaloes to do the work.

I brought up the question of the Khas. The Khas are the aboriginals of Laos and are, in fact, Moï tribes under another name. Several hundred years ago they were conquered and enslaved by the Laotian nation, and now Khas were to be seen hanging about the market places of Laotian towns and villages, utterly broken and degenerate; as helpless as the pathetic remnants of once powerful Indian tribes in North America. I asked if it was true that Laotians still possessed Kha slaves. Leveau smiled in his tolerant and sceptical Laotian way and said that it all depended what you meant by slavery. The slavery of the old West Indian plantation kind was unknown in the Far East. For superstitious if for no other reasons, the peoples of Indo-China always trod very gently when it came to oppression of others. The spirits of their ancestors had to be reckoned with, and they themselves if pushed too far might be forced to revenge themselves by the efficient, occult methods strangers were always imagined to possess. He cited the well-known fact of a collective bad-conscience on the part of the Vietnamese, who conduct special sacrifices and offer symbolical rent to the spirits of the unknown aboriginal possessors of the land they now occupy. Leveau believed that slavery did occasionally exist, but that it took more the form of a racial aristocracy maintaining a subject people in a condition of moral inferiority. The fact that a labourer happened to receive no money for his services hardly entered into the question, since we were not dealing with a money society and no one in Laos worked for more than his keep.

Leveau mentioned, as I had already heard, that there is evidence that the Khas before they were over-run possessed great artistic ability. He showed me as a proof a large bronze drum he possessed. This was identical with one in possession of the Musée de L'Homme which is described as being used by the Karens of Burma in the ritual conjuration of rain. A similar one illustrated in Maurice Collis's book *The First Holy One*, is represented as a Chinese War Drum of the Han Dynasty. The drum, which was cast by the *cire perdue* method, is decorated with an almost chaotic richness of design sometimes found in Chinese metal mirrors. It depicts in the greatest detail the activities of a primitive people, living by hunting, fishing and rice-growing. There are processions led by dancers with castanets and accompanied by musicians playing the *Kène*. Their long-houses are depicted as are crescent-shaped boats full of warriors in feathered head-dresses, carrying bows, javelins and axes. Birds and animals are shown in profusion, and the species are recognizable. According to the information of Monsieur Victor Goloubew of the École Française d'Extrème-Orient, these drums were found in large quantities in a burial ground in Tonkin and date from the period of Chinese domination, about two thousand years ago. The same authority affirms that the art in question is related to that of the Dyaks, and of the Bataks of Sumatra, while the technique of the workmanship is Chinese. This suggests that these people together with the Moïs, the Khas and the Karens may all once have been united in a homogeneous bronze-age culture — strongly influenced by the Chinese — which was probably at a far higher level than their present ones.

It remains to be said that such drums as have come into the ownership of citizens of Luang Prabang, in sad and symbolical descent from their original high function, now serve as cocktail tables.

288

It was fitting that at Luang Prabang the impetus of travel should have spent itself. Not even convoys ever came as far as this. Groups of unfortunate men occasionally set off on foot and walked for as long as three weeks through jungle trails to relieve isolated posts. Other arrivals and departures were by a weekly D.C.3 plying between Luang Prabang and Vientiane. It was booked up well ahead.

Down at the riverside the story was much the same as at Vientiane. There were pirogues which supposedly made regular journeys, but no one was prepared to commit himself to positive information about them. One authority went so far as to say that it was out of the question to hope to travel north by pirogue because the river was too low at this time of the year. I had just thanked him when the engine of what looked like a totally abandoned hulk, lying in an oily pool not far away, suddenly burst into wheezy activity. One of the crew of two said that they would be leaving in half an hour. Bound for where? — Vientiane? No . . . Xieng Khong — for the unnavigable north, of course. All the space had been reserved for a body of ex-pirates who had changed sides and had now, it was said, demanded to be sent back to fight their former allies.

While I was slowly piecing together this jig-saw of information in pidgin-French, the brand-new patriots arrived for embarkation; a most apathetic looking body of men. In their ill-fitting uniforms they were standardized; deprived of individuality by a common factor of misery, an ingrained habit of expressionless stoicism. Silently they filed up the gang-plank and filled the dim interior of the pirogue. It was difficult to believe that the fire of conviction burned in any of these breasts, and I felt sorry for the French N.C.O. who was being sent back in charge.

But Monsieur Leveau said that there would also be a pirogue going south one day, and to save me from being victimized by Chinese cat-and-mouse tactics he sent for the owner and asked him when the boat would leave. With gentle satisfaction the Chinese

289

immediately replied that the engine had broken down. Monsieur Leveau had been as ready for this as I had been, and said that he would send a mechanic down to inspect the engine. To this the Chinese replied that the repair was already in hand, and would be done by tomorrow — approximately. (The latter word, with which the Chinese protect their flanks in argument, corresponds to an equivalent in their own language — *Ch'a pu to* — and is never out of their mouths.) And after that? the Conseiller asked. The Chinese thought and said that he would have to give the boat a trial. This would take another day — approximately. And then? Well, then he would have to see about getting some cargo, which, after all, depended upon other people, and not on him. Shaking his head sadly, Leveau sent him away. There was something indomitable about this clearcut determination to have no truck with Western ideas about time and organization. Leveau told him to report every day as to the progress that was being made. But each day, the news of a difficulty resolved was accompanied by another protective imponderable, and then the trump card was slyly produced: the reported lowness of the water through the rapids which might make it impossible to go as far as Vientiane. It was quite clear that nothing short of the direct action of a War Lord or a Commissar could have compelled this man to go against his national tradition and commit himself to a definite promise.

And now there were other difficulties including money ones. Through the artificial pegging of the piastre at about two and a half times its real value, Indo-China is very expensive. The further one goes from Saigon the more expensive it becomes, because all supplies have to be brought by lengthy and laborious methods of transport. At Luang Prabang the bad, weak beer which cost about two and fourpence a bottle in Saigon, had reached eight shillings after a 15,000-mile trip up the Mékong. All other prices were in proportion. I was therefore becoming uncomfortably short of money, and it was an alarming thought that I might be stranded several weeks before the force of circumstance compelled the

Chinese pirogue owner to set out for Vientiane. Even when this date was fixed, and supposing that it were quite soon, there were the provisions for the voyage to be thought about. If everything went well it would take five days — or nights, as they say in Indo-China — downstream. But if a breakdown happened it might take two or three times as long. I was warned by Dupont that it would be impossible to buy anything in the Laotian villages: even to the number of eggs laid by the hens, everything was calculated so that no more than the bare essential was produced.

The other difficulty was that of a slow, progressive and hardly perceptible decline in health; a wasting away of the energy, and a seeping paralysis of the will. Comparing each day's performance with the previous one I could not measure the increase in lethargy. But when I remembered how I had felt and what I had been able to do a month previously; how even at Angkor I had walked mile after mile through the ruins in the rabid sunshine — it was by this that I could gauge the decline. Quite suddenly my strength had gone. I could only walk slowly and welcomed with relief the hour of the siesta. The siesta was slowly eating into the day, and now tended to last all the afternoon. It was as essential as eating and I could never imagine that I should ever be able to discontinue the habit, even in England.

I first put it down to the special kind of heat, to which even the natives of these countries never accustom themselves. It has greatly affected their history. The mountain peoples, attracted by the easy, abundant life of the hot river valleys came down, settled there and with the formidable gift of leisure, built, while their reserve of energy lasted, those brilliant, freakish civilizations that were never given the chance to grow up. Soon they relapsed into peaceful decadence, adopted religions which were suitable to their decline and which also fostered it, and became adepts of sleep. After the hour of the mid-day meal, Luang Prabang and all Laos is trance-bound. No living thing moves at this season until five in the evening.

But it was beginning to seem to me that, even allowing for the heat, something must be wrong. A hill rises sharply in the middle of the town, topped by a glittering pagoda. The climb up to this, long put off, was so thoroughly exhausting that it used up the day's supply of energy. The pagoda when I finally got there was very small and contained a collection of mouldering wooden Buddhas. The re-decorating bonzes had not been able to bring themselves to climb up here, so that most of the paintwork and gilding had weathered away, to the carvings' great advantage. But there seemed to have been a recent clear-out, perhaps in preparation for a re-furbishing to come. The images that were too far gone in decay had been stuffed into niches of the surrounding rocks, one of which bore a bright yellow poster which I supposed at first to have some religious significance, but which proved to be an advertisement for the Victory Brand Glorious Firecracker Company, and showed a Chinese nationalist soldier giving the V sign. The attraction of the pagoda lay in its doors, deeply carved with a graceful, swirling design of foliage, dancers and elephants. In either direction one looked out upon a very Chinese scene of mountains and rivers barely sketched in mist. It was viewed through the bare scrawny branches of frangipani trees planted round the pagoda, and at a lower level the slopes were clouded with the flowering trees bearing the blossoms which are called locally golden flowers of Burma.

After the descent from the pagoda I actually felt the need of a pre-lunch nap, and slightly alarmed I asked a French acquaintance's advice. Characteristically, he recommended me to a Sino-Viet-namese doctor, celebrated, he said, for his almost magical cures. This readiness to put one's faith in exotic medicine is another phase of going native. I have seen it happen before in Central America where people of European origin are quite ready to have themselves treated by Indian *shimans*, excusing themselves with a 'you never know; there may be something in it, after all'. In this case I had formed the private theory that amoebic dysentery might be the trouble, which, while it exhausts the vitality, does not always produce the familiar symptoms. Should this have been the doctor's opinion I was rather hoping, for the experience of it, that he would treat me, following the well-known Cambodian method, by an extract of the bark of the *pon* tree, which is only completely effective when the patient is allowed to cut the bark himself, removing it from the tree at a little above the level of his navel.

The Sino-Vietnamese doctor practised in a well-built single-roomed shack, with a good-sized garden and a river-view. The garden trees were decorated with offerings to the water spirits which naturally predominate in such a riverine town as Luang Prabang. They were contained in miniature ships made from banana leaves, with very high prows and sterns — far higher than those of the local pirogues. Since Laotian spirits have a highly developed aesthetic sense, they had also been offered red flowers. Egg shells had been thrust into the holes and cavities of the trees, perhaps for the benefit of landlubber genii. Unless this was the work of a domestic, the doctor evidently believed in doing in Rome what the Romans did.

Dr. Nam Tuan Thanh received me in his consulting-room, a curtained-off corner of his hut, which was adorned with flowers in brass vases, coloured photographs of members of his family and several framed diplomas. The doctor was dressed with extreme professional conservatism in a gown of dark blue silk decorated with the Chinese character for longevity. A few distinguished white hairs trailed from the point of his chin and the corners of his upper lip.

The doctor's manner was sympathetic but gently authoritarian. Grasping both wrists he quickly palpated the nine pulses recognized in Chinese medicine on each; corresponding in each case to an organ or group of organs. This was followed by a brief examination of the finger nails, after which the doctor pronounced me to be a classic example of a chronic excess of *yang* over *yin* — the positive and negative bodily humours — somewhat complicated by a minor obstruction of the *k'i*, or vital fluid. The condition thus originated in the liver — the most prominent *yang* organ, which, however, sympathetically influenced the *yin* organs corresponding to it — the spleen and the pancreas. The obstruction of the *k'i* said Doctor Tuan Thanh, with perhaps the merest hint of contempt, was of nervous or psychological origin, and would clear up of its own account. As for the lack of balance between *yang* and *yin*, it would need much treatment and he would content himself with providing me with a few pointers for future reference. I should limit myself, carefully avoiding the remedies classified as *pou, sheng, san, piao* and *yao*, to the category of medicaments known as *chiang* which comprised the metallic salts and oils of oleaginious seeds. Moreover I should remember that I was dominated by the number nine and the Western direction. The spirit should be refreshed as often as possible by the contemplation of white flowers. And I could expect to feel much better in the autumn.

In the meanwhile, he said, it might help matters, if only as a temporary measure, for an acapuncture to be performed, which, however, would not be completely effective owing to the overcast sky. Instructing me to lie on my side on his couch, the doctor removed a short metal needle from a lacquered case, gazed at it affectionately, and telling me to cough, thrust it into the back of each thigh. After that I was given a dose of what tasted like Epsom salts, and the doctor, examining the eighteen pulses again, told me that I was feeling better; which, owing to the natural stimulus of the circumstance, I of course was.

In one respect, at least, I found that the doctor had fallen into line with Western usages. In Cambodia, at any rate, the fee for successful treatment — and no fee is charged unless the treatment is successful — is a length of calico, four betel leaves, an areca nut, four handfuls of cooked rice and a wax candle stuck in a slice of bamboo trunk. The doctor had commuted such payment in kind to a simple sum in Indo-Chinese piastres.

Next day, Monsieur Leveau mentioned that he had news of a

military plane which had been parachuting supplies to a post somewhere in the north and which might stop at Luang Prabang on its
way back to Vientiane. At the military headquarters they told me
that it was not certain whether the plane would be stopping or not,
but that if it did, it should arrive at about three in the afternoon.
They had not been able to establish any radio contact with it. It
was not thought that any attempt would be made to land after that
hour because of the deepening haze and the fact that Luang Prabang
was in a basin in the mountains, which made the take-off a difficult
one.

I was beginning to feel an unreasoning horror at the prospect of
a long enforced idleness in Luang Prabang and this news filled me
with high hopes. But at three o'clock there was no plane, and as
nothing had been heard of it by four o'clock, all expectations were
given up. The sun had now disappeared again, smothered in the
thickening mist, and the town's edges had gone soft in the flat,
yellow light. One was imprisoned in air that felt like a tepid bath.
Breathing was an effort.

At five o'clock a vibration crept over the sky, swelling presently
into the waxing and waning of aero-engines. Within a few minutes
the plane was overhead, and seemed, always invisible, to be making
a slow, spiralling descent. Soon after, Dupont's red jeep came
tearing up through the mist. He said that the plane was coming in
to land but that if it took off again, it would do so immediately.
I threw my things into the jeep and waved goodbye to Leveau,
who said that it was too late for the plane to leave that night, and
that he would expect me to dinner. Dupont, an amateur of emergency, tore down to the river bank, hooting and gesticulating for
the ferry boat. By the time we were on the river we could see the
plane overhead, only a few hundred feet up and when we reached
the field, it had just landed; an ancient Junkers JU 51, palsied with
vibration as it lumbered up the runway, its three propellers slapping
idly.

It was now a quarter to six and in just over an hour the sweltering mist would deepen into night. The *droppermen* wanted to stay, but the pilot was determined to go on to Vientiane, and with thunder rumbling like heavy traffic beyond the unseen rim of the mountains, we took off. The pilot had no idea of how things were in Vientiane, because the radio wasn't working, and there was no time to circle to make height. Instead we were going to fly straight down the gorges of the Mékong, and as long, he mentioned, as we could see the river without being forced down so low as to be caught in down draughts, it should be all right. And so we went, charging into the heart of the mountains, which were usually veiled from us, but sometimes billowed out, grey and ugly, from the mist. There were crags and pinnacles that towered up and then suddenly sank down, leaning sickeningly away, as the pilot turned steeply from them; and once we passed quite near to a shrine perched on a rock jutting out of empty space. At last a *dropperman*, looking at his watch, said that we were through the mountains. Almost immediately, it seemed, the light went out. We were shrouded in the murk of a London railway terminus approach.

We landed at Vientiane at the beginnings of a tremendous thunderstorm; the crashing overture to the rainy season. The lightning was a continuous coloured display; an idle manipulation of theatrical lighting effects, through which one saw as in a spotlight the prodigious concussion of the rain that in a few days would clear the Laotian skies again — and wash away its roads.

CHAPTER XX

THE VIET-MINH

I BELIEVE that many political conspirators derive satisfaction from self-dramatization and that this taste for situations based on fictional models often complicates their lives unnecessarily.

As soon as I had returned to Saigon from Laos I was invited to meet an agent who had just come from the headquarters of Nguyen-Binh, the General in command of the Southern Viet-Minh armies. He was to be responsible for my safe conduct into Viet-Minh occupied territory. I was sure that the setting chosen for the meeting had been lifted from spy or detective fiction.

Visiting one of the Cholon dancing places in response to a note left at the hotel, I found there my dance-hostess friend. Excusing herself at the table where she had been sitting, she came over and gave me a piece of paper with an address on it. I was to go there at eleven next morning. There was no one I could ask for. She had just been given the address, and that was all she knew.

The address, I found, was that of a doctor's surgery in a crowded back street of Cholon. Soon after my arrival in Indo-China I should have been delighted by this jostling vociferous humanity; the children playing with bottle tops, the coolies limping under their loads, the rich men in sharkskin, the beggars and the dogs; but now I was hardened and immunized. When I found that the place was a surgery, I wondered if I had been given the right address. There was a pagoda on one side and a café on the other, but no signs of any private houses. I went in and found myself in a waiting-room with Oriental patients lining the walls. It was probably the first time a European had ever been in that room, and I felt awkward and conspicuous, but, as usual, no one looked up. After a few minutes a door at the end of the room opened, and a woman carrying a baby came out. A white-gowned doctor stood framed in the doorway behind her, beckoning to the next patient. He did not seem to see me. Another woman went in, and the door shut behind her.

There seemed to be nothing to do but sit down and wait. I sat down in a chair left vacant at the end of one line, after all the patients had just moved up one. The door opened again and the woman who had just gone in came out. Through the opening I saw an interior lined with gleaming gadgets. Now the doctor would come again and this time he would see me. I was already quarter of an hour late for the appointment. When the rather stern-looking, elderly figure appeared again I made a slight gesture, but was ignored. The patient at the end got up and went in and we all moved up one. I was beginning to be convinced that I had come to the wrong address and could imagine a ridiculous situation arising when it came to my turn to enter the surgery. A few passers-by came in to chat with friends in the waiting-room, bringing with them the tremendous din of the street. After them squeezed a blind beggar with a splendid, old-fashioned Tonkinese hat, a yard across, and then came a seller of iced sugar-cane juice and a goldfish-hawker. A china cuckoo-clock 'marque jazz' shrilled the half-hour, and one or two of the patients, glancing up, began to unwrap their snacks. The surgery door opened again, and just at that moment the young man sitting next to me spoke. 'Are you the foreigner who wants to go for a walk in the country?' he said. I said yes, I was.

He introduced himself as Dinh — an assumed name, he assured me, with a wry smile. I was interested to notice, in support of a theory I was beginning to form, that for a Vietnamese he was very 'unmongolian' in appearance. He was thin-lipped and cadaverous and there was an unusual narrowness across the cheekbones. If not a Frenchman he could certainly have passed for a Slav. There had been many Caucasian characteristics about the other Vietnamese intellectuals and revolutionaries I had met, and I was wondering whether whatever physcial mutation it was that produced this decrease in mongolian peculiarities encouraged at the same time the emergence of certain well-known Western traits, such as restless aggressiveness, an impatience with mere contemplation, and a taste for action.

Dinh informed me that all the arrangements had been made for my journey and that I should be taken wherever I wanted to go in Viet-Minh territory. The only difficulty would be in crossing the lines. He could not say exactly when we should be ready to start.

A young girl who had been sitting opposite now got up and came across to join us. Dinh introduced her as Gnuyet, adding that the name meant 'moonlight'. She made a face at this disclosure and apologized for the name's being so old-fashioned. She was the most beautiful girl I had seen in the Far East, and was sixteen. Dinh said that she would be travelling with me. She had been wounded and had been given leave to come to Saigon to convalesce with her parents. Having always understood that there were no women fighting in the Viet-Minh army, I asked her how she came to be wounded. She said that she had been caught in a parachutist's raid while giving a propaganda and theatrical show in a village. She had been prevented by her costume from getting away and had been shot and left for dead and had actually heard the order given for her burial, but had managed to crawl away after nightfall. She was obviously very proud to have been wounded, and anxious to get back. Her contempt for the frivolities of Saigon was measureless.

'In the *maquis* we only eat twice a day,' she said, with austere satisfaction. 'A little fish with rice. Some of our brothers and sisters who have been used to over-indulgence find it difficult at first, but they soon get used to it. But then, the life is very healthy. We start the day at five with physical exercises. And, of course, running and hiking are very popular. It is all good for the health. People are full of joy. They are always smiling. In the liberated territory there is a great deal of music. Everyone is expected to play a musical instrument. But not decadent music, of course. Beethoven and Bach — yes. We like them very much.'

And so, breathlessly, it went on. It was a revivalism, but an Asiatic brand of revivalism. An ultra-puritanical movement is launched at the drop of a hat in these countries. The prohibition of smoking ('some of our brothers and sisters do it in secret on the junks'), of gambling, of drinking, of feminine make-up; the rough standardized clothing, the communal pastimes, the obligatory sports, the compulsory culture ('in our spare time we volunteer to educate the peasants') . . . it is all repugnant to Western individualism and habits of freedom. But state interference in almost every aspect of the citizen's existence was the normal thing under the paternalistic system of government of Viet-Nam before the European's arrival. A modern communist state is libertarian by comparison with Viet-Nam under Gia-Long, the last of the great Emperors.

Dinh's enthusiasm was more reasoned than that of the girl, and when the girl had gone out he even allowed himself a slightly bitter reflection. I asked in a roundabout way if Viet-Minh losses had been very heavy, and he said that practically all those who were in the movement from the beginning had been killed. 'All except the intellectuals,' he then added. 'The intellectuals don't get themselves killed.'

I asked him why the Viet-Minh permitted minor acts of terrorism in Saigon, such as the nightly throwing of grenades into cafés and into cinema entrances. He said that the reason for this was that the owners had failed to pay their contributions towards Viet-Minh funds, and were therefore made an example of. In a way, it was also to show disapproval of such frivolities when there was a war on. He said that jobs of this kind were done by selected 'executioners', and, using the word, he grimaced with distaste.

These tentative arrangements fell through. It was unfortunate for me that at this time the Viet-Minh started several small, simultaneous offensives, the most serious of them being at Tra-Vinh, about thirty miles south of Saigon. Nothing could be done while the battle was going on.

After a few days I had another interview with Dinh; once again in the doctor's waiting-room. As it seemed as though I might be kept waiting for weeks to make the official visit to the General's headquarters on the *Plaine des Joncs*, I asked whether something less ambitious could be arranged. I mentioned a certain engineering firm I had heard of, which, although working on the French account, was actually allowed to pass unmolested in any way through Viet-Minh territory. The engineers used to travel every day in a private car down a road where not even a French armoured vehicle would have dared to show itself, and Viet-Minh soldiers sometimes strolled up to watch them at their work. It was another of those privately organized live-and-let-live arrangements, like the one by which foodstuffs are imported by Chinese go-betweens from Viet-Minh areas into Saigon. In this case, the construction work was allowed to go on because the Viet-Minh were clearly of the opinion that it was they who, one day, would derive the benefit from it.

I now asked Dinh whether, as I knew the engineers, and they had agreed to take me with them, it would not be possible to enter Viet-Minh territory in this way, and whether he could not obtain for me a safe conduct to allow me to move about freely once I got in. But the Vietnamese are formalists and bureaucrats by tradition. They revere the written word, documents that have been properly signed, stamped and counter-stamped, passwords, countersigns and standing orders. Having been governed for many centuries by a civil service into which it was the ambition of all to enter, they are respectfully familiar with all the delaying devices which such a system imposes. Behind the smoke screens of his excuses I was sure that the real trouble was that Dinh would have to refer back to higher authority for a decision.

The most important objection he raised was that the suggested area was cut off from the main body of Viet-Minh territory and that I should therefore miss all the show-pieces: the broadcasting station, the arms factories, the cloth mills, the schools, the 105 mm. howitzer recently captured from the French, and, most important of all, the 're-education' centres. I told him that as funds were running out and I should not be able to stay much longer in Indo-China, anything would be better than nothing at all. He agreed to inquire what could be done, and to give me the answer in two days.

When the two days had passed the Tra-Vinh battle was still being fought. The Viet-Minh had captured a large number of defence-towers and instead of withdrawing as usual with the captured equipment, they brought up reinforcements and awaited the French counter-attack. Ambushes were laid for the French troops rushed from other areas, and further diversionary attacks were launched in neighbouring provinces. Neither the French nor Dinh knew whether any of these might not develop into the general offensive the Viet-Minh had promised before the dry season broke. It was therefore agreed that I might go with the engineers to the town in question, where I was to wait at a certain hotel, and an attempt would be made to pick me up. If the worst came to the worst it would simply mean sleeping a night there and being brought back by the engineers – who made the trip daily – next day. Viet-Minh troops and partisans in the town would be warned of my presence.

Next afternoon I left Saigon in the car belonging to a director of the engineering firm. It was driven by one of the junior employees who had just arrived from Europe, was not a Frenchman and knew nothing whatever of the political situation. It was he who had staggered the French in Saigon by his description of how he had fraternized with a Viet-Minh patrol. He had been swimming in a river at the time and had found them waiting for him when he came out. A quite friendly chat followed and when the patrol found out he was a foreigner they shook hands and went off. My friend who still didn't know the difference between Viet-Minh and Viet-Nam believed his nationality a kind of talisman protecting him from dangers of all kinds. I told him that to a Vietnamese all

Europeans looked exactly the same, but he refused to believe it. He was quite sure that his extra ten per cent of Mediterranean characteristics was universally recognizable.

After Laos, Cochin-China was harsh and brilliant. It was as if the earth had gone to rust at the tail-end of the dry season. Sometimes there was a crystalline glitter where the sunlight shattered on the tiles of a flattened tomb. Buffaloes scrambled over the parched earth, bearing gleaming crescents of horns. The lagoons had blackened in stagnant concentration, and the peasants groping for fish were stained by the muddy water so that at a distance their circular hats seemed to float like brilliant money on the water. Junks were moving hull down through the canals and rivers, and only the sharks' fins of their sails could be seen cutting across the plains. An armoured car had nosed into a clump of palms, where several white-haired, pink-faced Teutons of the Foreign Legion hid from the sun.

The town contained a single, sordid, colourful little hotel. You went in through a café, passing under an awning of dried fish, to mount a narrow staircase in complete darkness. The rooms had swing doors like saloons, but the town must have lived through former days of grandeur as each chamber had a bath alcove. A Chinese lady was taking a bath in mine, but she soon dressed and came out and we smiled and bowed to each other in the passage. Radio sets appeared to be going at full blast in every room; all tuned in to different stations. Soon after my arrival the proprietor came up and asked me to pay. He brought with him a bottle of cherry-brandy and presented me with a drink on the house. The change was brought by a small oriental chambermaid, who sat on the edge of the brass bed, singing, while she counted out the incredibly filthy notes which she hoped that I would return to her in disgust.

A few minutes later the proprietor was back, with a Vietnamese girl of about twelve, who, he said, had come to take me to the house of a friend. Following this child I was taken to a gloomy little palace in a back street. Here I was invited to seat myself in a carved chair that was all the more throne-like from the fact that it was raised on a low dais, and left alone. A few minutes later the little girl was back again with a glass of lemonade and then once again with a saucer of nuts. The dragons and unicorns writhing through the mother-of-pearl-studded surfaces of the furniture gradually sank into darkness. It was night.

I was dozing when Dinh arrived. He was accompanied by a rather chinless and bespectacled youth called Trang and seemed cheerful and nervous at the same time. Both of them wore dungarees and carried Stens. Dinh had brought a pair of rubber boots which he told me to put on, but they were too small. He seemed worried about my white shirt and trousers, but when we got outside we found ourselves in brilliant moonlight. The dress made no difference. If possible they were more conspicuous than I was in their black against the broad, whitewashed surfaces of wall and road.

The streets were quite empty. Bao-Dai troops garrisoned two towers on the other side of the town, but Dinh said that they had orders never to leave the towers after sunset. We heard several distant rifle-shots which set the dogs barking, the barks ending in howls as the dogs were kicked into silence. We walked in the shadow of a wall; Dinh in front, followed by myself and then Trang. In a few minutes we were outside the town and scrambled down a low embankment into the rice-fields. We were on very low ground by the river, threading our way through a morass of quick-silver. Mist trailed in banks above the water. In the moonlight its surface was curiously solid. When we splashed through shallow pools a phosphorescence exploded round our boots. An enormous owl came flapping down to inspect us, and passed on with a strange, booming cry.

We reached a canal where a sampan awaited us, hidden among the water palms. Two soldiers standing in the boat held out their hands to steady us as we climbed aboard. They, too, were dressed in dark dungarees and wore Australian-type bush hats. We sat in the bottom of the sampan while the two soldiers, one standing at each end, began to row it along the canal. They rowed by a long single oar fastened to a post. After a short distance, one of them stopped rowing and tried to start up an engine. He had great difficulty, and Dinh held a torch while he took the carburettor to pieces. Trang said that the petrol was of very bad quality. They bought most of it from the Chinese who usually adulterated it with paraffin. In the end the engine was started. It was fitted with a very efficient silencing system, which Dinh said was of their own design. There were a few mechanical rattles, but no exhaust noise could be heard.

Little could be heard in fact along most of the reaches of water above the tremendous chirpings of frogs, which as we turned into narrow channels plopped into the water ahead of us in their hundreds. Twisting and turning through a maze of waterways we went on. The mosquitoes were very troublesome, biting through the three pairs of stockings I always wore, to get at their favourite area, the ankles, as well as feeding greedily on the neck, wrists and forehead. We passed clumps of water palms where fireflies were carrying on an extraordinary display, weaving a scroll-work through the fronds like the fancy terminals of the signatures of the Victorian era. In such a clump the sampan was stopped, with the engine switched off, while the soldiers listened to heavy mortar and machine-gun fire, which sounded, allowing for the water, as if it might be two or three miles away. A few hundred yards further on we stopped again. A dark shape, silhouetted by moonlight, lolled in the water ahead. Someone on our boat switched on a small searchlight and, as this happened, large aquatic birds flustered up with a great commotion from some low bushes among the reeds. The dark object was a sampan lying low in the water. We approached it slowly with levelled tommy-guns, but it was empty and partially waterlogged. Further down still, we ran into another obstacle; a log across the water. But this was the equivalent of a roadblock, and after an exchange of passwords with unseen guards on the bank it was pulled back far enough for us to pass through.

Soon after, a plane passed low overhead. It dropped a Very light a long way from us, so that the flickering reflection hardly imposed itself on the moonlight. The machine-gun and mortar fire started again. Dinh said in English 'exciting'. This was one of the three English adjectives he occasionally produced; the others being 'captivating' — used to describe any aspect of life in Viet-Minh territory — and 'regrettable' — reserved for the French and all their doings.

We stopped again when we overtook a sampan full of peasants. They were ordered ashore, where one of the soldiers, who it appeared was an officer, harangued them in angry tones. Dinh said that the brother officer had criticized them for failing to obey the curfew order; summary criticism being the lowest grade of disciplinary measures. And what came next? I asked. Arrest followed by public criticism, Dinh said. Although nobody wanted to be too hard on first offenders. I mentioned the old, Vietnamese simple correction of thirty strokes with the rattan cane, and Dinh said that naturally anyone would prefer that, as public criticism was so much less dignified. There had never been any stigma in a beating, because the offence was purged on the spot, but a public criticism took a lot of wearing down. People tended to say, there goes so-and-so who was publicly criticized. Psychological methods, besides being less barbarous, were more effective. A typical offence in the case of which such a punishment might be awarded, said Dinh, would be the failure, after warning, to build a proper outside latrine for the use of one's family.

We landed and went in single file up a lane through the palms. The moon was sinking now and the sound of the distant firing had ceased. In Indo-China the two sides seem to have reached an informal agreement to restrict their nocturnal combats to the early part of the night. Even the relentless chirping of the frogs had quietened. A few yards from the water's edge we came to huts made of branches and palm leaves. It was the local military headquarters.

Dinh explained that the unit, which had been newly established here, was chiefly occupied with observation of enemy movements, but that all male members were fully trained for combatant duties to which they could be transferred in emergency. It was one of a number of similar posts which formed an outside screen, interlinked by radio and sending back information to the army's headquarters in the centre of the *plaine des joncs*. Observers were sent out from here with portable signals equipment with which they kept a twenty-four-hourly observation of troop movements in a defined territory. This information was passed on regularly to the army signals centre where it was all pieced together and collated with the other information received, so that in theory a complete track was kept of the movement of every French patrol or operational group from the moment it left its barracks until it returned. A great deal of stress was laid upon the necessity for absolutely accurate information regarding numerical strengths and types of weapons carried. In this way army headquarters was able to decide whether the enemy was to be attacked or avoided. This particular post, Dinh said, owing to its perfect situation, was invulnerable, except from the air. It could only be approached by small, lightly armed craft which could be blown up in the narrow waterways by mines manufactured specially for this purpose. It was screened from the air by the method of building the administrative huts into the palms, close to the water's edge. Reconnaissance planes were never fired at, however low they flew. At a later stage — quite soon now, Dinh thought — these peripheral posts would throw out offshoots, further in the direction of French occupied territory, while they themselves would be transformed into battalion headquarters, with a purely operational function.

There was a second purpose which the post fulfilled. This was an educational and propaganda one. It was their job, for which they were allotted a certain time, to stamp out illiteracy in their area. From total literacy in the old pre-colonial days, when every man's ambition had been for his son to be able to compete in the civil service examinations, the literate minority of the population had dropped as low as twenty per cent. The people would now be educated, said Dinh, and in the interior of Viet-Minh territory where peaceful conditions prevailed it had been declared (with a touch of the old authoritarian sternness) a punishable offence to be unable to read and write. In frontier areas such as this it was left to public opinion. To be illiterate was unpatriotic, the Viet-Minh had told the peasants. And when they could read the Viet-Minh would of course supply their intellectual food.

By the time we arrived all the personnel of the post, with the exception of the duty staff, were already in bed. Dinh explained that the last meal was taken at five o'clock, and after that parties went canoeing, swimming or walking, or to their improving labours in the villages. But for the last week they had all been virtually confined to barracks owing to the fighting in the neighbourhood. Radio warnings had been received of several marine-commando raids in their area, and once they had been obliged to send men to create a diversion when a nearby post had been attacked. We had timed our arrival, it seemed, most unfortunately.

The commander of the post now came in. He had been out watching the attack which we had heard and which had been directed against a group of towers held by Bao-Dai forces. He was about twenty-five years of age, small, slight and grave, with features blunted with deep pock marks. He carried no badges of rank, but was the equivalent, Dinh said, of a captain. Officers were not saluted and were called brother, like anyone else. 'A respect for his superiors is second nature to any Vietnamese. It could not be increased by the addition of titles.'

Apologizing for being too busy to show me round in person, the commander said that there had been a flare-up of activity in all sectors and that Bao-Dai troops drafted into the area had just received orders to attack them. I asked how they knew that, and the commander smiling rather distantly said that it was their business to know. To forestall any such attack, it had, at all events, been decided to capture all the towers, and a combat team had been sent with the necessary assault equipment. Asked whether the towers would be held when captured, the commander said no, there was no point in it. They would be demolished. Two towers had been taken that night, but he thought that army headquarters might have decided to make a daylight attack on those that remained. Where possible they liked to have a camera-man filming such actions so that the staff officers could see how the commanders in the field were doing their jobs and correct their mistakes where necessary. Films of well-organized attacks also served instructional and propaganda purposes.

I asked whether it would be possible to see such an operation, and the commander, with a trace of coldness in his manner, said he thought it was extremely unlikely. He had no authority whatever to give permission. Regretting perhaps his somewhat blunt refusal, he then said that actions of this kind were sometimes dangerous. Usually the tower surrendered without opposition at all, or only a token opposition, because they were always attacked in greatly superior force. But on one occasion recently, after a surrender had been arranged by peaceful negotiation, and at the moment when the Viet-Minh party was advancing to take over, the tower had opened fire, killing the officer commanding and a high official who had been sent to observe from headquarters. That, said the commander, was a rare example of a bungle. But it went to show that accidents did happen.

Among the statistical charts with which the room was decorated was a propaganda poster. It consisted of a map of the world with China and the Soviet Union united in a huge red mass. Across were written words in Vietnamese, which the Commander said meant, 'These people are with you.' He added, 'Our enemies are slowly converting us to communism. If it is only by becoming communists that we shall achieve our liberty, then we shall become communists.'

We slept on bunks in the guard-hut. Mosquito nets were provided and there was a box of anti-malarial tablets open on a table. I was awakened before dawn by a bugle blowing but went off to sleep and awoke again when the sun was well up. Washing was done in a hut fitted with wooden bowls lined with sheet-metal. Large jars full of water were provided. Dinh, who was already up and came into the wash-room, said that filling the jars from the river was one of the rota fatigues, like cooking and other domestic tasks.

Afterwards he suggested a dip and we went down and swam about in a pool of warmish, yellow water. Dinh mentioned that this was reserved for males only and that the ladies' bathing pool was further along the river, modestly screened, I noticed, with an unusually dense growth of water palm. There had been a period, Dinh said, when 'naturism' and mixed sunbathing had received official sanction as cultural relaxations, allotted their half-hour in the day's approved activities. But now they were viewed with disfavour, along with the composition of lyrical poetry, as unfavourable to the development of a realistic attitude towards present problems. Love affairs, too, were detrimental to efficiency and were something to be kept, like smoking, for furtive indulgence in the bottoms of junks.

At ten o'clock the first meal was served; a Quakerish affair, girls on one side of the table, eyes demurely lowered, and men on the other, all dressed in black calico. The temptation to stare at the European must have been great. Dinh said that in the interior of Viet-Minh territory some of the young people have not seen a Westerner since early childhood, and that their first experience of the fierce, red, and often bearded features of the enemy was particularly terrifying.

The meal consisted of *tit-ca* — pork stewed in coconut milk — and balls of *riz gluant*. Gluant, which means sticky, is exactly what the rice is not, and it could not possibly be more unlike the boiled rice eaten in England. Each separate grain is firm, greyish in colour and practically dry; but the cooking is done in such a way that the grains adhere to each other and can be kneaded into balls. There was a poor quality *nuóc-mâm* to dip it in; thin, black and powerfully malodorous. The food was eaten rapidly and in silence, fifteen minutes being allowed. It would be followed by fifteen minutes rest and then a short period of calisthenics, Dinh informed me. The commander corrected him. Conforming to a new directive, the second morning period of physical culture had been discontinued, but could be replaced, if circumstances permitted, with community singing. A jug of water and a bowl stood at the door of the hut, and all washed their hands as they went out to their rather staid, oriental version of Strength through Joy.

The post had a prisoner they were very proud of. They excused themselves by saying that they had not had the chance to send him back to the army cage. But it was clear that they were really keeping him as long as they possibly could, and that he was regarded much as the pet boa-constrictor had been in the ideal French post — a fabulous monster which, once rendered harmless, had become a mascot; an object of amiable curiosity. He was a German legionary who had been found, more or less by accident, after his jeep had been blown up by one of their bamboo mines. The mine seemed not to have been very powerful as the other occupants of the car got away, leaving this man who had leg injuries. The Commander said that he had been found quite sympathetic to their cause, and undoubtedly had been compelled to fight for the French. He expected that after an indoctrination course and a period of observation he would be offered the chance to enlist in the Viet-Minh army. Dinh mentioned that the loyalty of suitable candidates of this kind was tested at the end of their indoctrination, by giving them every opportunity to escape. When commando raids were made in the neighbourhood of prisoner-of-war cages, the guards dispersed, telling the prisoners to stay where they were. Those who did so received good conduct marks and some small privileges.

No guard had been placed on the hut where the prisoner lay. Apart from his leg wounds, the Commander said, neither he nor anyone could ever hope to escape through the maze of waterways. The German was small, dark and slender; diminished, too, perhaps, by his misfortunes. He lay in the bunk in his uniform with his legs in paper bandages. When he found out that I was not another prisoner he was at first rather sullen and hostile. I asked him how he felt, and he said that his legs hurt him all the time and he would give a year's pay for a packet of cigarettes. At first he refused to give his name but later he said that it was Breczina. He was a Sudeten and had been an *unterscharführer* in the Waffen S.S. — a selected man, he said — and had been wounded on the Russian and Western fronts. To my inquiry as to the treatment he had received, he said that he couldn't complain, but that the food was filth. And was it true that he had been converted to the Viet-Minh's point of view? He made a face. I could imagine what he thought of reds, he said, but if the worst came to the worst, he would sooner be an officer in the Viet-Minh army — and they had told him that Germans from the Legion sometimes got commissions — than rot in a prisoner-of-war camp again. His fate was of little importance, since the defeat of Germany had proved for him that there was no purpose behind the universe. At the moment he was inconvenienced only by the loss of his spectacles, and his one sorrow was that what had happened to him had still further postponed the day when he would see his parents again. He had not seen them since he left school to enter the army.

Later in the day there was some air activity. A plane came over and circled the area several times, as if it were taking photographs. The temptation to fire at it must have been great as it flew very low. Dinh thought that there would have been a fifty-fifty chance of bringing it down with machine-gune fire. He said that the Viet-Minh were badly provided with anti-aircraft defence in the south and that there was a standing order that immediately a gun had been fired it had to be removed to another site. Soon after the plane appeared, a whistle was blown as a signal for all personnel to take cover, and later an order was issued that no one not on duty was to leave the huts for the rest of the day. Front line experiences, unless with an army on the move, are very restricted in their scope, and when the sector happens to be a small island screened by walls of vegetation in a swamp, one might as well be in a submarine for all one sees.

It was arranged that we should leave as soon as it was dark, since, as there had been no daylight activity, the night was expected to be a lively one. We boarded the sampan at dusk, and from the commander's last minute cordiality it was clear that he was relieved to see us go.

Once again the night was of a rare and perfect brilliance, with a sky of transparent gun-metal fenced in by a tall horizon of white palms. Through shining spear-hedged lanes we thrust forward with a gondola smoothness; pulling into a bank at last, where we left the sampan and climbed a low hillock. Here once had been a village, for although the shacks housing the living had disappeared a cluster of old substantial tombs remained; a stark revelation of bone-white stone in the neutral earth. On three sides stretched out a bleached-paper jungle of palms, but ahead was clear ground. In the centre of this cleared stage, about a mile away, a tower rose up; a small, neat, medieval shape, with its low girdle of bamboo; isolated in a plain which shone with the dull granularity of an ice-rink. 'I have a surprise for you,' Dinh said, looking at his watch. 'In fifteen minutes the attack will begin.'

But fifteen minutes later nothing happened. Another fifteen minutes passed and Dinh was getting nervous. The assault party would be there, he said, but undoubtedly hidden from us by some unseen dip in the terrain. And then a faint growling could be heard, the distorted ramblings of a radio set badly tuned in, or the un-natural bass of a gramophone running down. 'The loudspeakers,'

Dinh said, in triumph. The tower was being invited to surrender.

The growling stopped and there was a long silence. It was drama of a high order, its effect heightened by the setting and the strange theatrical lighting. There was the tower, a graceful well-made toy, solid and intact. At this moment the dozen or score of men who defended it would be cowering somewhere in its base, having crawled perhaps for extra protection, as one sometimes does in such emergencies, under quite unsubstantial pieces of furniture. And at any moment this would crumple before our eyes, dissolve or fall apart in the slow-motion that always seems to attend such violent dissolution seen from a distance. It was like the moment in the bull ring when the door of the pen is flung open and one awaits the bull's onrushing entry with excitement and a faint trepidation.

There was a slight disturbance in the plain at an enormous distance from the tower, which gathered itself into a silver puff of smoke, and then lost shape again. An explosion thumped in our ears. It seemed impossible that the mortar-bomb had been aimed at the tower. Another insignificant bubble of smoke formed and floated upward. It was much nearer than the first, but still a long way away. Dinh thought that this might be an inexperienced team who were being given some practice. It was clear from the violence of the explosions that an unusually heavy mortar was being used, but it was also clear that it was hopeless for this task. A quite small gun would have blown the tower off the face of the earth in a few rounds, but unless one of the mortar-bombs could be landed fair and square on the sloping roof of the tower it was clearly useless.

And now there was a faint, distant screeching as of a heavy iron gate turning upon its hinge, and we both ducked slightly. The screeching ended in an explosion that was sharper but less heavy than that of the mortar-bombs, and the puff of smoke was nearer to the tower than the others had been. The attackers were under fire from a French twenty-five pounder. Another whistle seemed to be coming straight at us, and we crouched down behind the low wall of a tomb as black earth fanned out half way between us and the tower. Dinh said in English, 'exciting'. At the same moment, almost, smoke spurted at the foot of the tower, and we saw pin-points of fire, which lasted for a few seconds and then went out. 'A direct hit,' Dinh said. 'They will surrender now.' And sure enough, we could just make out an insect movement beyond the stockade, soon absorbed in a fold in the earth. The garrison had given in. A few more twenty-five pounder shells came over, and then the silence closed in.

Asiatics could still be content, it seemed, to settle their differences, if left to themselves, with such a mild display of pyrotechnics. A whiff of powder and a face-saving show of resistance lasting half an hour, and it was all over. For the defeated it would be followed by a decent probationary period of indoctrination, and then a change of flag. All this was not so far removed from the old Sino-Annamese conception of warfare which had become so oddly picturesque now, so dilettante even, in its half measures and grotesque chivalries; the opposing generals meeting to agree over a pullet's entrails the date and place of battle; the warriors carrying lanterns at night to give their enemies a fair chance to see them; the battle suspended while the weather cleared up; the victory conceded to the side showing greater proficiency in the beating of offensive gongs. One is reminded of the military manuals — indispensable to old-style Vietnamese warfare — of those genial fire-eaters, General Dao and Marshal Khe; with their leisurely discussion of the best way to cook rice on horseback, while on the march, and their emphasis on the value of aggressive masks — or, in their absence, of merely pulling faces at the enemy.

Victory, as Pasquier observes, in his study of the Vietnamese army, was usually accorded, avoiding final resorts to arms, to the side recognized as possessing the moral ascendancy. It is all part of the essential pacifism and civilization — liable to crop out whenever given the opportunity — of a people who possess the proverb: 'The greatest honour any human being can possibly hope for is to return to his village with the degree of Doctor of Letters awarded at the triennial competitions at Hué. After that it is not a bad thing to come back as Marshal of the Empire, having won a great victory over the enemy'.

In the afternoon of the next day, I saw Saigon again, and for the last time.

I was driving back with the engineer. It had been a quiet night in the city, he said. That was to say, only an average number of grenades had been thrown. But he was afraid that more trouble was expected, because a shipful of Africans had arrived and the streets were full of them.

In fact, as we came into the suburbs we saw them, the Senegalese, wandering like lost children near the posts they had taken over — the black heads of processional giants carried jerkily above the oblivious Asiatic crowd.

The first strangers to arrive here, says Borri, were shipwrecked mariners, who 'took such an Affection to that Country that not a Man of them would go away; so that the Captain of the Ship was forc'd to drive them aboard with many Blows and Cuts, which he effectually did, loading the Ship with the Rice they had gather'd only by going about, crying, *I am hungry*'.

This, surely, was the end of the story; the completion of a cycle ... these frightened blacks and the sullen natives of the country with their averted faces. The successors of the shipwrecked Europeans had come back in increasing numbers, preaching, trading, worming their way into the organism of the country, changing it, remoulding it, and finally taking it for their own. And now they had withdrawn again into the port of their entry, where behind this African rampart they awaited the findings of Destiny.

I wondered whether it had all been worth it — the brief shotgun marriage with the West, now to be so relentlessly broken off. Had there been, after all, some mysterious historical necessity for all the bloodshed, the years of scorn, the servitude, the contempt? Could some ultimately fructifying process have been at work? And would the free Nations of Indo-China, in their coming renascence, have gained in the long run by the enforced rupture with the old, unchanging way of life, now to be replaced, one presumed, by a materialist philosophy and the all-eclipsing ideal of the raised standard of living?

These were questions, since there is no yard-stick for felicity, to which no final answer could ever be given. And even a partial answer would have to be left to an observer of the next generation.

INDEX

A VISIT TO DON OTAVIO

SYBILLE BEDFORD
A Mexican Journey

I am convinced that, once this wonderful book
becomes better known, it will seem incredible that it
could ever have gone out of print.
Bruce Chatwin, Vogue

This book can be recommended as vastly enjoyable.
Here is a book radiant with comedy and colour.
Raymond Mortimer, Sunday Times

Perceptive, lively, aware of the significance of trifles,
and a fine writer. Applied to a beautiful, various, and
still inscrutable country, these talents yield a
singularly delightful result.
The Times

This book has that ageless quality which is what
most people mean when they describe a book as
classical. From the moment that the train leaves
New York. . .it is certain that this journey will be
rewarding. When one finally leaves Mrs Bedford on
the point of departure, it is with the double regret of
leaving Mexico and her company, and one cannot
say more than that.
Elizabeth Jane Howard

Malicious, friendly, entertaining and witty.
Evening Standard

This edition is not for sale in the USA

If you wish to receive details of forthcoming publications,
please send your address to
Eland Books, 53 Eland Road, London SW11 5JX

Previously published by
ELAND BOOKS

THE DEVIL DRIVES

A Life of Sir Richard Burton.

FAWN M. BRODIE

Richard Burton searched for the source of the Nile,
discovered Lake Tanganyika, and, at great risk,
penetrated the sacred cities of Medina and Mecca.
But he was much more than an explorer:
he was also an amateur botanist, swordsman,
zoologist and geologist. He wrote forty-three books,
translated erotica, and spoke forty languages and
dialects. His life is probably the most fascinating
and outlandish of all the Victorians.

A model of what a life of Burton should be.
Philip Toynbee, Observer

No one could fail to write a good life of Sir Richard
Burton (not even his wife), but Fawn Brodie has
written a brilliant one. Her scholarship is wide and
searching, and her understanding of Burton and
his wife both deep and wide. She writes with clarity
and zest. The result is a first class biography of an
exceptional man…Buy it, steal it, read it.
J. H. Plumb, New York Times

*If you wish to receive details of forthcoming publications,
please send your address to
Eland Books, 53 Eland Road, London SW11 5JX*

Previously published by

ELAND BOOKS

THE
WEATHER
IN
AFRICA

MARTHA GELLHORN

This is a stunningly good book.
Victoria Glendinning, New York Times

She's a marvellous story-teller, and I think
anyone who picks up this book is certainly not
going to put it down again. One just wants to go
on reading.
Francis King, Kaleidoscope, BBC Radio 4

An authentic sense of the divorce between Africa
and what Europeans carry in their heads is
powerfully conveyed by a prose that selects its
details with care, yet remains cool in their
expression.
Robert Nye, The Guardian

This is a pungent and witty book.
Jeremy Brooks, Sunday Times

This edition is not for sale in the USA

*If you wish to receive details of forthcoming publications,
please send your address to
Eland Books, 53 Eland Road, London SW11 5JX*

A STATE OF FEAR

ANDREW GRAHAM-YOOLL
Memories of Argentina's nightmare

For ten hair-raising years Andrew Graham-Yooll
was the news editor for the Buenos Aires Herald.
All around him friends and acquaintances were
'disappearing'; and as an honest and brave
reporter he was under constant suspicion from all
sides in Argentina's war of fear.

Because of the author's obvious honesty and
level-headedness, we get an especially frightening
picture of life in a society where the slightest
deviation may cause you to disappear for ever.

'I have never read any book that so conveys what it
is to live in a state of permanent fear...'
Graham Greene, Observer

'Will become a classic document about 20th
century Argentina ... It is a small masterpiece.'
Hugh O'Shaugnessy, Financial Times

*If you wish to receive details of forthcoming publications,
please send your address to
Eland Books, 53 Eland Road, London SW11 5JX*

FAR AWAY
AND LONG AGO

W. H. HUDSON
A Childhood in Argentina

With a new preface by Nicholas Shakespeare

One cannot tell how this fellow gets his effects; he
writes as the grass grows.
It is as if some very fine and gentle spirit were
whispering to him the sentences he puts down on the
paper. A privileged being
Joseph Conrad

Hudson's work is a vision of natural beauty and of
human life as it might be, quickened and sweetened
by the sun and the wind and the rain, and by
fellowship with all other forms of life. . .a very great
writer. . .the most valuable our age has possessed.
John Galsworthy

And there was no one – no writer – who did not
acknowledge without question that this composed
giant was the greatest living writer of English.
Far Away and Long Ago is the most self-revelatory of
all his books.
Ford Madox Ford

Completely riveting and should be read by everyone.
Auberon Waugh

If you wish to receive details of forthcoming publications,
please send your address to
Eland Books, 53 Eland Road, London SW11 5JX

Previously published by
ELAND BOOKS

HOLDING ON

A Novel by
MERVYN JONES

This is the story of a street in London's dockland
and of a family who lived in it. The street was built in
the 1880s, and the Wheelwright family (originally
dockers) lived there until its tragic demolition in
the 1960s, when it was replaced by tower blocks.
  As a social document, the book rings with truth,
but it is much more than that: its compelling
narrative brings the reader right into the life of the
Wheelright family and their neighbours.

Moving, intelligent, thoroughly readable…
it deserves a lot of readers.
Julian Symons, Sunday Times

A remarkable evocation of life in the East End of
London…Mr Jones fakes nothing and blurs little…
It is truthful and moving.
Guardian

Has a classic quality, for the reader feels
himself not an observer but a sharer in the life of
the Wheelwrights and their neighbours.
Daily Telegraph

*If you wish to receive details of forthcoming publications,
please send your address to
Eland Books, 53 Eland Road, London SW11 5JX*

Previously published by
ELAND BOOKS

THREE CAME HOME

AGNES KEITH
A woman's ordeal in a Japanese prison camp

Three Came Home should rank with the great imprisonment stories of all times.
New York Herald Tribune

No one who reads her unforgettable narrative of the years she passed in Borneo during the war years can fail to share her emotions with something very like the intensity of a personal experience.
Times Literary Supplement

This book sets a standard which will be difficult to surpass.
The Listener

It is one of the most remarkable books you will ever read.
John Carey, Sunday Times

If you wish to receive details of forthcoming publications,
please send your address to
Eland Books, 53 Eland Road, London SW11 5JX

Previously published by
ELAND BOOKS

GOLDEN EARTH

NORMAN LEWIS
Travels in Burma

Mr Lewis can make even a lorry interesting.
Cyril Connolly, Sunday Times

Very funny . . . a really delightful book.
Maurice Collis, Observer

Norman Lewis remains the best travel writer alive.
Auberon Waugh, Business Traveller

The reader may find enormous pleasure here without knowing the country.
Honor Tracy, New Statesman

The brilliance of the Burmese scene is paralleled by the brilliance of the prose.
Guy Ramsey, Daily Telegraph

If you wish to receive details of forthcoming publications,
please send your address to
Eland Books, 53 Eland Road, London SW11 5JX

Previously published by
ELAND BOOKS

THE
HONOURED
SOCIETY

NORMAL LEWIS
The Sicilian Mafia Observed

New epilogue by Marcello Cimino

One of the great travel writers of our time.
Eric Newby, Observer

Mr Norman Lewis is one of the finest journalists
of his time. . .he excels both in finding material
and in evaluating it.
The Listener

It is deftly written, and every page is horribly
absorbing.
The Times

The Honoured Society is the most penetrating book
ever written on the Mafia.
Time Out

If you wish to receive details of forthcoming publications,
please send your address to
Eland Books, 53 Eland Road, London SW11 5JX

NAPLES '44

NORMAN LEWIS

As unique an experience for the reader as it must have been a unique experience for the writer.
Graham Greene

Uncommonly well written, entertaining despite its depressing content, and quite remarkably evocative.
Philip Toynbee, Observer

His ten novels and five non-fiction works place him in the front rank of contemporary English writers . . . here is a book of gripping fascination in its flow of bizarre anecdote and character sketch; and it is much more than that.
J. W. Lambert, Sunday Times

A wonderful book.
Richard West, Spectator

Sensitive, ironic and intelligent.
Paul Fussell, The New Republic

One goes on reading page after page as if eating cherries.
Luigi Barzini, New York Review of Books

*If you wish to receive details of forthcoming publications,
please send your address to
Eland Books, 53 Eland Road, London SW11 5JX*

Previously published by
ELAND BOOKS

LIGHTHOUSE

TONY PARKER

What is it that leads a man to make lighthouse-keeping his life's occupation? Why does he select a monotonous, lonely job which takes him away from his family for months at a stretch, leaving him in a cramped, narrow tower with two other men not of his own choosing?

Lighthouse-keepers and their families have opened their souls to Tony Parker, and his portrait of their lives is as compelling as any novel, and gives us an exceptional insight into the British character.

A very human book; and a pleasure to read.
John Fowles

Immediate, vivid, and absorbing... one of the most fascinating social documents I have ever read.
William Golding

A splendid book which has enriched my understanding of human nature.
Anthony Storr, The Sunday Times

If you wish to receive details of forthcoming publications,
please send your address to
Eland Books, 53 Eland Road, London SW11 5JX

Previously published by
ELAND BOOKS

A CURE FOR SERPENTS

THE DUKE OF PIRAJNO
An Italian doctor in North Africa

The Duke of Pirajno arrived in North Africa in 1924. For the next eighteen years, his experiences as a doctor in Libya, Eritrea, Ethiopia, and Somaliland provided him with opportunities and insights rarely given to a European. He brings us stories of noble chieftains and celebrated prostitutes, of Berber princes and Tuareg entertainers, of giant elephants and a lioness who fell in love with the author.

He tells us story after story with all the charm and resource of Scheherazade herself.
Harold Nicolson, Observer

A delightful personality, warm, observant, cynical and astringent. . .Doctors who are good raconteurs make wonderful reading.
Cyril Connolly, Sunday Times

A very good book indeed. . .He writes a rapid darting natural prose, like the jaunty scutter of a lizard on a rock.
Maurice Richardson, New Statesman

Pirajno's book is a cure for a great deal more than serpents.
The Guardian

In the class of book one wants to keep on a special shelf.
Doris Lessing, Good Book Guide

If you wish to receive details of forthcoming publications, please send your address to
Eland Books, 53 Eland Road, London SW11 5JX

Previously published by
ELAND BOOKS

NUNAGA

DUNCAN PRYDE
Ten years among the Eskimos

Duncan Pryde, an eighteen-year-old orphan, an ex-merchant-seaman, and disgruntled factory worker left Glasgow for Canada to try his hand at fur-trading.

He became so absorbed in this new life that his next ten years were spent living with the Eskimos. He became part of their life even in its most intimate manifestations: hunting, shamanism, wife-exchange and blood feuds.

This record of these years is not only an astonishing adventure, but an unrivalled record of a way of life which, along with the igloo, has vanished altogether.

He tells us stories, which he seems to have been born to do.
Time

One of the best books about Arctic life ever written . . . A marvellous story, well told.
Sunday Times

If you wish to receive details of forthcoming publications,
please send your address to
Eland Books, 53 Eland Road, London SW11 5JX

Previously published by
ELAND BOOKS

A FUNNY OLD QUIST

The Memoirs of a Gamekeeper
EVAN ROGERS
EDITED BY CLIVE MURPHY

An octogenerian gamekeeper tells us his story.
He has worked for sixty-eight years on the same
Herefordshire estate, and can remember the time
when wooden clogs were worn and young women
gave birth in the fields while gathering stones for a
shilling a ton.

Although he is a downright traditionalist who
dislikes new-fangled ways, he doesn't pretend that
life was always easy, and he is sometimes sharply
critical of his former masters. From this truthful
and vivid account, we get an unsentimental picture
of life on a semi-feudal estate – a way of life that
has almost completely disappeared.

A refreshing and informative book, a social
document of permanent value, as well as a
good read.
Times Literary Supplement

Extraordinary is the proper word for it.
Country Life

*If you wish to receive details of forthcoming publications,
please send your address to
Eland Books, 53 Eland Road, London SW11 5JX*

Previously published by

ELAND BOOKS

THE LAW

A novel by
ROGER VAILLAND

With a new preface by Jonathan Keates

The Law is a cruel game that was played in the
taverns of Southern Italy. It reflects the game of life
in which the whole population of Manacore is
engaged. Everyone from the feudal landowner, Don
Cesare, to the landless day-labourers are partici-
pants in the never-ending contest.

Every paragraph and every section of this novel has
been carefully cast and seems to be locked into
position, creating a structure which is solid and
formal, yet always lively. . .while we are reading the
novel its world has an absolute validity. . . *The Law* is
an experience I will not easily forget.
V. S. Naipaul, New Statesman

The Law deserves every reading it will have. It is and
does all that a novel should – amuses, absorbs,
excites and illuminates not only its chosen patch of
ground but much more of life and character as well.
New York Times

One feels one knows everyone in the district. . .every
page has the texture of living flesh.
New York Herald Tribune

A full rich book teeming with ambition, effort and
desire as well as with ideas.
Times Literary Supplement

If you wish to receive details of forthcoming publications,
please send your address to
Eland Books, 53 Eland Road, London SW11 5JX